The Aftershock Investor

The Aftershock Investor, Second Edition

A CRASH COURSE IN STAYING AFLOAT IN A SINKING ECONOMY

David Wiedemer, PhD

Robert A. Wiedemer

Cindy Spitzer

Published by John Wiley & Sons, Inc., Hoboken, New Jersey.
Published simultaneously in Canada.

For general information on our other products and services or for technical support, please contact our Customer Care Department within the United States at (800) 762-2974, outside the United States at (317) 572-3993 or fax (317) 572-4002.

Wiley also publishes its books in a variety of electronic formats. Some content that appears in print may not be available in electronic books. For more information about Wiley products, visit our web site at www.wiley.com.

Cartoons used with permission of Cartoon Stock, www.CartoonStock.com, and Cartoon Bank.

ISBN 978-1-118-73336-3 (Hardcover)
ISBN 978-1-118-73343-1 (ePDF)
ISBN 978-1-118-73345-5 (ePub)

Printed in the United States of America
10 9 8 7 6 5 4 3 2

Contents

Part III: Your Aftershock Game Plan

Acknowledgments

The authors thank John Silbersack of Trident Media Group and David Pugh, Laura Gachko, and Joan O'Neil from John Wiley & Sons for their relentless support of this book. We would also like to thank Stephen Mack and Jeff Garigliano for their help in writing this book. We thank Jim Fazone, Jay Harrison, and Nancy McSally for their work on the graphics; Michael Lebowitz for his help on the data; and Beth Gansner for her help in proofreading. We also want to acknowledge Christine Peglar's and Jennifer Schoenefeldt's help in keeping us organized.

David Wiedemer

I thank my co-authors, Bob and Cindy, for being indispensable in the writing of this book. Without them, this book would not have been published and, even if written, would have been inaccessible for most audiences. I also thank Dr. Rod Stevenson for his long-term support of the foundational work that is the basis for this book. Dr. Jeff Williamson and Dr. Lee Hansen also provided me with important support in my academic career. And I am especially grateful to my wife, Betsy, and son, Benson, for their ongoing support in what has been an often arduous and trying process.

Robert Wiedemer

I, along with my brother, want to dedicate this book to our mother, who died late last year. She inspired us to think creatively and see the joy in learning and teaching. We also dedicate this to our father, the original author in the family. We also want to thank our brother, Jim, for his lifelong support of the ideas behind this book. Chris Ruddy and Aaron De Hoog have been enormous supporters of *Aftershock*. It's been great to have such support. I also want to thank early supporters Stan Goldstein, Tim Selby, Sam Stovall, and Phil Gross. I also want to thank Dan Cohen and Michael Calkin for their support of this book. I am most grateful to Weldon Rackley, who helped my father to become an author and who did the same for me. A very heartfelt thanks goes to John R. Douglas for his very special role in making our books a reality.

Of course, my gratitude goes to Dave Wiedemer and Cindy Spitzer for being, quite clearly, the best collaborators you could ever have. It was truly a great team effort. Most of all, I thank my wife, Sera, and children, Seline and John.

Cindy Spitzer

Thank you, David and Bob Wiedemer, once again for the honor of collaborating with you on our fifth book. It is always an exciting experience, and I look forward to many more.

For their endless patience and support, my deep appreciation and love go to my husband, Philip Terbush, our children, Chelsea, Anya, and Zachary, and my dear friend Cindi Callanan.

I am also filled with a lifetime of gratitude for two wonderful teachers: Christine Gronkowski (SUNY Purchase College) and two-time Pulitzer Prize winner Jon Franklin (UMCP College of Journalism), who each in their own ways helped move me along a path exceptional.

My appreciation also goes to Beth Goldstein and Christie Chroniger for their ongoing help with all things great and small.

Introduction

We wrote our first book, *America's Bubble Economy*, back in 2004 and finished it in 2005, long before the housing bubble was visible to many people. We asked our publisher, John Wiley & Sons, to hold the book as long as they could because we were concerned that nobody would buy it. Few people believed there was a housing bubble at that time, much less a whole bubble economy. They wouldn't hold it any longer than fall 2006, and so it was published.

With that first book and *Aftershock* (Wiley, 2009 and 2011), we have built up a good track record of predicting much of what has happened since then, certainly better than most analysts. Almost no economists or analysts wrote an entire book about such issues at the time, although many have written books since. But many of those books are more historical than predictive. It's still scary to predict the future. It's much easier to review the past.

We have been criticized by some as being one-trick ponies—that we made one good prediction and that's it. Certainly, there have been cases of this in the past, such as Elaine Garzarelli, the market analyst who famously predicted the 1987 stock market crash. But we're not trying to predict a crash. What we are trying to do is predict a far larger change in the entire economy. Yes, an earlier real estate crash and stock market crash was part of that, but there is much more to what's going on in the U.S. economy and world economy. Anyone who reads our books will see that.

Some people may say we were right about one prediction, but in fact, it was a range of related predictions, many of which we predicted will not occur for years more. We'll have to wait to see if those come true. But even if we got only one prediction right, that's better than many people who get far more attention for their predictions than we do, such as Ben Bernanke. He predicted, after the Bear Stearns collapse in June 2008 and just four months before the biggest financial crisis in our history, that all was fine with our financial system. Well, it's better to be right once than never. At least it should give us more credibility.

But our forecasts are not meant to cheerlead or paint a rosy picture, and we know that leads many people to giving us less credibility, for obvious reasons. They would rather listen to a more bullish outlook, such as Mr. Bernanke's, especially on the stock market. As one of our good friends on Wall Street said, "Nobody likes a bear, especially when they're right!"

We're not trying to be a bear or a bull, we're just trying to help people better understand the economy. As another friend on Wall Street said, "What you're really doing is teaching people." And that's exactly what we want to do. Some people have said we are arrogant, but we try not to be arrogant. Of course, maybe in the act of teaching something very new that others aren't teaching, there is a certain inherent arrogance.

The best teachers have a passion for what they teach. And when you have a passion, you try to make strong points of great substance that will stick with the people you are teaching. If we have over-reached in some of our chapters and appeared arrogant, we apologize. We try to keep the book as nonarrogant and easy to read and enjoyable as possible, while still getting our message across. In fact, we think that is critical to good writing and good teaching.

We don't try to attack anyone personally. If we do make a reference to someone personally, it is to make a larger point about the economy or the way people look at the economy, not to personally put anyone down.

We try to be as fair as possible because we need to be as believable as possible. That is absolutely critical to teaching anything new.

In this book we hope to expand on what we have taught in the past, and we hope more people will benefit. The greatest joy of writing a book is that someone benefits from it—whether that's because they are entertained, or live a more financially secure life, or simply have a better understanding of the way our society works. It's all about feeling that you are somehow better off after reading the book than before.

We wrote this latest book, *The Aftershock Investor*, Second Edition, in response to our readers' demands for more details about how to put the ideas in *Aftershock* into action. The old ways of investing based on conventional wisdom are becoming increasingly ineffective and even dangerous. For those lucky enough to see what is coming, we need a new investing approach. Rather than passively waiting for things to get better, we need to actively manage our investment portfolios, based on the correct macroeconomic view of the current and future economy. For that, we now offer you *The Aftershock Investor*, Second Edition.

The Aftershock Investor

CHAPTER 1

This "Recovery" Is 100 Percent Fake

WHY THE AFTERSHOCK
HAS NOT BEEN CANCELED

As we write this second edition of *The Aftershock Investor* in mid-2013, U.S. stock markets have hit new highs, real estate prices are rising, and the economic cheerleaders are declaring once again that all is well or will be soon. The economy is in recovery and the coming Aftershock, our critics say, has been canceled.

How wonderful that would be—if only it were true. But nothing has happened to change our minds about our earlier forecasts. In fact, current events fall in line pretty well with our previous analysis and predictions, dating back to our earliest books, *America's Bubble Economy* in 2006 and the first edition of *Aftershock* in 2009. From the beginning, we said that in order to keep the stock, real estate, private debt, and consumer spending bubbles going, the government would inflate two more bubbles—the dollar and the federal debt bubbles—through massive money printing and massive money borrowing. That is the only way to keep this temporary bubble party going, and the government is doing all it can to keep pumping helium into the balloons so they don't fully fall. With the total national debt now nearly $17 trillion and the Federal Reserve flooding the economy with $85 billion in newly printed money *every month* (at the time of this writing), our predictions are looking pretty spot-on.

We never said the stock market wouldn't rise—in fact, it may go even higher. We never said the economy couldn't temporarily stabilize or that home prices couldn't rise a bit in some areas in the short term. We said this is a bubble economy and that the government will do anything it can to keep the bubbles going—and that is exactly what they are doing. But please don't confuse a temporary, artificially created recovery with the real thing. Any recovery that is created by massive government stimulus and can be maintained only with continued massive government stimulus is a *fake* recovery.

Why? Because the fundamental economic realities have not changed, and even massive government stimulus cannot permanently override the fundamentals. The fact is that since the early 1980s we have been living in a *bubble economy* (see Chapter 2 for why we say so), and bubbles don't last forever. We saw the beginning of the pop with the partial decline of the real estate bubble in 2007, which helped kick off the global financial crisis of late 2008. Since then, we've seen a mammoth effort to partially reinflate and maintain the sagging bubbles with an enormous amount of money printing and money borrowing.

This huge stimulus has been only marginally successful, as evidenced by the fact that the stock and real estate markets have not really grown much beyond their previous bubble highs prior to the 2008 crash, at best. This highly expensive, bubble-maintaining stimulus may work for a while—maybe even years—but it won't work forever. In the long run, the massive stimulus will be forced to end, and it will have made our problems even worse in the future.

So contrary to popular belief, this "recovery" is 100 percent fake and the Aftershock has *not* been canceled.

Isn't a Fake Recovery Better than No Recovery at All?

That seems true, but it really isn't. The massive money printing and borrowing that is creating this fake recovery and delaying the Aftershock will only make the coming crash all the worse later. That's why we say it's nothing to cheer about. A fake recovery may feel good now—like postponing a trip to the dentist with a strong painkiller—but it will only bring us much more pain later.

"These projected figures are a figment of our imagination.
We hope you like them."

Not only will the temporary painkiller eventually wear off, but the medicine itself will later become a poison as the massive money printing eventually causes *dangerous future inflation*. Why is that so dangerous? Because rising inflation will cause rising interest rates, and rising interest rates will cause markets to crash even harder than they would have had we not printed so much money.

And, of course, just like postponing a trip to the dentist, putting off dealing with our underlying problems only increases our future pain because it postpones the fundamental changes we desperately need to make in order to create a real economic recovery. What we need is not more government borrowing and more dollars created out of thin air to keep the party going. What we need is a true economic recovery based on fundamental changes that will boost real productivity (the subject of future books). Real productivity growth would generate real economic growth and real, nonbubble wealth that would not be vulnerable to bubble pops.

The problem is that those changes are difficult. No one wants to hear that we have to make tough choices and endure a lot of pain now to create real economic growth later. It's much easier to let the government borrow and print for now, and kick all the rest of it down the road to deal with later. Politicians might talk about fiscal and monetary responsibility, but the short-term consequences of stopping the current bubble-supporting machine would put their jobs in jeopardy. This is why we have been predicting since 2006 that our bubble economy will continue to be maintained until that maintenance is no longer possible. We will throw everything at it until we can throw no more. While marginally effective in the short term, eventually this strategy will fail. Until then, no one wants to pop the temporary bubble party.

Inflation or Deflation?

Nobel Prize–winning economist Milton Friedman in the 1970s famously said: "Inflation is always and everywhere a monetary phenomenon."

In fact, inflation and deflation are both "monetary phenomena," meaning they both result from changes in the money supply. Inflation results from increasing the money supply faster than the economy grows, devaluing the dollar and causing goods and services to cost more. Deflation results from decreasing the money supply relative to the economy, pushing up the value of the dollar and causing goods and services to cost less.

The Great Depression gave us deflation, not inflation. Too few dollars relative to the economic needs of the time caused the value of the dollar to rise, and the cost of goods and services to fall.

By sharp contrast, we are printing enormous amounts of new money, increasing the monetary base much faster than the economy is growing, which will bring us future inflation, not deflation. (Please see www.aftershockpublishing.com for more info on inflation versus deflation.)

Those who point to falling prices or the threat of future falling prices, and call it deflation, are making a fundamental mistake. Separate from inflation or deflation, prices also rise and fall because of changes in supply and demand. For example, when an asset bubble pops (such as real estate), falling home prices are not due to deflation; home prices fall because there are more sellers than buyers.

Just before and during the Aftershock, multiple popping bubbles will cause many asset prices (in inflation-adjusted dollars) to fall. That is not deflation; that is a price drop due to a bubble pop!

If the Aftershock Has Not Been Canceled, Why Hasn't It Happened Yet?

While we stand by our past and current predictions for the coming Aftershock, we admit that predicting exactly when the bubbles will fully burst is difficult. What we can do is look at the fundamentals of this economy, and they continue to look worse and worse as time passes. So while we cannot easily predict the timing of the coming Aftershock, there is no doubt that it will happen. It cannot be permanently avoided, only delayed.

To understand why the Aftershock hasn't happened yet, let's take a closer look at what is keeping this fake recovery going and how long we think it might last.

The Key to Creating and Maintaining the Fake Recovery: Massive Money Printing

Massive money printing is quickly becoming the key support of our multibubble economy. We are not talking about creating a modest amount of extra money to keep up with a growing economy, like we used to do. We are talking about a truly staggering amount of new money printing, more than we've ever done in U.S. history or, for that matter, the history of the world. If you think we are exaggerating, consider this: since the creation of the U.S. Federal Reserve almost 100 years ago, we have printed roughly $800 billion; now the Fed is printing more new money than that *in just one year* (see Figure 1.1)

Since the financial crisis of 2008, the Fed has increased the monetary base from about $800 billion to more than $3 trillion. This is a truly enormous increase. By making money so abundant and therefore cheap to borrow, money printing allows the government to run high deficits. And money printing keeps the stock market from collapsing and the bond and real estate markets from collapsing as well.

A government can boost the economy by running a large deficit. But eventually it will have to pay higher yields on its bonds as investors become more and more skeptical of the government's ability to pay its increasingly large debt obligations. The solution: money printing. The central bank uses printed money to buy government bonds in large quantities, thus creating an artificial demand for those bonds and keeping yields low.

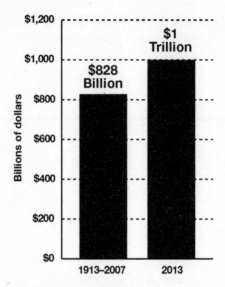

Figure 1.1   Massive New Money Printing

We will print more new money in 2013 than we created in total since the Federal Reserve was formed almost 100 years ago up to 2007.

Source: Federal Reserve.

The artificial demand for government bonds carries over to the rest of the bond market as well, where yields are often defined by the markup over the rate on sovereign bonds. The low interest rates in the bond market carry over into the mortgage market as well, keeping demand up for easy home loans and propping up the real estate market.

Low yields on bonds leave many investors chasing bigger gains. And what better place to increase their return on investment than the stock market? There's plenty of capital to put into stocks, too. After all, when the Fed prints money to buy bonds, it has to buy those bonds from somebody, and then they have to do something with it. Much of that newly printed money goes right from investors' bank accounts into the stock market, raising demand for stocks and boosting the overall stock market. The rising stock market further encourages the real estate market and general consumer spending, creating the fake recovery we have today.

So if money printing enables the government to run large deficits with little consequence and it boosts the stock, bond, and real estate markets as well, what's the downside? The answer is *future inflation.* Printing many more dollars while economic growth is very slow means they are less valuable. The resulting inflation ultimately pushes up interest rates. Higher interest rates in a bubble economy will mean collapsing markets and an exploding government debt problem. Rising inflation is something a bubble economy cannot afford.

When the first edition of this book was published in September 2012, the Fed had already completed two rounds of quantitative easing (QE1 and QE2), making the U.S. money supply roughly triple what it was in 2008. Soon after the book was published, the Fed announced yet a third round of quantitative easing (QE3). But this time, perhaps losing confidence in the economy's fundamentals, the Fed put no limits on its money printing operations, saying only that it would commit to *at least* $40 billion a month in bond purchases until unemployment figures had reached a satisfactory level. It didn't take long before that $40 billion commitment became a staggering $85 billion a month, with no end in sight.

That's a lot of artificial stimulus from the government to keep the markets up. It's working so far, as long as the money printing continues. But does anyone really think that endlessly creating dollars out of thin air is a path to real future prosperity? It's almost silly to believe in such a fantasy and yet the psychological drive to accept this as a safe and effective cure for our problems generally overrides logic. Investors love the easy-money fantasy that money printing supports and they want it to go on forever.

We are not saying that if we stopped the stimulus today, all would be fine. Just the opposite, ending the stimulus entirely would quickly throw the economy into severe recession. But our economic problems are not due to a lack of stimulus; therefore, the stimulus, no matter how massive, will not save us, it will only delay the inevitable economic pain and will make it all the worse when it happens later. This is a falling bubble economy (see Chapter 2 for details) and the money printing and money borrowing stimulus is simply delaying its further fall. But the more stimulus we throw at it now, the harder the crash will be later because inflation and interest rates will be that much higher.

In a Supporting Role: Cheerleading

Cheerleaders root for the home team. They won't tell you the quarterback has a weak arm, or that the offensive line is outmatched,

"Now we just have to sit back and wait for the Fed to bail us out."

or that the head coach is inexperienced. Their job is to be positive and cheer on the home team!

In recent decades we've seen the financial world take on a "home crowd" type of atmosphere, with financial pundits and economists assuming roles as cheerleaders rather than analysts. They won't tell you about the fundamental problems in the economy. They'll only assure you that everything is bound to get better, that recovery is right around the corner, or that it's already here. Never mind all the people out there looking for decent wages.

The cheerleading mindset is a big reason we ended up with a bubble economy in the first place. Brokerage firms needed to sell stocks in order to make money. Fundamentals didn't matter, as long as everyone played along. They cultivated a deep belief that prices were always going to go up, up, up. Remember how optimistic all the experts were before the subprime mortgage crisis?

The cheerleading mindset persists, as the analysts hype every little positive and ignore or downplay every negative. We can't possibly have inflation. It doesn't matter how much money the Fed prints. The unemployment rate is falling. It doesn't matter how many people are out of work. Home sales are on the rise. It doesn't matter how low they are compared to a few years ago.

Oh, but if gold prices drop, that's a "correction" on a fundamentally bad investment.

Ammo for the Cheerleaders: Inflation and Unemployment Numbers Still Appear Low

Our critics like to point to the current absence of rising inflation to show we are wrong about money printing causing rising future inflation and interest rates, which are key to our predictions for the coming Aftershock. They say, if we need inflation to push interest rates up and kick off the Aftershock and we have no inflation, then clearly the Aftershock has been canceled.

We disagree. To a large extent, the reason we haven't seen significant inflation yet in spite of massive money printing is that, as we'll explain in more detail in Chapter 5, there are some "lag factors" that create a delay between when money is printed and when inflation sets in.

But also keep in mind that we have seen *some* inflation. While inflation may not be 10 or 20 percent yet, the government's sub–3 percent figures are difficult to believe. Anyone who buys food or puts gas in their car knows that prices of many things have gone up in the past few years. So why doesn't the government's measure of inflation seem to more fully reflect this?

One important reason has to do with the way the government measures inflation, which they purposely changed in the last couple of decades in order to downplay the inflation rate. While manipulation of economic statistics is expected and accepted as an everyday occurrence in some other countries, the United States is not known for regularly manipulating our statistics. However, that doesn't mean it doesn't happen, albeit in subtle ways.

One of the easiest and most convenient statistics to manipulate is the inflation rate, and the United States is almost certainly massaging its chief measure of inflation, the CPI. This figure can easily be manipulated by making changes to the basket of goods and services measured over time and making subjective judgments about product substitution—for example, how a 2013 car model compares to a 2003 model.

We are not at all surprised that the government is taking steps to hide the real inflation rate. The stakes are very high, and the people generating the inflation statistics are likely under a certain amount of subtle pressure to produce statistics that are more supportive of current government economic policy. Aside from the danger that inflation leads to higher interest rates that can hurt the markets, inflation also puts a big strain on the government budget. The government has to make higher and higher payments for any inflation-indexed programs, including pensions and social security, and higher interest rates mean the government has to offer higher rates to finance its debt.

Worse yet, inflation eats away at gross domestic product (GDP) growth figures. If inflation reaches 4 or 5—let alone 10 or 20—percent, any growth in GDP has to be adjusted accordingly. With our economy right now *officially* only growing by about 2 percent annually (and likely the real number is less than that), it's very much in the government's interest to report low CPI inflation figures. That has no doubt played a role in the shifting standards for measuring inflation over the last couple decades.

The unreliability of government statistics makes it difficult for us to say exactly what inflation really is right now. But we don't see any reason to believe that the government's "new and improved" measure of inflation is more accurate than the measure they used 30 years ago. The evidence suggests that the changes to CPI were made out of self-interest, not a concern for accuracy.

Combine the inflation rate with the unemployment rate and you get the *misery index.* Generally speaking, the higher this number is, the more economic and social woes we face. So unemployment is another figure the government has a keen interest in understating. And while employment statistics are not as easy to manipulate as CPI, that doesn't mean we should take them all at face value.

More jobs were lost from 2007 to 2009 (almost 9 million), than during the previous four recessions combined. So employment statistics are important numbers for the media and the cheerleaders.

To be counted in the official "unemployment rate" a person has to be out of work entirely and actively seeking a job. This means those who have given up searching and whose unemployment benefits have lapsed—referred to as the *discouraged unemployed*—are not counted in the popular unemployment rate that gets reported so much in the news.

Also not counted in the typically reported unemployment rate are those working part time when they would rather work full time, or who are working well below their education and skill levels. In July 2013, Gallup reported that more than 17 percent of the workforce characterizes itself as "underemployed." Many previous full-time workers have been forced to take part-time work while they continue to look for better employment. When the media and cheerleaders tell us to feel good about the creation of new jobs, they rarely if ever mention that many of those new jobs are only part time (see Figure 1.2).

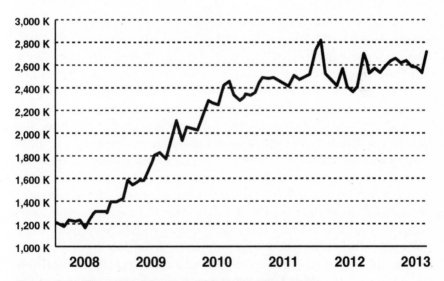

Figure 1.2   More Workers Forced into Part-Time Jobs

A growing number of people who would like to have full-time jobs have had to take part-time jobs instead. Many more workers have had their previously full-time hours reduced to part-time.

Source: BLS/Haver.

So while the typical unemployment rate reported in the media has recently held steady around 7 or 8 percent, it doesn't tell the whole story. For that, we need to look at what is called the U6 unemployment rate, which conveniently the government and the media avoid discussing too much. The U6 rate, which includes discouraged unemployed and those working part-time when they'd rather work full-time, is officially 14.5 percent. The actual number is likely higher.

It has become an increasingly common phenomenon to see the official unemployment rate figure remain flat or even go down slightly while the number of people dropping out of the work force goes up. In fact, according to the Bureau of Labor Statistics, the number of *working-aged* Americans who have now dropped out of the workforce is about 3 to 4 million. The majority of these folks are under 50 years old, so they aren't retiring. They are just giving up. There are typically some working-aged Americans out of the workforce—such as full-time parents—but this is an exceptionally high number. Recently, the employment-to-population ratio (in which "population" counts anyone 16 years of age and older) is down to 58.5 percent, when it had hovered around 63 percent for much of the previous decade.

And if you think job growth is bad, wage growth is in even worse shape. In fact, according to government statistics, real wage growth (adjusted for inflation) is worse now than it was during the Great Depression. Even with two people in the family working instead of one, the growth of household incomes has been essentially flat in the past few years (see Figure 1.3).

Between the underreported unemployment figures and the lack of income growth, much of the pain in the economy is quiet pain—meaning that it doesn't get much media coverage and few people are discussing it. But its impacts are widespread. Perhaps some of our readers know people who have lost their jobs and are looking for work, or who have dropped out of the workforce entirely, with little or no hope of finding a job. Or you might know some who have seen their wages or income fall, or their business suffer. And in spite of these realities we all see right in front of us, the government will still claim we are in a "recovery," trying to distract us with frivolous numbers that don't tell the true story. If this really were a recovery, we'd be seeing more jobs by now.

Figure 1.3   Household Incomes Are Languishing

Median household incomes, adjusted for inflation, have declined and not recovered much since the financial crisis of 2008.

Source: Sentier Research and the *Wall Street Journal.*

Money Printing = No Inflation = No Taxes!

We Are Fooling Ourselves—and We Know It

One of the craziest ideas that the cheerleaders promote can be summarized as "Don't worry, massive money printing is always perfectly safe!"

Really? If it's really so safe, why are we only doing it on an "as-needed" basis? Why not do it all the time, not just in a crisis? If it's really so safe, why ever stop?

And if it is really so safe, why not do a whole lot more of it? After all, if massive money printing doesn't cause future inflation, why are they so afraid of doing more? Surely, if $85 billion of new money per month is good, then $100 billion per month would be even better, right?

What the heck, if there's no downside to massive money printing, why not go for *$200 billion* per month? Think of how much that would boost the markets and the economy. It would be great! Why aren't we doing that right now? In fact, why do we need to pay any taxes at all? Let's just print all the money we will ever need, whenever we need it!

But you'll notice we don't actually do that, do we? How come? Because everyone knows that it can't work. If we didn't know, we'd be doing it, so obviously, we know. People know that massive money printing comes with a nasty future price tag (inflation). If it didn't, why should we limit it and why should we ever stop? Like smoking crack, we know darn well that this is a dangerous drug; we just can't kick our addiction to its short-term high.

How much crack can we smoke before we scare ourselves by the sheer quantity? Well, if we start out slowly and get ourselves used to it, our love of the short-term high can convince us that we are always printing the "just right" amount of new money. When we first started with limited quantitative easing (QE1) in early 2009, the idea of printing $85 billion/month without an end date would have seemed irresponsible. But by raising the amount of money printing gradually over time to create and maintain the fake recovery, each new round of QE was welcomed as perfectly safe and perfectly sized. Now $85 billion/month seems "just right."

In fact, any talk of even slightly reducing the money printing makes the stock market drop 100 points. We are addicted and we know it. And we are fooling ourselves and we know it.

Still Not Sure This Recovery Is 100 Percent Fake?

We've explained why this recovery is entirely fake and the coming Aftershock has not been canceled, but maybe you're still not convinced. Maybe you think the economy really is turning around, that employment will pick up once it catches up with the stock market, that China will carry the rest of the world out of this malaise, or that the fantasy of cheap energy will save us. If we haven't made the case yet that the fundamentals of the economy are not improving, and in fact are only getting worse, here are a few more facts to wake you up.

If This Recovery Is Real, Why Is Government Borrowing Outpacing GDP Growth?

While many people seem to cheer every little positive sign of growth in the economy (and ignore or downplay any negative news), what's really astonishing is just how little growth in the economy we've seen in spite of all the government intervention. Between 2008 and 2013, the cumulative increase in GDP in the United States was $2.8 trillion. Over the same period, government borrowing increased $4.7 trillion. In other words, government borrowing is outpacing GDP growth substantially (see Figure 1.4). That's a whole lot of borrowing for just a little bit of growth.

Such huge borrowing relative to GDP shows just how fragile the U.S. economy really is. Pro-intervention pundits and academics like to think of government intervention as a parent holding up a young child's bicycle, ready to pull the hand away as soon as the child can stay upright. In truth, the government is more like push-over parents who keep giving their children barrels of money well into their adult years, seeing less and less return on their investment as the kids become increasingly dependent. If the parents cut them off, they'd be out on the streets immediately.

It's the same for this economy. If you took away the huge money borrowing, we'd be thrown into an instant recession. At this point, the massive money printing and massive money borrowing are keeping the economy on life support.

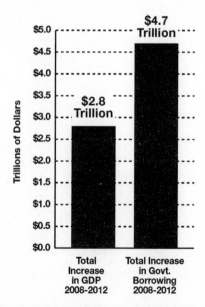

Figure 1.4   Increase in GDP Growth versus Increase in Government Borrowing

We are borrowing far more than the economy is growing.

Source: Bureau of Economic Analysis.

After Five Years of Emergency CPR, the Patient is Not Recovering

If the global financial crisis of 2008 was like a heart attack for the U.S. economy, then the massive stimulus (massive money printing and borrowing) needed to jump start this patient has kept the patient alive, but it certainly hasn't restored full health. Even after five years of massive stimulus, we are still getting nowhere.

If GDP is growing by 1 to 2 percent (the equivalent of $150 to $200 billion), even assuming that deficit spending is reduced to $800 to $900 billion this year, we are in fact buying very little GDP growth with a huge amount of debt—we are borrowing much more than the amount of GDP growth we get for the borrowing (see Figure 1.5).

In other words, we are stimulating nothing. It is all just fake bubble maintenance and no real growth. The only recovery has been in asset prices, not the economy. Only the assets are going up, while the economy is not.

Five years of CPR may keep some vital signs going, but the patient is not recovering. And with so much money printing and borrowing weighing heavily on our future, this patient will be sicker than before.

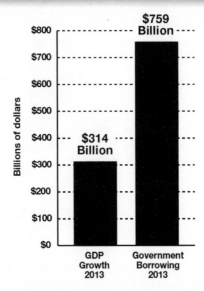

Figure 1.5   GDP Growth versus Current Government Borrowing

We are borrowing at a rate that is more than double our current growth rate. Apparently, we are not getting much of a bang for our borrowed buck.

Source: White House (Projected debt 2013), Bureau of Economic Analysis (GDP, calculated assuming 2 percent annual growth).

If This Recovery Is Real, Why Are Stock Prices Growing Faster than Company Earnings?

Lately, we have relied on the stock market for optimism. And while anyone can appreciate some healthy optimism, the kind of blind optimism we're seeing in the stock market right now helps no one.

A big reason for the stock market's record numbers is investors' outlandish expectations for future earnings. According to FactSet, industry analysts expect record earnings for the Standard & Poor's (S&P) 500 in the last two quarters of 2013. In fact, projections for the fourth quarter of 2013 are more than 15 percent above the fourth quarter of 2012. That would be an impressive rise for any period, and a great reason for people to want to own stock in these companies—if it actually happens, which is highly unlikely. Even a 15 percent year-over-year growth rate in earnings would be very impressive—and also very unlikely. Given that S&P 500 earnings grew less than 3 percent from the fourth quarter of 2011 to the fourth quarter of 2012, 15 percent growth would be a tall order for fourth quarter of 2013.

In addition, revenue growth is also poor. S&P revenues have been growing at only 1-2 percent for most of 2013. This is no surprise given that U.S. GDP growth will only be 2 percent for 2013 and most major world markets aren't growing much faster. But despite this, the market is apparently expecting an enormous jump in revenues (which drive company earnings and stock prices) in the second half of 2013.

This kind of freakish optimism isn't just calling the glass half full. This is like saying the glass is overflowing when there's barely a drop of water! The fact is that company earnings are not growing at the rate that stock prices are growing; therefore, you are paying more for the same earnings you could buy for less before. That's nothing to cheer about.

If This Recovery Is Real, Why Is the Global Economy Slowing?

One reason for slow earnings growth in the United States might be the situation around the world. For multinational corporations, like those that make up the S&P 500 and Dow Jones Industrial Average, a significant portion of their revenues comes from overseas operations. And the news from overseas has been pretty bleak.

In Europe, the north is in recession, while the south is in depression. Unemployment numbers in Spain, Italy, and Greece are staggering. In the north, even Germany is suffering from a slowdown, with big companies like Daimler abandoning their profit forecasts due to falling demand. France and the United Kingdom, Europe's second- and third-largest economies, are flirting with recession. And the Netherlands, a traditionally strong economy, is on the verge of economic crisis.

China, the engine many thought would pull the rest of the world out of this mess, is experiencing a slowdown in growth even by its own admission. The truth is likely even worse than the Chinese government lets on, as the enormous construction bubble that was built up in response to the 2008 financial crisis is becoming increasingly unsustainable. A *60 Minutes* report in March 2013 showed entire cities being built—high-rise luxury condominiums, expansive malls—with *no one living in them.* So much for the world's growth engine.

China's slowdown is taking a toll on the rest of the world, too. Brazil's impressive growth has slowed to a crawl (and possibly contraction if inflation is properly accounted for). Turkey, another country that seemed to be flying above the global earthquake, saw just 2 percent growth in 2012—down from about 9 percent in 2010 and 2011. Japan's government, unsatisfied with the country's sluggish economic activity, recently announced a money-printing campaign that would make even Ben Bernanke blush—printing $75 billion a month in an economy a little more than a third of the size of the United States. And while there's been a lot of talk about "emerging markets," it's becoming increasingly apparent that those markets were fueled largely by China's rise, and thus are suffering now that China is struggling to keep pace with its earlier gains.

This is important because the global slowdown has a direct impact on the U.S. economy and U.S. stocks, particularly those that collectively make up the S&P 500. That's because in this global economy, no country is an island. Some countries may fare better than others, but trends around the world operate as a large feedback loop. When the United States falters, the rest of the world slows down. When demand in Europe drops, exports in China drop. When China slows down, Europe sinks further, and other economies can't keep up their previous pace. Everyone depends on everyone else. We can turn our heads away from bad news all we want, but eventually there will be nowhere to hide.

How Do You Define a Bubble? Assets Up, Economy Flat

The only thing we are getting from all this massive government stimulus is more support for the bubbles, not real economic growth. This can clearly be seen in Figure 1.6. Only asset prices have been significantly rising, not GDP or jobs.

How Do You Define Insanity?

The classic definition of insanity is doing the same thing and expecting different results. That's exactly what we've been doing: applying the same stimulus (massive printing and massive borrowing) and expecting different results. More money printing, more money borrowing, more cheerleading, and more statistical smoke and mirrors are not going to give us the significant GDP growth, more quality jobs, rising wages, or anything else that comes with real economic recovery and growth.

The only thing we are buying with this ongoing stimulus is continued asset bubble maintenance—that's all.

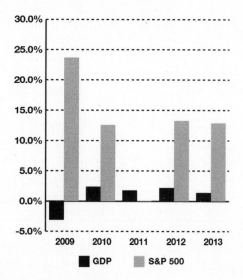

Figure 1.6   Assets Up, Economy Flat

Only asset prices are up, not the overall economy. By definition, that makes it a bubble.

Source: Standard & Poors and the U.S. Department of Commerce.

Don't Believe the Stimulus Has to Eventually End? There Is a Limit to What the Government Can Do

While the federal government does have much more power to affect markets and the overall economy than any private investor or company, even the federal government does have its limits.

The limit to continuing the stimulus of massive money borrowing is the government's ability to find investors willing to continue to buy our debt. In a way, we've already hit that limit. The fact that the Fed started printing massive amounts of money in 2009 was a clear indicator that the government's borrowing ability had essentially come to an end, or at least that it couldn't afford to pay competitive interest rates in order to borrow all the money it wanted. We had to print the money to enable the government to borrow more money.

The Fed is now printing about $1 trillion a year—money it uses to buy government bonds, creating artificial demand and keeping interest rates low. That's much more money than the $700 billion that the government is projected to borrow this year. In other words, the government's ability to continue borrowing is being entirely supported by the Fed's money printing. Would anyone be able to buy Treasuries at very low interest rates today if they weren't backed by the Fed's massive money-printing machine?

So what is the limit to the Fed's massive money printing? Technically, there isn't any. But history and the laws of economics tell us that the stimulating effect of money printing becomes increasingly ineffective over time. That's because increasing the money supply inescapably leads to inflation, as we will discuss in more detail in Chapters 3 and 5. In time, inflation cripples the economy when interest rates rise, ultimately canceling out the earlier positive effects that the stimulus originally provided.

The fact that there are lag factors between money printing and inflation is the only reason money printing can be so effective in the short term. After that, the negative consequences of inflation and interest rates kick in. That would be bad news for any economy, even a strong economy in a real recovery and with real growth. However, for a sagging multibubble economy in a fake recovery with almost no growth, the consequences will be very bad, indeed.

It's only a matter of time.

Wondering Why the Aftershock Hasn't Happened Already? "Animal Spirits" Are Keeping Us Going

For some of our biggest fans, the question isn't "Has the Aftershock been canceled?" but "What the heck is taking it so long?!" You might think, given the staggering amounts of money printing and borrowing, lack of jobs, overvalued assets, and low GDP growth, that the bubbles would have popped already and the Aftershock would be here by now. When is this thing going to blow?

That's a good question, and we don't have a precise answer. In a moment we will give you our best-guess answer. But first, let's look closer at why the money printing works in the first place.

The truth is that none of the money printing, cheerleading, or massaged statistics would be very effective at maintaining the fake recovery without one absolutely essential ingredient: *positive investor psychology*. Sometimes, the term *animal spirits* is used to refer to the emotional component of the economy, represented by consumer and investor confidence. Without positive animal spirits, the rest of the fake recovery maintenance activities simply would not work.

As long as the animal spirits stay positive, the activities to maintain the fake recovery will work for a while longer. People have to believe this recovery is real or all efforts to keep it going will fail. Once enough people stop having faith in the economy—once they stop believing in the strength of the dollar, the soundness of the markets, the good faith of the government, and the financial system—the game is over and the bubbles will pop. At that point, any additional money printing would translate immediately in to inflation, with no beneficial effect. Cheerleading will fall on deaf ears. Currency and market manipulations will fail to make people invest. And no amount of dumping gold on the market to lower its price will turn investors away from its perceived safety.

So when you ask "When will the Aftershock hit?" you are really asking: "When will positive psychology turn negative enough to pop the bubbles?" In the end, the timing of the turning point comes down to how people *feel*, not to economic statistics or sophisticated financial analysis.

While the final trigger won't be about numbers directly, in the buildup to the change in investor psychology some numbers will matter because they will begin to weigh heavily on investor optimism. One of these important, psychology-changing numbers will be the inflation rate, which currently is still low. How high does inflation have to rise to turn positive psychology negative? The exact figure is hard to know. We do know that as inflation rises it will undermine positive investor psychology, as will a continued lack of new, good-paying jobs. There may not be one defining moment or any particular CPI number that will suddenly tip the balance from positive investor psychology to more negative. But over time, that is where we are headed because with so much money printing, inflation will eventually rise.

Keep in mind, too, that as inflation moves up, interest rates will naturally move up as well. For example, if inflation goes to 5 percent, interest rates would have to rise to 6 percent just to bring lenders a 1 percent return after inflation. Higher interest rates certainly would be a big downer for stocks, bonds, and real estate, especially because all three are bubbles. Given the amount of money printing that has already occurred, inflation and interest rates could go even higher. It is possible that these bubbles will burst even before we hit the highest levels of inflation and interest rates, if investor psychology tips toward the gloomy side sooner. Again, we can't know the exact numbers, but we know rising inflation and interest rates will matter.

In addition to rising inflation and interest rates, a number of other potential triggers could turn investor psychology more negative (see Chapter 3), including simply the passage of time. But remember, no trigger in the world could turn most people negative if the underlying reality didn't back it up. Bubbles go up on wishful thinking, but they come down because of rational thinking. In the end, the final trigger will be the damning facts themselves.

The Fierce Fight to Save the Bubbles

In the meantime, as long as investor psychology is still good, it is in the government's and the financial system's best interests to keep animal spirits up *at all costs*. There is even some evidence that there may already be some government intervention in the stock and gold markets (see Appendix B). The motivations for this are strong because the stakes are so high. As long as the powers that be can convince people that the economy is recovering, that the markets will continue to fly high, that the dollar is strong, and that job growth is just around the corner, they can continue to keep the asset bubbles going.

Of course, all of this works only because most people are all too willing to believe the good news. Just like the government, they also have plenty to lose by facing reality. Jobs, careers, businesses, and lifestyles are in jeopardy. No one wants to face that our beloved age of easy bubble money cannot go on and on.

Could additional money printing and borrowing maintain the asset bubbles and positive investor psychology for a while longer? Most definitely, yes. Will more money printing and borrowing be able to keep the party going for another decade or more? Absolutely not.

Over time, as the economy continues to have minimal or negative growth despite massive government stimulus, people will start to wake up. That will mean changes in what they buy, save, sell, and invest in. Increasing negativity (just like positivity) will become self-fulfilling for the economy. As more and more investors become anxious enough to exit their bubble pumped investments other investors will want out, too (see Chapter 4 for details about each stage). Once enough investors try to exit, the U.S. bubbles will pop, and the global Aftershock will begin, impacting economies around the world.

When Will It Happen?

Our best guess about when the bubbles will pop and the global Aftershock will begin:

2–5 years   Probably
5–10 years   Possibly, but much less likely

Even if the bubbles don't all pop in the next 2–5 years, they certainly won't last another 10.

Please Prepare Now

So let's review. Right now, massive money printing (and the low interest rates it creates) are boosting the stock market, protecting the bond market, supporting the overall economy, and allowing the government to borrow massively. We like to tell ourselves it's all risk-free, but we know that's a lie. Massive money printing will eventually cause rising future inflation, which will push up interest rates, which will pop our multibubble economy (hurting stocks, bonds, and real estate).

No one enjoys thinking the current recovery is entirely fake—not even us. We are not permabears, always predicting the economy will get worse no matter what the situation. In the future, we look forward to telling you about how the economy is getting better, how real productivity is improving, and how to cash in on real economic growth. We just aren't there yet.

We're not writing this book to cheer the collapse of the economy, nor are we trying to rub it in that we were right in the past. We know it is uncomfortable to face these facts, and even scary because if we don't prepare correctly, we all have a lot to lose. But not facing facts will not serve you well.

Group denial may help delay the Aftershock for a while, but it can't delay it forever because the underlying fundamental economic forces cannot be permanently stopped—not by massive money printing, not by massive money borrowing, and not even by pervasive group denial. All these are only temporary.

Please prepare now, while you still can.

It may not be necessary to run and sell off all your investments today or tomorrow. But it is necessary that you pay attention to the fundamentals of the economy so that you can protect yourself and your investments before it's too late. In this updated second edition of *The Aftershock Investor*, that continues to be our goal.

Remember, we saw these problems coming prior to publishing our first book in 2006, back when many experts expected that home prices would rise forever. The fundamentals of our macroeconomic point of view were correct then and are still correct today. All we ask is that you listen to what we have to say and decide for yourself. The popping of America's Bubble Economy and the coming Aftershock will be like nothing we've seen before. The good news is that there's still time to prepare.

Along the way, if you're ever tempted to think that all is well, just remember these four damning facts:

- *Massive money printing.* We've *tripled* the monetary base and are printing $85 billion/month more, keeping the stock, bond, and real estate bubbles afloat.
- *Massive money borrowing.* We owe a staggering $17 trillion in total debt, and are borrowing another $700 billion each year—four times more than what we borrowed in 2007.

- *Paltry GDP growth.* We're growing at only 1 to 2 percent per year which means we are borrowing almost three times more than the economy is growing.
- *Pitiful job growth.* New jobs are barely keeping up with population growth and not even close to replacing the more than 7 million jobs lost from September 2008 to February 2010. Also, an very large number of the newly created jobs are only part time.

This recovery is 100 percent fake and the Aftershock has not been canceled. Please don't stay asleep with the sheep. If you want to protect yourself, you have to wake up before everyone else does. Chapters 2 through 5 will show you how we got ourselves into this mess, and Chapters 6 through 14 will help you prepare for and even profit from it.

PART

I

AFTERSHOCK

CHAPTER 2

Bubblequake and Aftershock—A Quick Review of How We Got Here and What's Next

WHY READ THIS BOOK? BECAUSE WE WERE RIGHT; NOW YOU CAN BE RIGHT, TOO

We are not Ben Bernanke, chairman of the Federal Reserve. We are not economic Nobel Prize winners, like Paul Krugman. We don't run huge investment firms, such as Goldman Sachs or Merrill Lynch. *But they were all wrong, and we were right.* That is why this book is worth reading. We don't have a crystal ball—no one does. But we do have something even more reliable over the long term: the *correct* macroeconomic view of what is occurring and what's coming next. Once you have this correct Big Picture, too, you can be just as right as we have been. With this book, you and your family and associates will likely have a better chance than most to cover your assets, protect yourself, and perhaps even find profits in the coming Aftershock.

The purpose of this book is to move you closer to that with every page.

Please note: If you have not yet read any of our previous books, the chapter will serve as your quick executive summary. If you already know why we say we have a multibubble economy, you could just skip this chapter. However, you may want to stay around for the quick review. If nothing else, it will help you hold up your end of the discussion with some people who may still be in the dark about what is really happening.

Not Asleep with the Sheep

Back in 2006, when the U.S. economy was still looking pretty good, our first book, *America's Bubble Economy*, accurately predicted the future popping of the real estate bubble, the fall of the stock market bubble, the decline of the private debt and consumer spending bubbles, and the widespread pain all this was about to inflict on our vulnerable, multibubble economy. Of these bubbles, we said the real estate bubble would be the first to go, kicking off the fall of stocks and the decline of private debt and consumer spending— exactly what occurred in the financial crisis of 2008. We also predicted the eventual bursting of the dollar bubble and the massive government debt bubble, which are both still to come.

Other bearish analysts have also predicted some of our current economic troubles, but very few did so as early as 2006. Even those who did see parts of this mess coming are still failing to connect all of the dots. They don't fully understand what's happened so far, and they can't tell us what will happen next. *America's Bubble Economy* was the only book to *both* warn about the current economic problems here and around the world, and also to go way out on a limb by predicting in substantial detail what would occur, why it would occur, and when. Not too many authors have been willing to go that far out on a limb, mostly because they can't. They don't yet see the whole story, and they don't dare take a chance on making inaccurate predictions that may come back to haunt them later. We went out on a limb, and it turned out to be rock solid.

Of course, back in 2006, our prescient predictions were largely ignored. Our next two books, *Aftershock* (2009) and *Aftershock*, Second Edition (2011), further fine-tuned our forecasts, explaining in more detail how massive stimulus spending by the federal government and massive money printing by the Federal Reserve would temporarily boost the falling multibubble economy, particularly the stock market, but would only kick the can down the road and later make our bubble economy crash even harder later.

This time, with the memory of the 2008 financial crisis still painfully fresh, more people began to take notice. In 2009, *Aftershock* was named one of *SmartMoney*'s Best Books. And in 2011, within weeks of publication in August, *Aftershock*, Second Edition, became a *New York Times* business bestseller, a *Wall Street Journal* business bestseller, and the number one Amazon personal finance book and number one Amazon economics book. Since then, the book has been translated into Japanese, Chinese, Polish, and Korean, becoming a Korean bestseller. The book was made even more accessible in the form of an audio book, beautifully read by Christopher Kipiniak, which was nominated for an Audie Award. By the end of 2011, *Aftershock*, Second Edition, was named by *The Economist* magazine as Amazon's third bestselling personal finance book, not just in the United States but in the world.

What a difference a crash makes! Some people were clearly starting to wake up.

But despite all the kudos and recognition our books have gotten, our basic macroeconomic message is still falling mostly on deaf ears—or, more accurately, on *denying minds.* Most people simply do not want to wake up and fully face the truth of what is really happening. Even the bear-oriented analysts are missing the bigger picture. This is not merely a "down cycle" that will eventually be followed by a bullish "up cycle." *This economy is evolving.* We are not going back to how it was before. We are going forward to something new.

For a fuller explanation of our macroeconomic views, we encourage you to take a look at *Aftershock*, Second Edition. For your convenience, we are also summarizing the key ideas of that book in this chapter.

But before we get to that, we would like to take a moment to congratulate you, the person who is reading these words right now—not just for opening this book, but more importantly for *opening your mind,* if not to our entire macroeconomic point of view, at least to the *possibility* that something is not quite right with this so-called recovery. Perhaps we are headed not back to the prosperity of the past, but forward, toward something entirely new, highly dangerous, and potentially profitable. You are part of an elite, early group of people with their eyes open and their lights on. You may not know everything about what is occurring or exactly what to do about it, but you, dear reader, are not asleep with the sheep!

"Tell me the fairytale about the economy."

Bubblequake! First, a Rising Bubble Economy; Now, a Falling Bubble Economy

The first thing you need to know about our current and future economic problems is that they didn't start yesterday. It all started decades ago with a combination of declining productivity growth beginning in the 1970s, coupled with a growing propensity to run big government deficits beginning in the 1980s.

Please understand that, in and of itself, running big deficits is not necessarily a bad thing. In fact, there are times when borrowing big money is really quite smart. For example, you might borrow a large sum of money to start a profitable business or to go to medical school, which among other benefits can increase your real wealth in the future. But this big government borrowing was not the equivalent of starting a profitable business or going to medical school, and it did not lead to increasing the nation's *real* wealth in the future. Instead, we just borrowed money to buy things we wanted without having to raise taxes—the equivalent of being able to go shopping with a credit card without having to get a better-paying job.

Now, to be fair, the $1 trillion federal debt in 1982 really wasn't that much compared to today's nearly $16 trillion federal debt, but the relatively small annual federal budget deficits in the 1980s were significant because they were the early beginnings of the big federal borrowing and big deficit spending that would come later.

Of course, at the time, no one was too worried about the beginnings of big federal borrowing and deficit spending in the 1980s. In fact, the U.S. economy grew nicely over the next couple of decades, with a 260 percent increase in U.S. gross domestic product (GDP) from 1980 to 2000. And asset values, such as stocks, bonds, and real estate, grew even faster.

However, there was a hidden driver behind much of this rapidly rising abundance: *bubbles!*

What Is a Bubble?

This should be a relatively easy question to answer, but, believe it or not, there is no academically accepted definition of a financial or economic bubble. For our purposes, we define a bubble as an asset value that temporarily rises and eventually falls, primarily due to changing investor psychology rather than due to underlying, fundamental economic drivers that are sustainable over time.

Before it is a bubble, an asset value may first begin to rise because of real fundamental economic drivers, such as when population growth pushes up the demand for housing and therefore the price. But at some point, the impact of the underlying fundamental driver has a diminishing effect and hopeful investor psychology takes over, pushing the asset value temporarily higher, creating a bubble.

In the course of history, asset bubbles have varied greatly in their causes, duration, height, and crash impact, but one thing has remained absolutely constant about all bubbles of every type and size: *they all eventually pop.* By definition, if it is a bubble, what goes up must come down. That is the economic reality that no bubble can escape. *Gravity happens.* It's only a matter of time.

Because bubbles go up primarily due to investor psychology rather than due to fundamental economic drivers, all it takes for a bubble to fall is a significant enough change in investor psychology. What makes investor psychology change significantly? Investor psychology changes when enough people figure out that they have bought into a bubble, leading to a sell-off and a bubble pop. If it weren't really a bubble, the deep sell-off wouldn't last. Nonbubble asset values can certainly drop, but the underlying fundamental economic drivers would still be in place, and eventually investors would soon return to buy back the asset, stopping its fall. Only bubbles pop; nonbubbles may fall but eventually recover.

Is it possible to stop a bubble from falling or to reinflate it once it falls? The short answer is no. You cannot indefinitely prevent a popping bubble from popping, nor can you push it back up and keep it up once it fully pops.

However, the longer, more nuanced answer is yes and no. While we can't permanently prevent a bubble from popping, we can *delay* it from falling and even push it back up a bit with a lot of resources and artificial stimulus. As we will see later in this chapter, that is only temporary and often leads to a much bigger bubble crash down the road.

Why doesn't artificial stimulus work to *permanently* reinflate a bubble? Because, generally speaking, you cannot fool the same people twice, and even when you can fool the same people twice, you cannot fool them for as long. For example, if you were among the investors who lost money when the Internet bubble popped, how willing have you been since then to buy stock in technology companies that show no profits? Investors do generally learn and move on.

However, with massive amounts of artificial stimulus (like massive money printing by the Federal Reserve), it is possible for a falling bubble to defy gravity and temporarily rise again. But because of the enormous costs, massive stimulus cannot continue forever. Eventually, the stimulus has to stop and gravity wins. So, for various reasons, including artificial stimulus, a popping bubble may not go down in a straight line. Instead, it may pause in its descent or even lift up for a while, but in the end *down* is its destiny.

How to Spot a Bubble

How can we know if an asset value is rising primarily due to positive investor psychology (speculation leading to a bubble), rather than due to underlying, fundamental economic drivers that are sustainable over time (real growth)?

While it is not always easy, it is possible to analyze and identify a not-yet-popped bubble if you are willing to stay rational and objective, and not get caught up in wishful thinking. It is human nature to want to believe in a rising bubble, especially when it is a bubble that you profit from or depend on. The only way to see a bubble that has not yet fully popped is to make a firm commitment to clear-eyed logic. *You cannot stay asleep with the sheep.*

As we pointed out in our earlier books, there are two important truths about bubbles:

Bubbles Are a Lot Easier to See *After* They Pop

and

The Hardest Bubble to See Is the One You're In

Throughout the ages, asset bubbles have always been largely invisible right up until the end. For example, no one could see the Dutch tulip bubble before it popped in 1637. Virtually no one saw through the appealing South Seas stock bubble until it burst in 1720. Investors were not the least bit worried about the great Florida land boom in the 1920s until the property values crashed back to earth, just as few people concerned themselves about the intoxicating stock market boom of the 1920s until it evaporated into the crash of 1929 and the Great Depression. And, more recently, precious few investors and analysts recognized the irrational exuberance of the Internet stock bubble in time to get out before it popped in 2000.

Looking back, these examples of past bubble booms and busts seem so obvious now, don't they? Of course, it makes no logical sense to overpay for tulips, buy swamp land in Florida, or invest in dot-com companies with no profits, but at the time, all these seemed perfectly plausible, even desirable to investors. Regardless of the time, place, or type of asset in question, all bubbles share this common feature: positive investor psychology pushes the bubble up, and negative investor psychology pushes the bubble down.

Here is the typical bubble-up, then bubble-down pattern:

- An asset value begins to rise due to some underlying, real economic drivers that begin to boost demand and therefore the price.

- As the asset value begins to rise, investor psychology begins to rise as well, leading to some investor speculation about the future value of the asset.
- Investors become even more interested in owning the rising asset, pushing up the price.
- More and more investors take notice and want to buy in before the asset price rises even further.
- As the bubble approaches its peak, some investors become anxious about future growth and sustainability, which leads some investors to increase their profit taking (selling the asset).
- Other investors take notice and become anxious or at least do not feel as positive about owning the asset, also deciding to sell.
- The asset price no longer rises and begins to decline.
- Positive investor psychology is increasingly replaced with neutral or negative investor psychology, sparking a larger sell-off.
- A critical level of negative investor psychology is reached, a mass exit begins, and the bubble pops.
- Most people cannot exit quickly enough, and most of their assets go to Money Heaven.

After the fact, it all seems so terribly obvious, doesn't it? However, this pattern is anything but easy to recognize *before* a bubble pops. Not-yet-popped bubbles are amazingly difficult to see. Why? Because we don't want to see them! We want the big run-up in prices to be real and sustainable, not a bubble. It takes a firm commitment to logic to see a bubble before it pops.

Now let's take a clear-eyed look at our current bubbles, the ones that have been working together to help push up the U.S. economy over many years, and more recently have started to deflate and lean heavily on each other, helping to push down the falling U.S. economy as they pop.

America's Bubble Economy

The U.S. economy has been such a strong and prosperous powerhouse for so long, it's difficult to imagine anything else. Our goal is not to convince you of anything you wouldn't conclude for yourself, if you had the right facts. Most people don't get the right facts because most financial analysis today is based on preconceived ideas about a hoped-for positive outcome. People want analysis that says the economy will improve in the future, not get worse. So they look for ways to create that analysis, drawing on outdated and incorrect ideas, such as repeating "market cycles," to support their case. Such is human nature. We all naturally prefer a future that is better than the past, and luckily for many Americans, that is what we have enjoyed for many years.

Up until a few decades ago, we grew our rising economic prosperity the old-fashioned way: by increasing real productivity. We laid railroad track from coast to coast that led to an explosion of trade. We invented cars and airplanes that changed how we lived and did business, and that impacted economies around the world. It wasn't all perfect, but rising productivity growth worked like Miracle-Gro on the rising U.S. economy.

Then something changed. Instead of rising productivity growth, real productivity growth began to slow down in the 1970s. In addition to declining productivity growth (and perhaps in some ways because of it), we also began to borrow massive amounts of money. Please do not waste precious time assigning political blame. Over the years, presidents and congressional leaders from both parties participated in this orgy of borrowing and deficit spending. Love or hate what we spent the money on, the fact is we have been borrowing and spending a whole lot of OPM (other people's money) since the early 1980s.

And please don't just blame the politicians. All this public borrowing and spending by governments was accompanied by plenty of private borrowing and spending by businesses and consumers. Plus, there were plenty of investments in what would eventually become asset bubbles, all combining to give us what we call America's Bubble Economy (spurring us to publish a book by that name in 2006).

To quickly review, we identified six colinked, economy-boosting bubbles that together helped boost the rising multibubble economy in the 1980s and 1990s. Since 2006 (with the popping of the real estate bubble), these bubbles have been deflating and falling, each putting increasing downward pressure on the others. These are . . .

The Real Estate Bubble

Now that it is partially popped, the real estate bubble is easy to see. As shown in Figure 2.1, from 2000 to 2006, home prices grew almost 100 percent.

Income Up 2%   Housing Prices Up 80%

Figure 2.1   Income Growth versus Housing Price Growth, 2001–2006

Contrary to what some experts say, the earlier rapid growth of housing prices was not driven by rising wage and salary income. In fact, from 2001 to 2006, housing price growth far exceeded income growth.

Source: Bureau of Labor Statistics and the S&P/Case-Shiller Home Price Index.

If nothing else, looking at Figure 2.2 on inflation-adjusted housing prices since 1890, created by Yale economist Robert Shiller, should make anyone suspicious that there was a very big real estate bubble in the making. Note that home prices barely rose on an inflation-adjusted basis until the 1980s and then just exploded in 2001.

According to the Case-Shiller Home Price Index, while the inflation-adjusted wages and salaries of the people buying the homes went up only 2 percent from 2000 to 2006 (according to the Bureau of Labor Statistics), home prices shot up during that same time period. The rise in home prices so profoundly outpaced the rise of incomes that even our most conservative analysis back in 2005 led us to correctly predict that the vulnerable real estate bubble would be the first to fall.

We will have a lot more to say about what's ahead for the housing market in Chapter 8, and it's not what the economic cheerleaders want you to think.

The Stock Market Bubble

The stock market bubble is one of the easiest, most obvious bubbles to spot, yet so very difficult for most people to see. Stocks can be analyzed in many different ways. We find the state of the stock

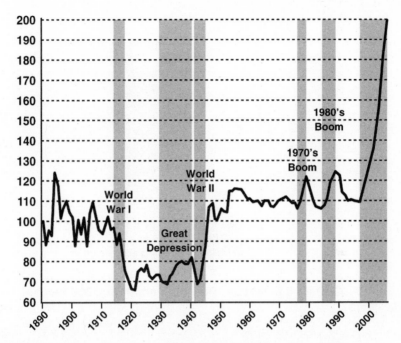

Figure 2.2   Price of Homes Adjusted for Inflation since 1890

Contrary to popular belief, housing prices do not ordinarily rise rapidly. In fact, until recently, inflation-adjusted home prices haven't increased that significantly, but then shot up after 2001 (1890 index equals 100).

Source: Robert J. Shiller, *Irrational Exuberance*, 2nd ed. (New York: Crown, 2006).

market is easier to grasp by looking at Figure 2.3. If this doesn't convince you that there was a stock bubble, we don't know what will. From 1980 to 2000, GDP rose a very decent 260 percent. However, the U.S. stock market, as measured by the Dow Jones Industrial Average, leaped up an astounding 1,100 percent!

We call that a stock market bubble! It looks even more out of line when you consider that the population of the United States grew only 25 percent from 1980 to 2000. Given that population growth is one driver of GDP growth, and given that GDP growth is the fundamental driver of corporate earnings growth and therefore stock prices, we would more or less expect to see the Dow rise about as much as GDP, which was about 260 percent. A 1,100 percent rise in the Dow is a giant flag, spelling out the word *B-U-B-B-L-E.*

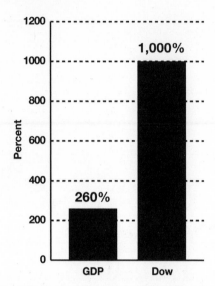

Figure 2.3   GDP Up 260 Percent, Dow Up More than 1,000 Percent, 1980-2000

The stock market rose almost four times as much as the economy grew from 1980 to 2000. That's a good indicator of a bubble.

Source: Dow Jones and Federal Reserve.

Shown in a different way in Figure 2.4, the value of financial assets as a percentage of GDP held relatively steady at around 450 percent from 1960 to 1980. But starting in 1981, financial assets as a percentage of GDP rose to *more than 1,000 percent* by 2007, according to the Federal Reserve. We call that prima facie evidence of both a stock market bubble and a real estate bubble.

The Private Debt Bubble

We can simplify the complex private debt bubble by seeing it as essentially a derivative bubble, driven by two other bubbles: (1) the rapidly rising home price bubble; and (2) the rapidly rising stock market bubble, which combined to make for a rapidly growing economy. In both cases, lenders of all forms (not just banks) began to feel very comfortable with the false belief that the risk of a falling economy had been essentially eliminated, and the risk of any type

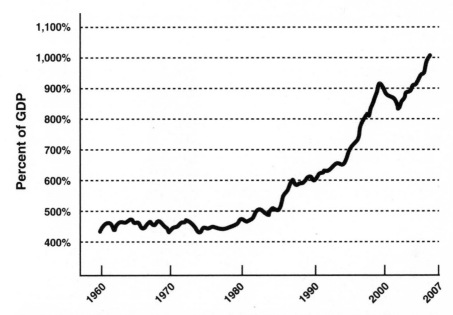

Figure 2.4   Rise of the Financial Assets Bubble: Financial Assets as a Percentage of GDP

The exploding value of financial assets as a percentage of GDP is strong evidence of a financial asset bubble.

Sources: Thomson Datastream and the Federal Reserve.

of lending in that environment was minimal. This fantasy was supported for a time by the fact that very few loans went into default. Certainly, at the time we wrote our first book (one year before its publication in 2006) commercial and consumer loan default rates were at historic lows.

The problem was not so much the amount of private debt that made it a bubble, but taking on so much risky debt under the false assumption that nothing would go wrong with the economy. For us, it was easy to see even in 2006 that if the value of housing or stocks were to fall dramatically (as bubbles always eventually do), a tremendous number of loan defaults would occur. We felt the private debt bubble was an obvious derivative bubble that was bound to pop when the real estate and stock market bubbles popped.

The Consumer Discretionary Spending Bubble

Consumer spending accounts for about 70 percent of the U.S. economy. A large portion of consumer spending is discretionary spending, meaning it's optional (how big a portion depends on exactly how you define *discretionary*). Easy bubble-generated money and easy consumer credit made lots of easy discretionary spending possible at every income level. When the real estate, stock market, and private debt bubbles began to pop and people started losing their jobs or were increasingly concerned that they might, consumers began to reduce their spending, especially unnecessary, discretionary spending.

This is typical in any recession, but this time the effect has been much more profound for two key reasons. First, the private debt bubble allowed consumers to spend like crazy because of huge growth in housing prices and a growing stock market and economy, which gave them more access to credit than ever before, via credit cards and home equity loans. As the bubbles popped, that credit started drying up, and so did the huge consumer spending that was driven by it.

Second, much of our spending on necessities has a high discretionary component, which is relatively easy for us to cut back. We need food, but we don't need Whole Foods. We need to eat, but we don't need to eat at Bennigan's or Steak & Ale (both now bankrupt). We need refrigerators and countertops, but we don't need stainless steel refrigerators and granite countertops. The list of necessities that can have a high discretionary component, complete with elevated prices, goes on and on. And, of course, there is a lot of other discretionary spending, beyond necessities, such as entertainment and vacation travel.

The combined fall of these first four bubbles—housing, stock market, private debt, and consumer spending bubbles—make up what we call the Bubblequake of late 2008 and 2009. Unfortunately, our troubles don't end there. Two more giant bubbles are about to burst in the coming Aftershock.

The Dollar Bubble

Perhaps the hardest reality of all to face, the once mighty greenback has become an unsustainable currency bubble. Due to a rising bubble economy, investors from all over the world were getting huge returns on their dollar-denominated assets. This made the dollar more valuable but also more vulnerable. Why? Because we didn't really have a true booming economy based on real underlying, fundamental economic drivers. We had a rising multibubble economy. Therefore, the value of a currency in a multibubble economy is linked not to real, underlying, fundamental drivers of economic growth (like true productivity gains), but to the rising and falling bubbles. For many years our dollars rose in value because of rising demand for dollars to make investments in our bubbles. More recently, demand for U.S. dollars has remained pretty strong, especially in light of the current European debt crisis. But that strength will wane as the falling bubbles lead to falling demand for dollars, despite all kinds of government efforts to stop it.

In our effort to stop the fall of our multibubble economy, the government has created two giant "airbags" to cushion the falling bubbles. The first airbag is the dollar bubble, created by massive money printing by the Federal Reserve. The Fed has been printing massive amounts of new money through their program of quantitative easing (QE). Three rounds of massive money printing (QE1, QE2, and QE3) have increased the U.S. money supply from $800 billion in March 2009 to $3.1 trillion as of this writing in mid-2013 (see Figure 2.5). This massive amount of money printing (the dollar bubble) will eventually cause significant rising inflation.

Future Inflation Will Cause Rising Interest Rates

In and of itself, rising inflation would not be so bad if the only consequences were rising prices and wages. But rising inflation also eventually causes *rising interest rates* (see *Aftershock*, Second Edition, for more details), and rising interest rates will have a very negative impact on the rest of the bubbles and the economy.

Rising interest rates will certainly be a big downer for the bond market (bond values drop as interest rates rise), as well as the real estate market, which will be hurt by higher mortgage rates (housing is only marginally improving now, even with mortgage rates at record lows).

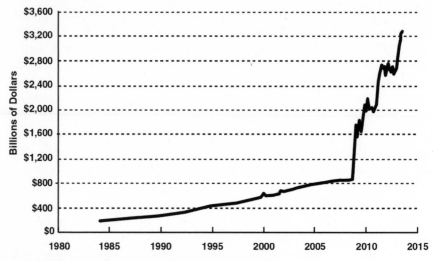

Figure 2.5   Growth of the U.S. Monetary Base

Money printing basically kept pace with economic growth until the financial crisis, when it exploded in 2009.

Source: Federal Reserve.

Higher interest rates also mean consumers will buy less on credit, if they even qualify for credit cards and loans, further depressing consumer spending, on which 70 percent of the U.S. economy depends.

And, of course, rising interest rates will also mean that businesses will borrow less money, buy less inventory, hire fewer workers, and generally expand less. That will negatively impact employment, which will negatively impact consumer spending, reduce company earnings, and lower stock values.

Even without the already falling bubbles, rising interest rates would not be good for a nonbubble economy recovering from a recession. For a falling bubble economy, rising interest rates will be the beginning of the final multibubble pop. While that is still off in the future, when it finally occurs, it will not take long for U.S. stocks, bonds, real estate, and other dollar-denominated assets to drop. Many investors, including many foreign investors who now own an enormous amount of U.S. assets (see Figure 2.6) will not want to hold on to as much of these declining investments. Foreign investors don't have to all run away at once to cause a big downward drop in dollar-denominated assets. Any significant decline

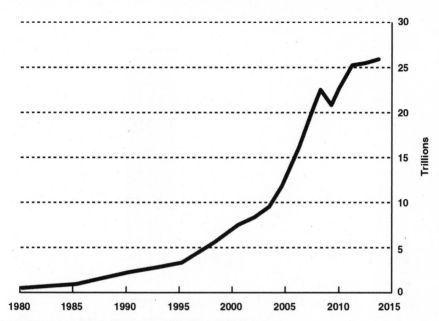

Figure 2.6   Growth of Foreign-Held U.S. Assets

Part of what fueled our bubble economy in the 1980s and 1990s was massive inflows of capital from foreign investors, which grew from less than $1 trillion in 1980 to $25.9 trillion in the first quarter of 2013. We remain highly dependent on their continued support.

Source: Bureau of Economic Analysis.

would do the trick. And, of course, domestic investors will not want to stick around either.

With inflation and interest rates rising, and even more money printing likely in the future as the Fed tries to support the falling bubbles with more quantitative easing, it is only a matter of time before the big dollar bubble pops.

The Government Debt Bubble

In addition to massive money printing (the dollar bubble), the government has pumped up another enormous airbag to temporarily cushion the falling bubble economy. Weighing in at more than $8.5 trillion when our 2006 book was published and now (mid-2013) nearly $17 trillion, the whopping U.S. government debt bubble, as shown in Figure 2.7, is currently the biggest, baddest bubble of all. Much of this debt has been funded by foreign investors, primarily

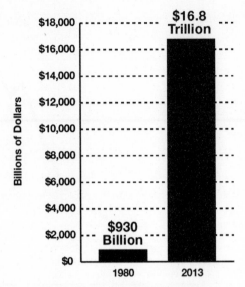

Figure 2.7   Growth of the U.S. Government 's Debt

The U.S. government 's debt is massive and growing rapidly. With no plan and little ability to pay it off, the debt is quickly becoming the world 's largest toxic asset.

Source: Federal Reserve.

from Asia and Europe. But as our multibubble economy continues to fall and the dollar starts to sink, who in the world will be willing— or even able—to lend us more?

From Boom to Bust: The Virtuous Upward Spiral Becomes a Vicious Downward Spiral

On the way up, the six conjoined bubbles described earlier helped co-create America's booming multibubble economy. In a seemingly virtuous upward spiral, the inflating bubbles helped the United States maintain its status as the biggest economy the world has ever known, even in the past few decades, when declines in real productivity growth could have slowed our expanding economic growth. Instead, these bubbles helped us ignore slowing productivity growth, boost our prosperity, disregard some fundamental problems, and keep the party going.

Not only did the U.S. economy continue to grow and remain strong, but the rest of the world benefited as well. Money we paid for rapidly increasing imports boosted the economies of developing countries like China and India. First World economies benefited from America's Bubble Economy, as well. Because of our rising bubbles, developed economies, such as Japan and Europe, were able to sell us lots of their cars and other high-end exports, which helped their home economies prosper. The growing world economy created a rising demand for energy, pushing up oil prices, which made some Russian billionaires, among others, very happy. Growing demand for minerals, like iron, oil, and copper, pumped money into every resource-producing country. For example, China's and India's expanding appetite for steel boosted iron ore exports from Australia, lifting their economy. All combined, America's rising bubble economy helped boom the world's rising bubble economy.

Now, as our intermingled global party bubbles are beginning to deflate and fall, the virtuous upward spiral has become a vicious downward spiral. Linked together and pushing hard against each other, each time a bubble begins to sag and pop, it puts tremendous downward pressure on the rest.

First, the Bubblequake; Next, the Aftershock

As we said earlier, the first four of the six bubbles—real estate, stock, private debt, and discretionary spending—have begun to pop, creating the beginning of what we call the Bubblequake. In response, the federal government and the Federal Reserve have been pumping up the remaining two bubbles—the dollar and government debt bubbles—with massive money printing and massive deficit spending since early 2009 in a dramatic attempt to stop the falling bubbles and to boost the overall economy. This massive stimulus spending and especially the massive money printing have been helping *in the short term* to temporarily boost the stock market and keep the overall bubble economy from sagging further.

But this massive stimulus cannot continue forever, and in the longer term, the bubbles will continue to fall. Not only will the massive stimulus eventually have to end, it will actually make our bubbles crash even harder when they finally do pop. Continued use of massive stimulus is like using a powerful short-term drug that will later become a toxic poison. The stimulus itself will later make the future crash all the worse.

It is important to understand that the Bubblequake problems we are now facing are due to much more than merely a popped real estate bubble. If all we had was a burst real estate bubble, it would not have created so much financial pain here and around the globe. In addition to the real estate bubble, the private debt bubble and the stock market bubble also began to fall. These Bubblequake problems are not going to be permanently resolved anytime soon, not even with the temporary boost from massive stimulus spending and massive money printing. Rather than a real economic recovery, the combination of sagging bubbles and the future poisonous consequences of the massive stimulus will put increasing downward pressure on our entire bubble-based economy.

Once our last two bubbles—the dollar and government debt bubbles—finally burst, we will enter the next phase, what we have dubbed the Aftershock, in which all our asset bubbles will burst and the U.S. economy will fall dramatically.

It's Not Just America's Bubble Economy—The World Has a Bubble Economy, Too

When America's Bubble Economy fully pops, so will the world's bubble economy. Why? Because all these bubbles are *linked together*. On their way up, each supported and fueled the others; and on the way down, each falling bubble will put increasingly downward pressure on the rest.

For example, the real estate boom in the United States created a consumer spending orgy here that helped fuel China's rapid economic growth and boomed China's own real estate bubble. To keep up with growing demand for their exports, China in turn has been buying more natural resources from other regions, such as South America. But when our real estate bubble began to pop and U.S. consumer spending dropped a bit, China's growth also began to cool down over the past few years, although it is still growing, just at a slower rate. In the coming Aftershock, when U.S. consumers will buy much less than they do today, China's bubble economy will take a deep hit, which will then spill over to South America, Australia, and other places that currently supply China's commodities demand.

Meanwhile, back in the United States, stocks, bonds, real estate, consumer spending, and government spending will be down, inflation

A Whole Lot of Money Will Go to "Money Heaven"!

People often ask where the massive amount of investment capital in stocks, bonds, and real estate will go in the future. The answer is Money Heaven, a place where wealth goes to permanently disappear. Most investment money will go to Money Heaven in the future because most people won't pull their money out of falling stocks, real estate, and bonds soon enough. Anyone who doesn't move money out early won't be able to move it out at all. That's because other people will have moved their money out of those investments earlier, most importantly, and there will be little demand for those investments afterwards. Hence, the values of most people's investments will decline dramatically.

At that point, most people will realize they should have moved their money out, but it will be too late. Their portfolios will have been automatically rebalanced for them, heavily weighted toward Money Heaven. For the money managers and financial advisers who will preside over this reweighting of investors' portfolios into Money Heaven, it's going to feel a lot less like Money Heaven and a lot more like Money Hell.

and interest rates will be up, and the bubble economy will be over. In the coming Aftershock, the global multibubble crash will kick off a deep, long-term downturn here and around the globe.

Please understand that we are not intrinsically pessimistic or doom-and-gloomy by nature. We are not driven by any particular political agenda, left, right, or sideways. We are not fanatical gold bugs (although we think gold will do quite well). And we are not paranoid survivalists who think you should run out and build a fallout shelter filled with two years' worth of food. We are just calling it as we see it, based on facts and rational analysis, and we would like to help you see it, too, while there's still time to protect your assets and prepare.

Why Don't We Have the Aftershock Right Now? Two Temporary "Airbags" Are Supporting the Other Partially Popped Bubbles

Question: We have four falling bubbles but they are not yet fully popped. What is keeping these bubbles partially inflated?
Answer: The pumping up of the final two bubbles!

The easiest way to understand the economy right now is to look at it as a set of deflating bubbles (stock, real estate, private credit, and consumer spending) whose fall is being cushioned by the rapid inflation of the two final airbag bubbles: the dollar bubble and the government debt bubble. By rapidly pumping up these two bubbles, the government is temporarily postponing the fall of America's multibubble economy. Because they are cushioning and supporting the other bursting bubbles, we like to think of these last two yet-to-pop bubbles as America's Airbags—they are preventing a dangerous crash for a while, but eventually they, too, will fall. When these final airbags overinflate and burst, the rest of our bubble economy will burst, too, bringing on the global Aftershock. But, these airbags aren't going to pop immediately, and that's why we don't have the Aftershock right now.

Airbag 1: Massive Government Borrowing

Massive government borrowing (the government debt bubble) is boosting the economy. In fact, most of the growth in the economy since the financial crisis has been directly related to the massive 500 percent increase in federal government borrowing since 2007. And let's not forget that the U.S. deficit wasn't exactly tiny in 2007, when it was already weighing in at $170 billion. Now it's $800 to $900 billion in 2013. That is a big fat government debt bubble becoming a truly colossal government debt bubble.

Naturally, with the country awash in so much deficit spending, the not-yet-popped government debt bubble is acting like a still-inflated, protective airbag, keeping the other bubbles from fully falling. Surely, had we not borrowed and spent all that extra money, the U.S. economy would be in far worse shape today. The problem is, airbags eventually pop, too. By pumping up this protective airbag so gigantically, it will only make the future crash all the bigger.

Airbag 2: Massive Money Printing

Massive money printing (the dollar bubble) by the Federal Reserve, mostly in the form of quantitative easing or QE, has also been acting as an airbag, keeping the United States and world economies protected from the popping bubbles. Massive money printing has

worked like Viagra to reinvigorate the stock market bubble whenever it shows signs of deflating. This temporary lift to the stock market also indirectly boosts the rest of the consumer-based economy.
Stock investors spend more when their portfolios are up, and studies show that even people who own no stocks spend more when the
stock market is doing well. So massive money printing has been
doing its temporary airbag job, first with QE1 and QE2 (2009–
2011), and more recently with QE3—or QEternity, as we like to call
it, because it has no end date. More on this later in the book.

But the Airbags Only Postpone the Inevitable

The trouble with pumping up America's airbags (the dollar bubble and government debt bubble) is that it is just a short-term fix.
And worse than being just a short-term fix, it is a short-term fix that
comes at an incredibly high long-term price. We're not just kicking
the can down the road, we're piling up sticks of dynamite in that
can and it is going to cause an even more massive explosion later,
when we can kick the can down the road no further.

Rising Future Inflation Is Key

When the airbags fail, all the bubbles will pop. What will cause the
airbags to fail? *Rising future inflation.* In a terribly ironic twist,
the very things we are doing to support the economy (by printing
money and borrowing money) will lead to what eventually pops
these airbags and causes the rest of the bubbles to fall even harder.
(For more details about inflation, please see *Aftershock*, Second
Edition.)

Right now, we can keep on borrowing (pumping up airbag 1,
the government debt bubble) as long as we can keep on printing
money (pumping up airbag 2, the dollar bubble). Massive money
printing keeps interest rates low so we can keep borrowing. We will
keep printing money to fund our borrowing for as long as we can
print money *without creating inflation.* As long as inflation remains
low, as it is today, America's airbags can continue to keep America's
Bubble Economy from fully popping. Rising future inflation (and
the rising interest rates it will cause) can be avoided for a while longer, but it cannot be avoided forever. We simply cannot increase the

money supply threefold, with even more money printing to come, and not eventually get some very significant inflation.

Rising inflation will force interest rates higher, whether the Fed likes it or not. The Fed can't control interest rates once we have significant inflation. Printing money can solve many of our ills short term, but one ill it can never solve is inflation. That inflation will push up interest rates, and rising interest rates will devastate the stock, bond, and real estate markets, and all the bubbles will fall.

Chapter 3 will give you a deeper understanding about the coming inflation, why we don't have it now, and why we won't be able to avoid it later. For now, the point we want to make clear is that future inflation is key. When rising inflation and rising interest rates force the airbags to fail (i.e., when we can do no more money printing and borrowing), all the bubbles will fall. Until then, the airbags will hold off the coming Aftershock right up until they no longer work.

Why Don't Most Conventional Investors See This Coming?

The reasons for the current widespread bubble blindness by conventional investors are many. They include:

- A deep faith in "the myth of the natural growth rate" that is supposed to guarantee us continued economic growth no matter what. (The myth of the natural growth rate is described in detail in Chapter 4.)
- Denial: Human psychology makes it difficult to think rationally in the face of things we don't want to be true. (Investor psychology is also addressed in Chapter 4.)
- What we call the "Hamptons Effect": Conventional investors and analysts desperately need the current status quo (from which they greatly benefit) to continue; otherwise, they will lose everything: their jobs, wealth, homes (in the Hamptons, for example, for wealthy New York investors), social status, and so on. These people will fight to the end to keep what they have, even if that means complete bubble blindness. If you are counting on bubble-blind people to guide you, we suggest you keep your expectations low.

What's a Savvy Aftershock Investor to Do?

The deadly combination of declining productivity and the multi-bubble economy is giving us massive debt, massive money printing, future rising inflation and interest rates, falling asset bubbles, and an increasingly dangerous investment environment. Conventional wisdom on investing, such as the buy-and-hold value investing practiced by Warren Buffett, for example, will not hold up well under these worsening conditions. Instead of conventional wisdom, we need a new kind of Aftershock wisdom (see Chapter 4) for a new way of investing (see Chapters 6 to 14) that will guide you to and through the coming Aftershock. Ignore this new Aftershock wisdom at your peril.

The key to Aftershock wisdom for successful investing is to ignore the economic cheerleaders and stay focused on what really matters: *inflation*. Rising future inflation and future rising interest rates pose the biggest threat to the future health of your portfolio. Not too many people are worried about inflation and interest rates right now because both are remarkably low and pose no immediate threat. But rising inflation and rising interest rates will strike the final blow to the vulnerable dollar and government debt bubbles, and will send your hard-earned assets to Money Heaven faster than you can log onto your online brokerage account and hit "Sell!"

The rest of this book is entirely focused on helping you protect your wealth, whether it is $200 or $200 million. But there is only so much we can tell you in a book. This is an evolving economy and investment environment, and therefore the actions you take must also evolve over time. Beyond our books, you can keep up with us through our newsletters, or invest with us, and you will see each step we take as the Aftershock approaches. With or without our help, please understand that you must actively keep up with changing economic conditions in order to correctly manage and protect your assets in this increasingly dangerous investment environment.

CHAPTER 3

Aftershock Update: They Read Our Playbook—The World Is Printing Money

As we have said before, massive money printing can solve almost any financial problem. Money printing allows governments to borrow more massively, it calms nervous stock and bond markets, and it helps boost investor confidence and general economic activity. Except for that one pesky problem (future inflation), money printing seems to be good for what ails us in the short term and, just as we predicted, that is exactly what many countries have decided to do.

Central Banks Gone Wild

To keep interest rates low, boost investor confidence, and stimulate their economies, governments around the world have opened the floodgates of newly printed money.

In addition to the $85 billion per month we now print (as of mid-2013), which has increased our monetary base by 373 percent, Europe has increased its money supply by 206 percent to support its economies and markets. This has also taken pressure off the U.S. financial markets as well and helped pave the way for the U.S. stock market rally in the first half of 2013.

Not to be left out of the party, England has also continued to print, increasing its money supply by 343 percent since the global financial crisis of 2008.

Meanwhile, China's massive government-controlled banking machine also continues to stimulate its economy with a whopping 500 percent increase in its money supply (more on China later in this chapter).

And Japan, with an economy of only about a third the size of the United States, is now printing an astonishing $75 billion per month. To put that into perspective, it would be the equivalent of the United States printing $200 billion per month—more than twice our current rate, which is already very huge.

All this adds up to a truly enormous amount of worldwide money printing (see Figure 3.1). According to JPMorgan Chase, the U.S. Federal Reserve, the European Central Bank (ECB), the Bank of England, and the Bank of Japan combined have collectively printed more than $3.9 trillion since 2009. By comparison, the entire money supply of the United States, the world's largest economy, was only about $800 billion in 2007.

Interestingly, the earlier discussions about an "exit strategy" for the Fed to pull back some of the new money out of the system, which was quite in vogue a couple of years ago, seems to have been *completely* forgotten. Not only are we not pulling back any of the new money, we are printing more and more new money with no end in sight. As of the printing of this book, there was talk that the Fed would slightly decrease the enormous amount of money it was printing but it turned out to be just talk. The Fed decided not to reduce money printing at all.

All of this money printing has helped boost economies and especially financial markets around the world. It may not appear like much of a boost because world economic growth has been so slow. But it is working, especially on the financial markets. Without this massive money printing, financial markets could melt down.

In the case of Europe, it is easy to see that bond yields on Spanish and Italian debt would have quickly spiraled out of control without massive ECB intervention to keep them lower. Out-of-control interest rates in such large countries as Spain and Italy would rattle financial markets around the world, taking the European, U.S., and Japanese economies down with them. So the money printing madness may not look like it's helping because European, U.S., and Japanese economic growth is so slow, but it is most certainly helping keep the financial

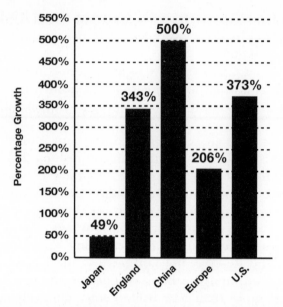

Figure 3.1   Around the World, Central Banks Are Printing Money

In response to the 2008 financial crisis, central banks around the world, not just the U.S. Federal Reserve, have responded by printing money as shown by central banks' balance sheet growth since 2008. This is supporting the world's bubble economy.

Source: Bloomberg.

markets from deteriorating dramatically, which would have a severe negative impact on all of those economies.

But, of course, massive money printing, while supportive in the short term, is simply another bubble, not a solution. And just because other countries are doing it, too, doesn't mean it won't have negative impacts on each economy. Money printing in each country will still drive up inflation in that economy, regardless of how many other countries are also printing money.

In the United States, the world's biggest bubble economy, pumping up the huge dollar bubble with massive money printing is going to cause significant inflation and rising interest rates, which will make the bubbles crash even harder and more uncontrollable later. Rising inflation and interest rates will pop what is left of the first four partially popped bubbles (stocks, real estate, private debt, and consumer spending) and will fully burst the last two: the dollar and the government debt bubbles.

In the meantime, no one wants you to think about that.

Economists Continue to Ignore the Risks of Money Printing

As with any bubble, the key to its short-term success is *ignoring it.* If you don't ignore the bubble, it is a lot harder to keep it going. So part of the key to the short-term success of this money-printing madness will be for cheerleading financial analysts and economists to overlook the bubble it is creating. For help in overlooking bubbles it is always good to have some academic support. And, sure enough, as if on command, there is growing support for a new economic theory called New Monetarist Theory.

The group of economists who support this theory think that deficits are good and cannot cause economic problems. Actually, deficits help solve economic problems. They say governments can borrow massive amounts of money and never have to default on their debt because their central banks can always buy their debt with more printed money. But these economists don't just believe this will help in the short term, they see it as an acceptable, even desirable, long-term solution because they don't see any long-term problems with it. They believe that this printed money won't cause inflation because the new money is simply a "balance sheet adjustment" in the economy. Like a magic trick, it doesn't really count and it won't hurt us in any way.

New Monetarist Theory is like Keynesian economics on steroids. And, to a large degree, at least in the short term, it is true. Government borrowing *does* help the economy. And, yes, the Federal Reserve, with printed money, can buy *every single* government bond Congress wants to sell if need be. Hence, there is no possibility of a failed Treasury auction and no possibility of default even if government debt became incredibly massive.

Of course, as we have been pointing out for years, there is a giant flaw in this plan. Using printed money to buy bonds will eventually cause rising future inflation!

Unlike Most Current Economists, the Federal Reserve Actually Knows that Printing Money Causes Inflation

According to the Federal Reserve's own analysis—which mainstream economists seem to want to ignore—there is a very close correlation between the amount of money printed and the amount of future inflation created. According a report published by the Federal Reserve Bank of Minneapolis in 1995, the historical correlation between inflation and money printing is nearly 1-to-1. In other words, if you increase the money supply by X percent, it will eventually cause about that same percentage increase in inflation.

The authors of the report, George T. McCandless Jr. and Warren E. Weber, concluded: "A central bank can be confident that over the long run a higher growth rate of the money supply will result in a *proportionately higher* inflation rate." Table 3.1, taken from the Fed report, shows just how strong they found the correlation to be.

This isn't the only study to show a high correlation between increasing money supply and rising future inflation. In fact, the same Fed research report cited above also references many additional studies that show this same high level of correlation between money growth and inflation in many countries, including the United States, over many years (see Table 3.2).

Yet somehow, our learned economists don't point out that increasing our monetary base by more than 300 percent will likely bring us nearly the same percentage of future inflation, and they don't see this as a huge future threat to the U.S. economy—or if they do, they are not sounding the alarms and trying to stop it. They want the short term benefit no matter what the long term price because if they didn't do it, we'd be in a deep recession today. Perhaps more importantly, the as asset bubbles would pop.

Table 3.1   Correlation Coefficients for Money Supply Growth and Inflation

21 OECD countries, including the United States, Japan, Israel, Canada, Australia, and many Europe countries (from 1960 to 1990)	M0 .894	M1 .940	M2 .958

Inflation is defined as changes in a measure of consumer prices.
M0 is defined as currency plus bank reserves.
Source of basic data: International Monetary Fund.

Looking at data from 21 countries from 1960 to 1990, every measure of the money supply, including M0, M1, and M2, shows a near 1.0 correlation between money printing and inflation.
Source: Federal Reserve Bank of Minneapolis.

Table 3.2 Many Studies Confirm the High Correlation between Money Growth and Inflation

Author (and year published)	Money	Inflation	Countries	Time Period	Finding
			Study Characteristics	Time Series	
Vogel (1974)	Currency + demand deposits	Consumer prices	16 Latin American Countries	1950–1969	Proportionate changes in inflation rate within two years of changes in money growth
Lucas (1980)	M1	Consumer prices	United States	1955–1975	Strong positive correlation: Coefficient closer to one the more filter stresses low frequencies
Dwyer and Hafer (1988)	NA	GDP deflator	62 countries	1979–1984	Strong positive correlation
Barro (1990)	Hand-to-hand currency	Consumer prices	83 countries	1950–1987	Strong positive association
Pakko (1994)	Currency + bank deposits	Consumer prices	13 former Soviet republics	1992 and 1993	Positive relationship
Poole (1994)	Broad money	NA	All countries in World Bank tables	1970–1980 and 1980–1991	Strong positive correlation
Rolnick and Weber	Various	Various	9 countries	Various	Strong positive correlation for fiat money regimes

NA = not available.
Seven separate studies analyzing data from more than 100 countries from 1950 to 1991 confirm the Fed's assertion that there is a strong correlation between money printing and inflation.
Source: U.S. Federal Reserve

We would like to ask today's economists: What is so different this time that all these studies are no longer valid? Have the laws of supply and demand suddenly stopped and now we can print all the money we want with no negative consequences?

If it is true that massive money printing will magically no longer cause future inflation, then, using the logic of the New Monetarists, the government could simply eliminate all taxes and borrow all the money it needs by selling bonds to the Fed, who will buy them with newly printed money. No taxes and lots of government spending (funded with printed money) certainly would boost the economy! And if all that printed money doesn't cause inflation, we have created the perfect solution to any economy's ills. It would truly be "Money from Heaven," and it could basically move any economy in the world into hyper-drive.

But, of course, Money from Heaven does not really exist. As we like to say, Money from Heaven is the Path to Hell. It is amazing that such a line of economic thought is getting increasingly greater attention. It is also a reflection of the sad state of the economics profession that this nonrigorous line of thinking represents cutting edge nonmainstream economists. That's a big problem because over the next few decades, almost all real change in economic thought will come outside of the mainstream. That this represents current nonmainstream thinking shows how far the field of economics has yet to go.

The miserable failure of the whole economics profession to see any of this coming is a key reason we are in this current economic mess and, more importantly, it will be a key part of the reason we will have so much trouble getting out of this mess after the Aftershock hits. Moving economics into a much more sensible direction is so important that we devoted a whole chapter to this issue in a previous book *Aftershock*, Second Edition (Chapter 9).

Why Isn't Inflation Higher Now?

We are often asked why we keep harping on the dangers of future inflation (and the rising interest rates it will cause) when inflation is still quite low. If money printing is so bad for us, why hasn't it caused inflation yet?

What Exactly is Money "Printing"?

When we say money printing, we don't mean the actual *printing* of the dollar bills in your wallet. That task is handled by the Bureau of Engraving and Printing, and has little to do with the money supply.

Money printing, or perhaps we should say money *creation*, is done through the Federal Reserve's open market operations. Based on guidelines set by the Federal Open Market Committee (FOMC), the trading desk at the Federal Reserve Bank of New York will contact a handful of dealers (banks and investment banks like Citibank or Morgan Stanley) to purchase bonds from bank clients.

Since the Fed's open market operations generally deal with US government bonds, and since the Fed is the central bank to both the Treasury Department and banks around the country, the transactions are very easy to record. The bonds are debited directly from the dealer's electronic bonds account at the Fed, and the funds to buy the bonds are credited to the dealer's Federal Reserve account. The dealer will then adjust the accounts of its clients accordingly.

Here's the catch: Before the transaction takes place, the funds did not exist. The simple act of entering it onto the Fed's balance sheet is all it takes to make money out of thin air.

First, we need to point out that the current inflation rate is not zero, so we do have *some* inflation already. The government's conservative inflation statistics put the Consumer Price Index (CPI) at around 2 percent.

But so far, inflation has not been high enough to increase interest rates, which is the big negative effect of inflation in a bubble economy. And inflation likely won't be high enough to increase interest rates for at least the rest of 2013 and probably longer, even though the U.S. monetary base has already been increased more than threefold and more new money is pouring into the economy at the current rate of $85 billion per month.

So, why isn't inflation higher?

Lag Factors and "The Fool in the Shower"

Inflation isn't higher now due to what are called lag factors. There is always a lag time between printing money and inflation. We discussed lag factors in more detail in *Aftershock*.

The easiest way to understand lag factors is the "fool in the shower" analogy first used by Nobel Prize–winning monetarist economist Milton Friedman. The fool in the shower turns on the hot water and at first, all he gets is very cold water. So he turns the knob higher to get hot water, and still nothing, so he keeps turning it up more and more, rather than waiting for the hot water to arrive. Then, all of a sudden, the hot water hits and scalds him.

That's what will happen with future inflation and the current lag factors. We don't get inflation immediately, so we see no harm in "turning up the hot water" by increasing the money supply. All we see are the short-term benefits, so we keep printing more money without getting burnt. In fact, as we have said before, the reason inflation could be very high in the future is not because of the money we have already printed, but, more importantly, because of the money we will likely print in the future. More money printing will go from being somewhat discretionary to being mandatory due to the need for increasing support of financial markets here and abroad. Since we are simply trying to support falling bubbles in housing, stocks, private credit, and consumer spending, there will be a continuing need to keep printing more money, otherwise the bubbles will again fall. Not that the money we have already printed won't create inflation—it will. But the greatest contributor to future inflation will be *future* money printing.

However, even with massive money printing, a lot can go wrong long before we get high inflation. Printed money helps to solve some of our economic problems short term, but it doesn't work perfectly and it isn't a one-stop cure-all. Governments can print money, but that doesn't mean they have an economic steering wheel, accelerator, and brake that allows them to drive the economy perfectly. Much of the economy is entirely out of their control. So even if we don't have high inflation, we can still have financial crises, falling stock markets, and sluggish real estate markets.

In all fairness, it is true that if we were really willing to open the money-printing spigot, we probably could solve all our problems at least in the short term ($10 trillion would likely do the trick). But few people would support it. And, that tells you that they actually know more than they are saying—they know that printing lots of money will eventually create inflation—otherwise, why not print $10 trillion right now? They know full well the dangers; they are just hoping beyond hope that somehow $2 trillion dollars won't be dangerous and won't cause future inflation.

Another Reason We Don't See More Inflation Now: Massaged Statistics

As we mentioned in Chapter 1, another key reason that many investors are not too worried about massive money printing causing high future inflation is because the government's official measures of current inflation are deliberately designed to hide the real inflation rate. We are not the only ones who think this way. A popular web site called www.shadowstats.com attempts to calculate a more complete measure of inflation. Beginning in the late 1980s, the government changed the way it calculates inflation so that the CPI would appear lower than it had in the past. According to shadowstats.com, if the current CPI was calculated the way it used to be in 1980, today's inflation rate would be closer to 8 to 9 percent.

The Good Doctor

Some people say that we are anti-American because we talk about America's Bubble Economy, but we most certainly are not. As we have so often said, this is not just America's Bubble Economy, it is the World's Bubble Economy. China is an excellent example of this. In fact, we try very hard to be *anti-nothing*. We try to be unbiased,

(continued)

although we know that many people say that and are not. But we hope we are. Given our very pointed assertion in *America's Bubble Economy* and *Aftershock* that the United States will absolutely perform the best after the Aftershock because of the inherent flexibility of its economy and the structure of its economy, which encourages growth and innovation, it seems that would indicate that we are not anti-United States. In addition, we also say that China and its non-market, heavily government-controlled economy will do the worst (with Japan doing the next worst and Europe doing the best outside of the United States). We further say that it will be so bad that there will ultimately be a popular revolt against the government (a Tiananmen Square that succeeds) that will move the country to a more democratic state.

The point of this example is that we try not to have any bias, although after reading this, some people would say we are too pro-United States. It's hard to please everyone, and we certainly do not try. We try to call it as we see it, just as any good doctor should in diagnosing and treating a patient. We strive to be the best and most unbiased economic doctor in the house. Short term, that may anger some people—investors, economists, and financial media members—and it may please others. Long term, we are absolutely sure it is the best, and only, approach to take if we are to truly understand and solve our economic problems.

Even Before We Get High Inflation, Other Potential Triggers Could Accelerate a Downtrend in the U.S. Economy

There are many possible situations that could accelerate a downturn in the economy. Some are more likely than others and some are less probable but are still possible, depending on unpredictable wildcard events. Potential triggers include:

- China's Slowdown and Possible Construction Meltdown
- Continued Recession in the Eurozone
- Collapsing Growth in Emerging Market
- The Passage of Time

China's Slowdown and Possible Construction Meltdown

China may be considered one of the strongest and fastest growing economies, but don't be fooled: China is now a bubble economy. It wasn't earlier, although much of their growth prior to 2008 was dependent on our own rising economy. But more recently, especially since the global financial crisis in 2008, China has been self-inflating its own bubbles.

Just as in the United States, China is pumping up two giant air bags to try to support its bubble economy: massive money printing and massive borrowing. But in China, the story is a little different. Their government doesn't borrow money at the rate we do, instead they print massively, give the money to the banks, and the banks lend it out to stimulate the economy. This is creating a massive Chinese debt bubble. Debt, both public and private combined, as a percentage of GDP, has grown substantially since 2008 indicating an increasing reliance on greater amounts of debt for economic growth (see Figure 3.2).

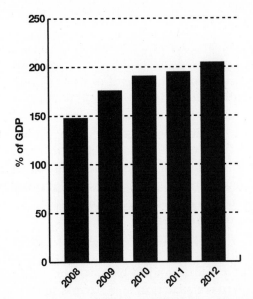

Figure 3.2 China's Increasing Debt-to-GDP Ratio (Combined Public and Private)

For years, China maintained a stable ratio of debt to GDP, despite big rises in both. However, since 2008, lending has exploded relative to GDP.

Sources: People's Bank of China, State Administration of Foreign Exchange, CEIC, CLSA Asia-Pacific Markets.

As in our own multibubble economy, one bubble pushes up another. In China, their massive debt bubble is fueling a huge and unsustainable real estate construction bubble. In the last decade, China's construction boom is unprecedented in human history. By some estimates, as much as 50 percent of their GDP is now driven by fixed investment, a large part of which is in construction. That is almost an inconceivable amount of new construction.

By comparison, at the height of the U.S. housing bubble, construction represented only about 17 percent of our economy. During the height of Spain's housing bubble, it was 23 percent. And in Dubai—the world's former poster child for supersized real estate—construction approached about 30 percent of GDP at the peak of its speculative construction boom. China seems to be exceeding them all.

China's massive construction bubble is driven not by real economic demand but heavily by massive bank lending. The government prints money, gives it to Chinese banks, and then forces them to lend it out—often for construction projects that will never see a dime of profit. For example, they built the stunningly huge South China Mall which is twice the size of the Mall of America (our biggest one), but now sits more than 90 percent vacant. More recently, loaned money was used to build the mammoth New Century Global Center, three times the size of our Pentagon.

All this tremendous lending with little chance of full repayment puts China's banks in a very vulnerable position. China escaped a credit crisis in June 2013 with government intervention and has since recovered. This seems eerily familiar to our own Bear Sterns crisis: we dealt with it quickly and declared all was well, only to later face an even bigger crisis with the loss of Lehman Brothers. The recent Chinese financial crisis, although resolved for now, may very well signal more trouble ahead.

It is hard to see it going any other way, given the huge level of debt and the unlikeliness of repayment. So we think there is a good chance that China will face a bubble pop and economic meltdown due to a collapse in construction and a banking crisis.

For the world's bubble economy, a meltdown by China would have unusually harsh consequences. That is part of the reason so many people are cheerleaders for China's construction bubble, even though they wouldn't normally support such extreme non-market intervention in their own country.

China is not only the second biggest economy in the world; it is providing almost *all* of the growth in the world since 2008. So, any big slowdown or meltdown in China will have a big impact on the world and on the United States, depressing the exports of many countries. In addition, any major problem in China's banking system will impact many countries and will hurt our banks, as well.

Like so much about China and its economy, it is hard to know exactly what is happening or when such a meltdown could occur. But it is likely we will see a more pronounced slowdown in the next couple years. Just like our own government, the Chinese government will fight this with even more money printing, but they have been doing this for a while now, and at some point it simply won't work. China is already a huge economy, and maintaining its high growth rates will become increasingly difficult under any circumstances. And when that growth stops, it won't go gently into the night, but rather will likely go from dream straight to nightmare.

Jim Chanos—A Realistic View of China

There are a few voices out there saying that China's problems are far greater than most economists and financial analysts realize, most notably hedge fund manager Jim Chanos of Kynikos Fund, which is why we give him an ABE Award for Intellectual Courage (ABE stands for the name of our first book, *America's Bubble Economy*).

Jim Chanos is the founder and president of Kynikos Associates, a hedge fund with a particular focus on short selling. While the practice of short selling has been somewhat controversial, especially in recent years, one value of companies like Kynikos is that they can point out critical flaws in the market long before most people see them. For example, back in 2000, Kynikos took short positions in a huge energy company, one that *Fortune* had consistently labeled America's most innovative company. Within the next 14 months, the stock had lost 99 percent of its value and the company ended up in bankruptcy. You've probably heard of Enron.

Chanos admits that he's not a "macro guy." His focus is intensive fundamental research and analysis to find stocks that are overvalued. But that hasn't stopped him from seeing some big picture problems,

(continued)

too, and in recent years he has pinpointed a major bubble in the world economy: the Chinese construction bubble.

Chanos noticed several years ago that property development in China was reaching unsustainable proportions. If the average Chinese couple makes a combined $8,000 or so a year, how can they afford condominiums that can easily cost up to $150,000? It didn't add up. Much of this growth was driven by bad loans pushed by the government. In fact, Chanos found that many new apartment buildings stay empty and are flipped from speculator to speculator on the greater fool theory.

Mr. Chanos' insights aren't especially popular in a financial community that's counting on China to lead the global economic recovery. He has been publicly berated by some, though the attacks against him tend to be very short on data. Jim Chanos deserves big kudos for ignoring the cheerleaders and letting the facts speak for themselves.

Continued Recession in the Eurozone

Europe has been in recession for almost 2 years. The Netherlands is in its third recession since 2008. Spain and Greece's unemployment rates are now about 27 percent. Eurozone automobile sales are the lowest in 20 years. And even Germany, the largest and strongest economy in the Eurozone, is facing sluggish exports and little growth.

Yes, Europe's Purchasing Managers' Index (PMI) has recently turned slightly toward the positive as of this writing in mid-2013, indicating a change from declining to nearly flat growth. Britain's GDP is now growing 0.6 percent annually, barely avoiding its third recession since 2008. But that's hardly a big turnaround, and Europe's continued economic troubles far outweigh the small improvements.

With the world's largest consumer market flat or declining, the drop in consumption has put downward pressure on U.S. and Chinese exports. This has contributed to the slowdown in economic growth in the United States and other countries, which also decreases multinational company earnings.

Europe has no immediate solution to these problems, other than to print more money, just as we are doing. And just as we are experiencing, money printing in the Eurozone is unlikely to create a significant recovery. Instead, it will just keep the problems from worsening or from worsening more quickly.

Continued flat or falling growth in the Eurozone could accelerate the economic troubles in the United States by further depressing manufacturing and reducing our exports. This helps explain why Caterpillar—considered a bellwether indicator of global business activity, construction, and mining—recently downgraded its forecast for the pace of the global recovery for 2013 and 2014.

As much as some Americans may like to think that what happens in Europe stays in Europe, that just isn't true. Continued economic malaise there affects us here, and any future downturns will continue to impact U.S. exports and growth. That wouldn't be so bad if we didn't already have a multibubble economy with troubles of our own. But with our current fake recovery, any future economic or banking crisis in Europe will have negative consequences for our economy and banks.

Collapsing Growth in Emerging Markets

The emerging markets—such as India, Russia, Korea, Mexico, Taiwan, Brazil, and others—have economies that are highly dependent on their exports of commodities and manufactured goods. During the more recent years of the rising U.S. and world bubble economies, these economies were growing rapidly from relatively low levels, hence the term *emerging*. But now that our bubbles are no longer rising as they did before and, in some cases are falling, much of the growth in the emerging markets is slowing down too.

Brazil provides a good example. Through most of the 2000s prior to 2008, Brazil's economy (now the fifth-largest in the world) grew as much as 6 percent per year, fueled in part by China's demand for its natural resources.

Then after the global financial crisis hit in late 2008, Brazil's GDP nearly came to a standstill in 2009. Its exports and GDP soared again in 2010 due to China's initial burst of massive bank lending, but have steadily and dramatically declined each year since, as China's growth has continued to slow (see Figure 3.3).

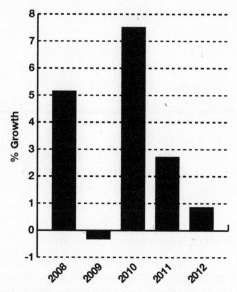

Figure 3.3   Brazil's GDP Growth Rate since 2008

Emerging markets such as Brazil are slowing dramatically, in large part due to China's slowing growth.

Source: World Bank.

And the problem is not just in Brazil. Russia, where enormous profits had been and are still being made due to high oil prices, is now seeing near zero GDP growth. Although not an emerging market, Australia is also feeling the pain. A major supplier of iron, copper, and coal to China, Australia's exports have dropped and growth has slowed dramatically.

As each county's economy has slowed down due to falling exports, they in turn import less from other countries and so the contagion spreads.

The United States is not immune. It is certainly true that when the U.S. bubble economy bursts, the rest of the world will feel the pain because we will buy a whole lot less from various countries. But the converse is also true: when the emerging markets suffer, our U.S. exports worldwide will decline.

As we've said before, it's not just America's Bubble Economy but the world's bubble economy that will burst. A sharp downturn in emerging markets could speed up the bubbles bursting in the U.S.

*"We're still the same, great company we've
always been, only we've ceased to exist."*

The Passage of Time

While we tend to focus on possible future dangers that could kick off the coming Aftershock, the most likely trigger will simply be the passage of time. It would be quite wonderful if we really could print all the money we wanted forever, without ever having to face bad consequences. Think of all the problems we could solve! Think of all the fun we could have! But such nonsense is the stuff of childhood dreams. Of course, we cannot print money endlessly without a future cost.

Even if, by some miracle or magic trick, high future inflation is somehow avoided, what about all these bubbles? In what universe do rising bubbles never fall? Sooner or later, *bubbles always pop.* That is why, regardless of what triggers may or may not occur, regardless of what manipulations may be deployed, even regardless of what marginal economic growth we may be able to produce, *time happens.* The passage of time, alone, will be enough to make the colinked multibubble U.S. and world economies eventually burst.

Remember, smart reader, this recovery is 100 percent fake (see Chapter 1), and fake is never permanent. It isn't a question of if this will end, only a question of when.

Do the math. A little bit of new money will eventually cause a little bit of inflation. A large amount of new money will eventually cause a large amount of inflation.

It's just a matter of time before that happens.

Staying Afloat in a Sinking Economy

We did not write our series of books in order to get you to buy something from us. All our current products and services grew out of reader demand over many years. For those who want to prepare for, not just read about, the coming Aftershock, we offer the following:

You are welcome to visit our web site, www.aftershockpublishing .com, for more information as we approach the Aftershock. While you are there, you may sign up for a two-month free trial of our popular **Aftershock Investor's Resource Package** (IRP), which includes our monthly newsletter, live conference calls, and more. Or you may reach us at **703-787-0139** or info@aftershockpublishing.com.

We also offer **Private Consulting** for individuals, businesses, and groups. Please contact coauthor Cindy Spitzer at **443-980-7367** or visit www.aftershockconsultants.com for more information.

Through our investment management firm, **Absolute Investment Management**, we provide hands-on, Aftershock-focused asset management services on an individually managed account basis. For details, please call **703-774-3520** or e-mail absolute@ aftershockpublishing.com.

The Market Cliff

NOT YOUR FATHER'S DOWN CYCLE

Remember the "Fiscal Cliff"? At the end of 2012, the media was all abuzz about an artificial deadline previously set by Congress after which a slew of budget cuts and tax hikes would go into effect unless lawmakers could reach a budget agreement. Congress had the power to create the artificial Fiscal Cliff deadline, and Congress had the power—although not necessarily the immediate internal agreement—to avoid this artificial cliff, which eventually they did.

The kind of cliff that we want to introduce you to now is not a cliff that can be avoided by an act of Congress, the Federal Reserve, or by any part of the U.S. government. In fact, this new kind of cliff cannot be avoided at all because it will be the natural and unavoidable result of years of enormous government borrowing and money printing. This new cliff is what we will inevitably end up with when massive government stimulus to support a multibubble economy ceases to be effective or even possible, and instead fundamental economic gravity kicks in and the bubbles pop. This is what we call the Market Cliff, and the United States is headed straight for it.

The Market Cliff Won't Be Just a "Down Cycle"

The mantra we often hear in a down market—but rarely during a boom—is that markets are cyclical. Every valley, say the cheerleaders, is just a precursor to the next peak, and every new peak will be even higher than the last. There is some historical truth to this. In a healthy, growing economy (like we had up until the late 1970s), market up cycles do tend to follow market down cycles. And during the rising bubble economy that began in the early 1980s, every market down cycle was reliably followed by an up cycle sooner or later because the overall movement of a rising bubble is generally up.

Even now that the rising bubble economy has been replaced with a sagging bubble economy being held up by massive money printing and borrowing, we can continue to expect more up and down swings in the stock and bond markets. But over time, as the artificial stimulus supporting the economy and the markets becomes increasingly ineffective, we'll likely see these up and down swings happening more frequently. With each downswing, the cheerleaders will surely declare that it's just a temporary dip triggered by irrational panic, and of course they will claim vindication when the markets temporarily rebound.

But there will be no immediate rebound once we hit the Market Cliff. This downturn won't be soon followed by an upturn because it won't be based on irrational panic but on legitimate fear of a falling multibubble economy and a stock market that simply isn't worth what investors used to think. This time the downturn won't be cyclical. Going over the Market Cliff will be the end of the bubble economy.

When the Medicine Becomes Poison: Inflation and Rising Interest Rates Will Push Us over the Market Cliff

Fake recoveries and upbeat investor psychology can keep the stock market and the general economy on the upswing for a substantial amount of time, especially in an economy as large and as traditionally solid as ours. And we could easily relax and think this party could go on indefinitely, if there were no future downside to massive money printing. But, sadly, there are certain economic truths that cannot be forever avoided, and one of them is the economic fact that massive money printing eventually does cause inflation. Inflation, in turn, eventually does lead to higher interest rates, and rising interest rates are highly poisonous to a bubble economy.

Of course, as we already know, the markets have largely turned a deaf ear to the possibility of inflation, in spite of enormous amounts of money printing by the Fed. But avoiding reality doesn't permanently defer it. As with any bubble, the biggest enemy to the status quo is *time*. When it takes increasing amounts of new money just to keep the economy from falling, sooner or later people begin to lose faith.

At the same time, the medicine of money printing will become the poison of inflation and rising interest rates. That will create increasing downward pressure on the fake recovery, as it would even in a real recovery. But for a bubble economy in a fake recovery, the consequences are far greater because the increasing downward pressure of inflation and interest rates will force the bubbles to pop. For the stock and bond markets, this will be the Market Cliff.

Exactly when we will hit and go over the Market Cliff is hard to predict. Even after a bubble pops, people don't know the moment it happened. Prior to a bubble bursting, there are always people who recognize the problem early, but they tend to have little effect. (The fact that we have so many concerned readers is testament to that.)

But at some point, enough people get scared and pull out, and that sets the dominoes in motion, spreading fear throughout the markets and collapsing asset values. Sometimes this happens due to irrational fears—or at least it *begins* as irrational fears—for example, back when irrational fear used to drive occasional runs on a bank, followed by rational fear that the bank could go under. Or sometimes the initial fear can be very rational, as it will be in this case when people begin to wake up to the fact that the current bubble-based economy is no longer sustainable.

Why Hasn't the Market Cliff Happened Yet?

The Market Cliff hasn't happened yet because there is so much at stake. The coming multibubble pop will be bigger than any previous bubble pops and therefore far more devastating to the U.S. and world economies when it bursts. Because the stakes are so high, the current bubble economy is being heavily supported by the government. By contrast, the popping of the Internet bubble in 2000 was significant, especially if you were invested in dot-com stocks, but that bubble was only a small part of the economy and we could afford that inevitable correction, even if a bit painful.

However, the price of losing a whole series of conjoined bubbles that now support the our entire economy will be *much, much more* costly. This is something that everyone wants to avoid, and thus governments, institutions, and investors all around the world are highly motivated to keep the U.S. multibubble economy going. Because of that, we can be sure that the Market Cliff will not occur until all their firepower is fully spent.

The unfortunate reality is that the only way to change the fundamental problems with our economy is to hit and go over the cliff. That will end the worldwide delaying tactics and eventually move us into a period of actually trying to improve the basic drivers of real economic growth.

"What should you do? Here's what you should do: invent a time machine, go back sixteen months, and convert everything to cash."

Hitting the Market Cliff

The events leading up to the Market Cliff won't necessarily lend themselves to a perfectly organized timeline, but we are going to do our best to give you our current predictions of how it will happen— something few books would dare to do because the likelihood of getting the future wrong is so high. We are willing to do it anyway because our macroeconomic view has been so reliable for so many years (our first book came out in 2006).

In the following timeline, many events will overlap and some may occur simultaneously. The general idea is that what begins very slowly can snowball very quickly. As an investor, the odds of your timing any market perfectly are near zero. With the stakes so high, we always say it is better to get out too early than too late.

Stage 1: 2006 to 2009

Stage 1 is the Bubblequake. This has already happened, much in line with what we predicted in our first book, *America's Bubble Economy*, back in 2006.

> **Stage 1, Step 1**. *The real estate bubble pops.* After reaching historic levels in 2006, home prices in the United States saw their biggest year-to-year drop on record in 2008, according to the Case-Shiller Home Price Index.
> **Stage 1, Step 2**. *The stock market bubble pops.* In *America's Bubble Economy*, we predicted the stock market would fall to about 8,000 over a period of a couple years. In fact, it fell below 7,000 in early 2009, less than half what it was at its high in 2007.

Stage 2: You Are Here

The government intervenes with massive monetary stimulus and borrowing. The Fed buys bonds to pump up the stock and real estate markets. Putting money into bonds keeps interest rates low, encouraging more mortgage lending. It also frees up money investors had been keeping in bonds and encourages them to buy stocks in search of higher yields. A huge increase in government borrowing stabilizes the economy, keeping the gross domestic product (GDP) from shrinking precipitously. Government intervention stabilizes the economy, but it's a Band-Aid—not a real solution.

Stage 2 can last a long time—years, even. We have been in Stage 2 since shortly after the Financial Crisis of 2008, and are still here today.

Currently, inflation is still relatively low. Because people and businesses have little incentive toward wage and price increases, inflation can remain low for some time in spite of massive money printing. Low inflation allows the Fed to continue printing money while the public takes little notice. Remember, as we mentioned in Chapter 1, inflation numbers are being misrepresented, which helps keep the public's mind off of it.

Some key indicators to pay attention to that may indicate we are leaving Stage 2 and entering Stage 3:

- The stock market doesn't rise as consistently.
- People become more aware of massive stimulation, misleading statistics, and stock market intervention by the government.
- People become increasingly aware of and concerned about inflation.
- People take notice of economic malaise worldwide and the more and more extensive stimulus (especially more money printing here and in other countries) need to keep global economy stable.

These indicators can be gauged by a close reading of the financial press, and more media coverage of these points to a shift in market sentiment. We are now leaving Stage 2 and entering early Stage 3.

Stage 3: Increasing Instability

In early Stage 3, which we are now in, we have an oscillating stock market and continued money printing that will at first keep the market from falling significantly.

As Stage 3 advanced, investors will become increasingly worried about an economy that is taking too long to recover and people will begin to lose faith. The premise that the economy will recover if we can just keep up the stimulation for a few more months or years is losing traction, and that moves us closer to the rapid multibubble pop in Stage 4.

Stage 3 starts slowly and then moves quickly. Therefore, some steps may overlap or happen simultaneously.

Stage 3, Step 1. *The stock market falls gradually in spite of intervention.* We see an oscillating trend, within an overall downward trend.

Stage 3, Step 2. *Interest rates rise in spite of actions by the Fed.* Bondholders are getting more worried about risk. Government intervention begins to lose its effectiveness, as even the Fed can't keep interest rates down. Some people expect the bond market to fall before the stock market, but it's unlikely because bonds are easier to manipulate and support than stocks. Currently, bonds are slowly falling, while stocks are doing better. Later, stocks will sharply fall, followed by bonds falling sharply.

Stage 3, Step 3. *More government stimulus by foreign countries, as well as interventions in foreign currencies and foreign economies.* As the situation in other countries—Spain, Italy, and even China, for example—becomes increasingly problematic, more drastic measures of stimulus and intervention need to be taken by their governments, possibly with U.S. support, to keep their economies afloat and their governments in good standing.

Stage 3, Step 4. *Gold manipulation ramps up.* Government manipulation in gold markets becomes more serious, shifting from paper gold futures to physical gold. This move is limited by the government capacity to unload physical gold. As such, manipulation becomes increasingly ineffective, leading to rising gold prices. This is a very strong indicator that the Market Cliff is near.

Stage 3, Step 5. *People increasingly begin to see the connection between money printing and inflation, which radically decreases the positive impacts of money printing.* As the public increasingly sees money printing as a negative rather than a positive for the economy, monetary stimulus rapidly loses effectiveness in boosting the markets, and stocks, bonds, and real estate begin to fall.

Stage 3, Step 6. *Dollar outflow.* U.S. assets are not performing well, and the lack of good investment opportunities here, coupled with increasing risk awareness, motivate foreign investors to move out of their U.S. assets to greater safety in their own countries. This will not only contribute to U.S. stocks and bonds falling, but will also crash the dollar in the foreign exchange markets and boom some foreign currencies that will be seen as relatively safe compared to the falling dollar. This will be very damaging to U.S. asset markets and economy.

Please note that the foreign exchange rate is different from inflation. While they are certainly related, inflation is an internal phenomenon based on prices of domestic goods and services. Foreign exchange rates come from international demand for a currency and demand for investments based on that currency. In other words, the value of any currency on the foreign exchange markets is based on the extent to which investors around the world want to buy and hold that currency. When investors around the world want fewer U.S. dollars, the foreign exchange value of the dollar will fall.

Stage 4: Rapid Collapse

Stage 4 will occur very rapidly. Rising interest rates and the anticipation of future rises in interest rates due to rising inflation alarms investors. Much of the following could take place in just a matter of weeks, days, or even hours, with most people getting caught on the wrong side and going over the Market Cliff.

> **Stage 4, Step 1**. *Manipulation fails in gold market.* Gold prices soar, leading the U.S. government to levy a significant tax on gold purchases. This keeps some money in stocks, bonds, and real estate in the United States, but has little effect on gold prices around the world.

> **Stage 4, Step 2**. *Manipulation fails in the stock market.* The oscillating market—and its downward trajectory—is impossible to ignore. Discomfort with the stock market leads to many more sellers than buyers. Stock prices are plunging deeply on a daily basis, leading to the government's declaring short stock market holidays—first, for a couple hours and later, for much longer. **This is the Market Cliff**.

> **Stage 4, Step 3**. *The bond market collapses.* Rising interest rates will cause big drops in bond prices. With few investors wanting to sell at a huge discount and even fewer investors willing to buy, the bond market will essentially shut itself down. The government may also choose to shut it down, just as with the stock market, in an attempt to soothe the markets with a little "time out."

> **Stage 4, Step 4**. *The real estate market collapses.* High interest rates and little mortgage money means nearly no home purchases. Real estate prices are devastated.

Stage 4, Step 5. *The dollar collapses.* Collapsing assets leads to a massive exodus of foreign money. No one wants to hold dollar-based assets. By now, most foreign investors can't find sellers and are stuck with their losses. The pullback collapses the value of the dollar, spreading economic disaster around the world. **The Aftershock begins.**

The Last Resort: A Stock Market Holiday

As we approach and go over the Market Cliff, the Fed will be entirely unprepared. Instead, officials at the Fed will make decisions moment by moment. And when faced with a free-falling market, officials will need to take fast action. The old way of doing things—massaging numbers, manipulating prices, and flooding the market with printed money—will be powerless to stop the plunge. At this point, the government won't own enough gold to sell to drop the gold price and prevent a flight to safety. So the last resort will be to temporarily shut down the stock market entirely.

At first, the idea would be to shut down the market for only a few hours and address whatever immediate issue is causing the plunge in prices. In this case, we might see this initial shutdown last up to a day before reopening. Of course, the problem in this case is a bubble economy. That's not something that can be fixed overnight. So when the market does eventually reopen, the plunge continues, and the government will need multiple additional shutdowns, eventually having to shut it down for longer and longer periods.

In 1933, Franklin D. Roosevelt declared a national bank holiday in order to shore up the problems that had been leading to runs on banks throughout the country. During that time, the Emergency Banking Act was passed, and when the banks reopened the following week, depositors came rushing back with renewed confidence. Likewise, when the stock market has to be shut down, the government will be frantically looking for whatever reform it can implement to send investors rushing back to stocks.

But without being able to assuage investor fears, the name of the game here will be finding ways to encourage purchases and discourage sales. Brokerage firms will have no qualms about playing along, and what we might see for some time is that clients who want to sell their stocks have a difficult time getting past their broker's secretary or voicemail, while those who want to buy will get top priority. Whatever happens, the government and the financial industry will surely go to great lengths to prevent anyone from selling stocks when the market reopens, and they will also very likely get rid of high-frequency trading and shorting. There may be other reforms as well, mostly ineffective in stopping the mass exit out of stocks and other assets.

What we will *not* hear from the Fed, or from most of the financial industry, is that stocks and other assets have been in a bubble all this time, and that going over the cliff was inevitable and is irreversible. Instead, we'll hear all kinds of excuses, perhaps blaming the crash on activities such as high-speed trading, which may have irresponsibly flooded the market with sellers. Then, of course, there are the short sellers, among the favorite scapegoats from 2008, and fear mongers. We'll almost certainly hear that it's a temporary irrational panic, and that everything will be fine once people come to their senses and renew their confidence in the U.S. markets again. Anything to convince the public—and themselves—that the market cliff is just an anomaly.

A big problem with selling this narrative is that, even with the U.S. stock market shut down, the Fed can't stop the trading of U.S. stocks overseas. So even while officials in the government and financial industry are selling the idea that real stock values are strong, even a mildly curious investor will be able to log on to the Internet and see the bottomed-out prices of U.S. stocks overseas.

Try as it might, the Federal Reserve won't be able to reverse this downturn. And eventually it will have no option left but to shut down the stock market indefinitely. At best, stock sales might be allowed in cases of extreme hardship, but such sales will be of little value to anyone. Investors who weren't able to sell their stocks before the cliff will have little left in their portfolios. When the market finally does reopen, probably one to two years down the road, those basement prices will be essentially permanent.

Will the financial industry—or what's left of it, anyway—admit at this point what the problem really was? We're not optimistic. They will continue to blame the wrong things, like irrational fear, political mistakes, and other nefarious forces. It's the earlier prices that were the correct ones, if only everyone would realize it. Expect that drumbeat to continue for a long time.

But sooner or later, people will understand what happened: we had a bubble economy, the bubble is not coming back, and the road to recovery is a long and difficult one. This time it will not be fueled by low interest rates and overextended debt, but by slow and steady real growth.

What About Bonds, Real Estate, and Gold?

Like the stock market, the bond and real estate markets will have their own temporary shutdowns, but not solely because of government action. With soaring interest rates that the Fed can no longer control, lending will dry up, and the bond market will effectively shut down on its own. The Fed may try to keep the bond market going with more money printing, but with inflation rising due to money printing, it is simply too costly to keep this up.

When the bond market shuts down, there will be no mortgage money available, and thus essentially not much of a real estate market left to speak of.

The one oddity will be the gold market, which will behave in exactly the opposite way. With assets tanking across the board, people will rush to what they consider the intrinsic value of gold and precious metals. This is the last thing the Fed wants, and so measures will be taken to try to discourage gold purchases. A prohibition is remotely possible, but more likely we might see a punitive tax, such as 50 percent tax on gold purchases. The Fed might even prohibit the redemption of paper gold, such as through gold exchange-traded funds, into physical gold, and may stop the option of buying gold on margin and may even stop the delivery of physical gold from gold depositories. The idea is to prevent investors from leaving traditional assets and rushing to gold instead.

But once investor confidence is lost, it will be very difficult to gain it back. And the reason why discouraging gold purchases won't be too successful is the same reason that shutting down the stock market won't be too successful in trying to control asset prices: the United States is not the only country in the world. The U.S. government can pass all kinds of regulations and restrictions on market activity, but it cannot prevent those same transactions in overseas markets. Gold, of course, will be easy to buy and trade elsewhere in the world regardless of what the U.S. government does. And any restrictions and tax increases on buying and selling gold in the United States will only drive underground transactions. There won't be much the government can do to prevent the exchange of bullion coins and bars underground.

When Is the Best Time to Get Out of the Stock Market?

You won't like our answer: 1999.

Had you exited the stock market at its peak in 1999 and bought gold instead at that time, you'd be very happy today. Despite missing the stock rally of 2013, you would not have missed much because the market hasn't really gone anywhere since 2000 (see Figure 4.1). Actually, the stock market is *way down* since its peak in March 2000—as much as 25 percent—in real terms, meaning adjusted for inflation.

Meanwhile, despite its volatility, gold would have made you about 300 percent. It's too late to do that now, but there is still plenty of time to profit from the big run up in gold in the Aftershock. However, before then, there is something very important for you to focus on: don't go over the Market Cliff!

With stocks on the rise and the Market Cliff still a ways off, it's perfectly understandable that some readers will want to maximize their profits before pulling entirely out of traditional assets. If the stock market is going to continue to rise, or if there is still money

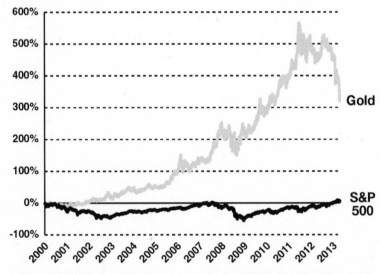

Figure 4.1   S&P 500 Up 8 percent, Gold Up 300 percent since 2000

While the cheerleaders have spent many years touting stocks and dismissing gold as a pointless investment, in fact the stock market is only up about 8 percent since 2000, while gold is up more than 300 percent.

to be made from flipping real estate properties, why would anyone want to miss out on those potential gains?

The problem comes from not knowing how long you can safely push your luck. And that is why we wrote this book: to help investors make intelligent decisions between now and the Market Cliff. Our best advice is to just get out now and don't play chicken with the approaching crash. However, we know that a good deal of you simply will not do that. Instead, even those who believe there is a Market Cliff ahead will still stay in the markets for a while longer and try to squeeze out a bit more profits.

If you are in this group, we ask you to please maintain a sober perspective. First, get real: you are not going to get 15 percent every year in every market. This is going to be a bumpy ride with plenty of ups and downs that could help or hurt you, and increasingly more hurt than help.

Second, whenever you do get out of stocks, bonds, and real estate, keep in mind that if you want to do that before you go over the Market Cliff, you will be going against the vast majority of investors, and that is not easy to do. Some people will give you a hard time and maybe even make you question your sanity. Remember, back in 1999 when the markets were booming and the Internet bubble was at its peak, few people thought that the best thing to do then was to pull out of stocks and get into gold. In 1999, most people would have told you it was crazy to get out. And yet, if you had, you'd be in outstanding shape today.

But here's the rub, no matter when you get out, at the peak or no peak, getting out *before* the Market Cliff is absolutely essential—far more important than when you time your move. At this point, timing your exit is trivial compared to simply exiting. For example, even if you had exited the stock and real estate markets at what appeared to be the very worst time—during the depths of the global financial crisis in 2009—you would *still* be far better off in the long term than you will be if you stay with the majority of investors as they go over the Market Cliff. In fact, if you invest wisely before and during the Aftershock, you won't just be better off, you will be quite prosperous.

The point is this: even if we can't convince you to get out now, please do not get caught holding on to traditional assets when we hit the Market Cliff. The last thing you want at that point is to be a seller when everyone else wants to be a seller, too. You want to be a seller much sooner than that, when there are still plenty of buyers (even if some people think you are crazy to sell).

If you want to push your luck a little further and stay in stocks, bonds, and real estate a bit longer, the rest of this book can be your guide. But keep in mind that the road to the Aftershock will be a bumpy one. The stock market will not keep going up dramatically every year until one day it suddenly crashes. It's not like we will have perfectly smooth sailing and then abruptly go over Niagara Falls. There will be plenty of potential for losses even before the final crash.

So, when is the best time to get out of the markets? Probably 14 years ago.

When is the second best time to exit? Any time *before* we go over the Market Cliff.

CHAPTER

5

Conventional Wisdom Won't Work This Time

INTRODUCING AFTERSHOCK WISDOM FOR INVESTING

For years, conventional wisdom (CW) money gurus have been telling us that buy-and-hold investing is the way to go. All you have to do to grow yourself a nice future nest egg is to get some high-quality stocks and bonds in the right mix to match your age and goals, and then like those infomercial ovens on TV, you can "just set it and forget it."

This easy CW approach to investing naturally worked very well in an overall rising multibubble economy. As long as you stayed well diversified with a collection of average-performing stocks and bonds, you could count on earning a good profit in the stock market and a steadily rising total return in the bond market, especially from the 1980s to 2000. With the Dow rising more than 1,000 percent in 20 years and falling interest rates pushing bond prices ever higher, investors could practically throw a dart at a stock page and end up with some good gains eventually. CW investing in a rising bubble economy is nearly effortless.

Then, beginning in 2000, all that started to change. Bonds still did okay, but that 1,000 percent growth in stocks got replaced by a big fat zero percent growth for the Dow and a 50 percent decline in Nasdaq stocks over the next decade. Nonetheless, the CW gurus seemed unfazed, plowing ahead with their CW investing as if America's multibubble economy would always continue to rise. They didn't see the bubbles, only the growth. And if that growth happened to occasionally experience a bit of a "down cycle," they could always just relax and wait for an inevitable "up cycle." That's because the rising bubble economy had convinced them that economic growth was virtually guaranteed if you just had patience and waited for a while. CW has faith and CW doesn't quit.

So when the real estate bubble started to pop in 2007 and kicked off a global financial crisis in 2008, along with a stock market drop of nearly 40 percent, many CW investment experts were quite shocked and confused. Without the correct macroeconomic view of what was occurring, they held even more tightly to their faithful buy-and-hold mantra. CW investing had simply not prepared them for moments like this. They used phrases like "Black Swan event" and "highly unpredictable" to describe the 2008 stock market crash and global economic downturn, when in fact it was all *very predictable* (and, by the way, was predicted in our book *America's Bubble Economy* in 2006). CW, however, saw the entire global financial crisis as unpredictable and beyond our control—as if an unexpected asteroid suddenly hit us out of the blue in late 2008, not something we systematically created ourselves over the course of decades.

Then, just when it looked like economic Armageddon, the U.S. Federal Reserve came to our rescue—at least for the short term—with massive money printing beginning in early 2009, as well as massive federal government borrowing. The enormous expansion of the money supply directly boosted the stock market and helped support the overall economy—so much so that the Dow and Standard & Poor's (S&P) hit new highs and real estate prices began to move up a bit in 2013. However, it also left us with the specter of future rising inflation and rising interest rates dangling over CW investing like an unseen guillotine hanging by a thread.

So now the question is *what's next?* Should we stick with the CW folks, like Warren Buffett and other previously highly successful investors, or does this new and evolving economy call for a new and evolving approach? Hmmm, can you tell which way we are going with this?

Before we get to the details of our Aftershock wisdom on how to invest in the new and changing economy, let's take a close look at CW investing and why it's so very, very hard for most people to give it up.

The Key to Conventional Wisdom: The Future Will Be Just Like the Past

The key assumption behind all CW investing is pretty simple: What worked well in the recent past will work well today. It's easy to understand, it's easy to follow, and, most of all, it's *very comfortable.* And for a very long time, it was also very true. Let's look at some recent history to see why CW investing still has such powerful appeal.

Over the past century or so, the U.S. stock market has experienced solid, albeit slow (by the standards of the 1980s and 1990s) growth. Even in the Great Depression—a big economic collapse by any measure—most major corporations survived (many major corporations such as Caterpillar were even able to maintain profitability), as did most major banking and investment banking firms. The government entered the Depression with relatively little debt and little inflation. In fact, they probably printed too little money, contributing to deflation during the Great Depression.

Also, for the first half of the twentieth century, the economy was much less capital dependent and, hence, much less vulnerable to changes in interest rates. Leverage was less common for corporations and was certainly less common for consumers buying homes or cars. Most of our grandparents would not have even considered having more than a 10-year mortgage on a home, and they did not use credit to buy cars (even though that was becoming increasingly common). Use of debt had grown enormously since the late 1800s, but it was far less than today. In addition, there was much less consumer spending, partly due to less credit for such activities. As an example, credit cards really weren't in heavy use until the 1970s and especially the 1980s. Thus, with less consumer spending, the earlier economy was more resistant to downturns in consumer spending.

The economy had also experienced only a few major bubbles prior to the Great Depression. The 1920s stock bubble was the biggest, but even that bubble was accompanied by huge real growth in the economy. Relatively speaking, it was a much smaller bubble than the combined stock, housing, private credit, and consumer spending bubbles that rose up beginning in the 1980s.

The inflation and flat stock market of the 1970s (due in large part to declining productivity growth) was a harbinger of future problems, but not enough to offset almost a century of solid growth. Gross domestic product (GDP) growth was still fairly good, even in the 1970s. Except for the period of the Depression, down cycles were limited. Any down cycles during the century were relatively modest and were far outweighed by the good to great up cycles.

All of this enormous growth in the economy provided a strong basis for solid but slow growth in the stock market, which helped people like Warren Buffett and others do very well (see Figure 5.1).

Then, beginning in the 1980s, all that slow and steady growth driven by real fundamental economic drivers was replaced by rapid growth driven by another kind of driver: rising bubbles. As we reviewed in Chapter 2, during this time we saw the rise of the . . .

- Stock market bubble
- Real estate bubble
- Private debt bubble
- Consumer spending bubble
- Government debt bubble
- Dollar bubble

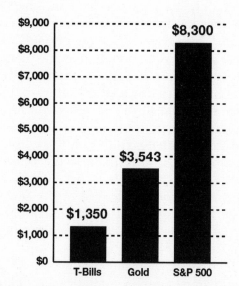

Figure 5.1   Stocks versus Three-Month T-Bills and Gold, 1965–2013

What $100 invested in 1965 would be worth in June 2013.

Source: Bloomberg.

The first four of these six bubbles began to pop in 2008, and the last two bubbles (the dollar and government debt) have been expanding rapidly to help keep the other bubbles afloat. This has created and maintained the current fake recovery, but it has not fully reinflated the sagging bubbles or pushed them up much further:

- The S&P index has risen only about 8 percent (when adjusted for inflation), while the Nasdaq is down 35 percent.
- Home prices in the top cities on average are still 25 percent below their peak, according the Case-Shiller Index.
- Consumer spending has shown marginal improvements, but has not returned to previous highs.

How does CW account for the changes described above? They say, "Don't worry, be happy. Just be patient and eventually everything will get better."

What in the world is giving CW so much sustained confidence? The answer is . . .

The Myth of a Natural Growth Rate

Inherent in CW is the deep faith that the U.S. economy possesses a reliable "natural" growth rate. This is somehow fundamental to our very existence and will never end. Hence, anytime we deviate from that natural growth rate and go into a recession temporarily, we will also, at some point, usually quickly, automatically return to our natural growth rate. That means that we can count on always having a rebound after every recession or, more to the point, after the recent financial crisis. This is also the fundamental basis for CW's thinking about investments in stocks, bonds, and real estate. CW says the economy has a natural growth rate and, hence, stocks, bonds, and real estate all have a natural growth rate, too. That is why buy-and-hold investing is at the heart of conventional investing: just get in and hang on, and eventually that natural growth rate will kick back in.

CW makes no acknowledgment that we could be in a bubble economy or that the world could be in a bubble economy. All bubbles eventually pop, and they don't automatically reinflate. There is no "natural" growth rate that we can always count on to pull us through. Something has to actually *cause* a recovery; we don't just get one automatically if we wait long enough, like winter turning into spring.

The United States does not have a natural growth rate that is in effect at all times and will always save us. In fact, there never has been a natural growth rate—not for any country, not in the past, and not in the future. There is simply no such thing as "natural" economic growth. All economic growth has to be caused by something; it doesn't just happen automatically. That is why not all countries experience economic growth all the time.

Real (nonbubble) economic growth is driven by two forces: population growth and productivity growth. These two are related to some extent because higher agricultural productivity will lead to a larger population. However, our focus should be on productivity since we are primarily interested in becoming wealthier *per person*, not just having a larger economy with lots and lots of poor people. So, *productivity growth* is the source of economic growth. Hence, economies will grow only when productivity grows. An automatic increase in productivity is not natural or automatic. It has to come from changes in the way we produce goods and services. This involves changes in the way we do business, and that often involves changes in government and changes in technology.

China is a great example. What was China's "natural" growth rate in the 1960s? What was its "natural" growth rate in the 1990s? We all know China's growth rate was much higher in the 1990s than in the 1960s. Hence, there is no "natural" growth rate for China (or for any other country). It varies—quite a bit actually—depending on governmental and business actions. Growth was higher in the 1990s for China because they had made numerous important changes in the way they conducted business and in the way their government worked. Entrepreneurship was encouraged, free markets were encouraged, and more input from foreign investors and businesses was encouraged.

So, if China, or any other country, wants its economy to grow, it will have to continue to increase productivity. Yes, some of that productivity will continue to improve due to changes made in the past, but eventually the impact of those past improvements will diminish and economic growth will plateau if people don't continue to make *more* improvements in productivity.

This may sound a lot like us telling you "there's no free lunch," and that's true. But it has enormous importance for how many economists are looking at the economy. Many economists are assuming that any downturn in our economy is simply a diversion from our "natural" growth rate. In fact, you will even see that term used in many financial and economic articles. Nobody asks the most basic question: where is that growth coming from? Instead, they simply assume it is *always there* and that our economy will naturally bounce back into its natural growth mode. They are assuming that productivity is naturally growing all the time, even when history clearly shows it is not also growing.

Curiously, the economists also don't seem too interested in asking, If there is a natural growth rate that we can always count on to eventually return, why doesn't that happen all over the world, in every country? Why do only we get to have this magical natural growth rate?

There is no "natural" or automatic growth rate, not here in the United States and not anywhere in the world. Wherever it occurs, real economic growth has to be earned. It comes from real productivity growth.

Real Productivity Growth Is Slowing Down, Here and Around the World

Rather than staying the same or accelerating, productivity growth in this country and in the other major industrialized nations in Europe and in Japan has been slowing dramatically. Productivity growth in the last quarter of the twentieth century was much slower than in the first three quarters. These are long periods of time. That's how real productivity improvement works. It is a very long term process.

By the way, you should almost completely ignore the government "productivity" statistics or "output per man-hour." Not that they are biased or wrong, but they don't give you a true idea of *real* productivity growth. For example, productivity by that measure can be improved enormously by simply stopping all research and development. That is a dumb measure of productivity.

So, instead of looking at misleading government figures of output per man-hour (although not intentionally misleading as much as just bad information), let's look at *real* productivity growth over a very long period of time. That's the only way to look at it, since significant productivity growth is a relatively slow process. For example, when we look at the productivity growth of food production in the United States over the longer term, we see that two centuries of advancements have made it possible for the number of people required to grow food to drop from 90 percent of the U.S. population to just 3 percent. Now that's real productivity growth!

Across many sectors, we had that kind of robust productivity growth in the United States for many decades. However, beginning in the 1970s, just before the bubbles started to inflate in the 1980s, overall productivity growth began to slow significantly (see Figure 5.2).

Here is another way to look at productivity. Under normal conditions, income generally goes up when productivity goes up. As Figure 5.3 shows, real income growth ("real" because it is adjusted for inflation) has slowed dramatically since 1970. The lack of large increases in real income is another indicator that productivity has not significantly grown since the 1970s.

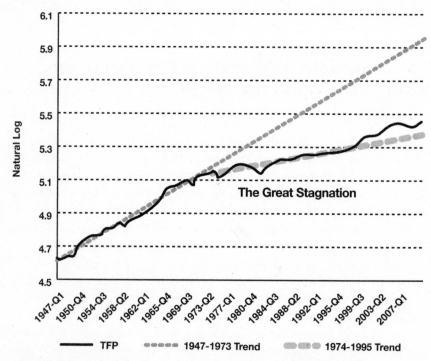

Figure 5.2   Slowing Productivity Growth (Using Total Factor Productivity)

Productivity growth was very rapid until the early 1970s and then grew very slowly afterward.

Source: John Fernald, San Francisco Federal Reserve.

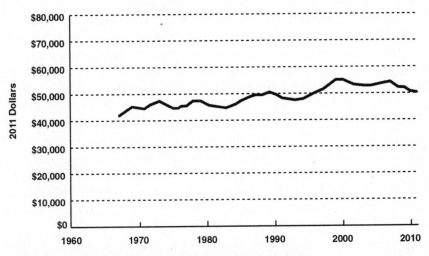

Figure 5.3   Real Median Family Income, 1965–2012

Slowing growth in real (inflation-adjusted) family income after 1970 is another indicator of slowing productivity growth.

Source: U.S. Census Bureau.

By focusing on the big picture of productivity—which is the real fundamental driver of economic growth—it is easy to see that the CW idea that we are merely in a market "down cycle" that will soon be followed by an "up cycle" is wrong. This is not a short-term down cycle; it is a longer-term productivity slump and the more bearish analysts have it right when they say we are not going to get out of this economic downturn anytime soon.

But even the bears are wrong, too. They are correct to see doom and gloom ahead, but they don't see what is behind the doom and gloom, only that things are bad and will get worse. Having the *correct macroeconomic view* about stalled productivity growth is what separates the brains from the bears, and from CW, as well.

Warren Buffett: Master of Conventional Wisdom

Without a doubt one of the best, if not the best, CW investors is Warren Buffett. He is truly a CW master, and his incredible success attests to that. If you invested $1,000 in his investment firm, Berkshire Hathaway, in 1987 it would be worth about $17,000 by the beginning of 2000, before the Internet bubble popped. That's pretty impressive!

However, after the beginning of 2000, his growth slowed considerably. Assuming you invested at the beginning of 2000, a $1,000 investment would grow to about $3,000 at its recent peak in 2013. That's still very good growth but nothing like the earlier growth of the booming 1980s and 1990s stock market.

Some people would say Warren has lost his touch. We don't think so. We think he just lost his bubbles. Warren is still an excellent investor, but he tends to do very well during stock market bubbles and not so very well when there is no bubble.

So is it any wonder that Warren doesn't want to believe we are in a bubble economy? Is it any wonder that he so fervently pushes stocks as a good investment? Remember Figure 5.1 at the beginning of this chapter that showed how well stocks had performed relative to gold and T-bills? He needs to push stocks because he desperately needs a bubble economy and a bubble stock market in order to show good growth. Now, of course, he doesn't say that, but clearly that is true.

And if the stock bubble were to continue to rise, you couldn't make a better choice than putting your money with Warren Buffett. But if the stock bubble does not continue to rise or if it pops, then you could be in real trouble betting on Warren. You could even end up like those who invested in another master of CW investing, Bill Miller (see the sidebar that follows).

Buffett's reliance on CW is already showing problems because the stock market bubble is no longer rising. As Figure 5.4 shows, stocks don't look nearly as good now, while gold has been looking far better, even with recent declines. Mr. Buffett would say this is simply a diversion from the longer-term pattern. We say the pattern is changing for all the reasons we discussed earlier in this chapter and in our previous books.

Another Example of Conventional Wisdom Put to the Test: Hedge Funds

The people managing hedge funds are some of the best investors in the business. That's the conventional wisdom, and this time we agree with conventional wisdom. So, if CW is working, they would be some of the best practitioners of CW and would have some of the best returns to show for their CW investing.

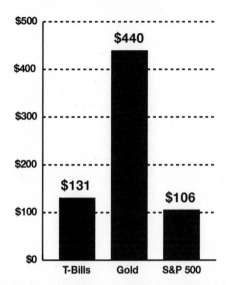

Figure 5.4   Stocks versus Three-Month T-Bills and Gold, from 2000 to July 1, 2013

What $100 invested in 2000 would be worth in mid-2013 in stocks, in T-bills, and in gold.

Source: Bloomberg.

So, let's take a look at hedge fund returns. To do this we will rely on another John Wiley & Sons author, Simon Lack, who recently published a book about hedge funds called *The Hedge Fund Mirage* (2012) that reviewed the actual performance of hedge funds. Before we go on, we should clarify that not all hedge funds use conventional wisdom. Many are truly hedge funds and use a variety of non-CW strategies to get high returns.

However, most hedge funds are surprisingly unhedged and very conventional. Their returns are highly correlated to the stock market. They are essentially leveraged stock funds. Hence, they really do make a good case study of the best in CW investing.

So what did Simon Lack find in his research on hedge fund returns? Basically, what he found is that hedge funds did very well when they were first created in the early 1990s. They were smaller, which made it easier to find a good niche from which to extract higher profits. As they got bigger—much bigger—it became harder to find more or larger niches to properly invest their funds. Plus, there was more opportunity when the stock bubble was just starting. Also, like any new industry, they may have been a bit more creative when the industry just starting its rapid growth—they had to be creative to attract capital to a type of investing that was not well accepted.

So returns fell over time. However, fees did not.

That wasn't a big issue until the stock market collapsed in 2008. At that point, hedge funds lost an enormous amount of money. They weren't really hedged at all. Or at least a large number of them weren't. Let's keep in mind we're looking at an entire industry. There always have been outstanding performers and likely will be in the future. But, as an industry, it wasn't looking very good in 2008.

Mr. Lack found that, after deducting fees, hedge funds had lost almost *all* of the profits that the industry had *ever* made for investors in the stock market crash of 2008–2009. That's right, *over 15 years of profits lost in less than 6 months!* Please note that this does not take into account "survival bias" (when companies go under) and other reasons why these numbers are actually more conservative than reality. In other words, it was even worse than this.

So much for the best of CW investing. They had bet heavily on a rising stock market, and when the market took a big fall, they lost everything they had *ever* made. And these people are the best in the business. The bottom line is that it's increasingly tough to make money with CW investing.

This short summary of Mr. Lack's groundbreaking work does it little justice. It's a great book, whether you have any interest in hedge funds or not. It's an honest and fascinating look at how the best American investors operate.

Will the United States Become Energy Independent?

Many people ask this question. It is important to point out that we actually are energy independent in the production of coal and natural gas, which is much of our energy usage. Only in oil are we not independent. That is changing. Oil production in the United States has grown from 5 million barrels per day in 2009 to 6.5 million per day in 2013. But given that we consume 18 million barrels of oil per day (about 20 percent of the world's total oil supply), even if we can increase production of oil by 1 million barrels per day every year, it will still take us roughly 10 more years to produce all the oil we consume.

However, there is one big problem with counting on that: we haven't added a single oil-drilling rig in more than a year. In fact, the number of rigs drilling for oil has actually dropped since mid-2012. Yes, the number of oil drilling rigs increased from about 200 in 2009 to 1,400 in mid-2012, but since then there has been no growth at all. Oil production is still increasing, but without the massive increase in oil drilling rigs that we had in the past, the rate of increase in production is likely to slow down. Also, the new shale wells have very short lives—their production often declines by 70 to 90 percent in their first three years, so we need to drill lots of wells just to replace the ones that are dying.

It's worth noting that the increased oil drilling has come largely at the expense of natural gas drilling. Active natural gas–drilling rigs have fallen from about 1,600 at the start of 2009 to about 350 in mid-2013. That means the total number of active rigs, both gas and oil, has actually fallen from about 2,000 in late 2008 to 1,800 by mid-2013. Also, as a result of falling natural gas drilling, the price of natural gas has almost doubled since its lows in spring 2012 and could go higher in 2014 given the very low number of active gas-drilling rigs.

Although the increased activity in oil drilling has certainly helped the economy, the decline is natural gas drilling has muted the gains. In fact, there was a gain of only about 27,000 new jobs related to oil and natural gas extraction from January 2009 to June 2013, according to the Bureau of Labor Statics. This is largely due to the lack of any increase (actually a decline) in the total number of oil- and gas-drilling rigs during the past four and a half years.

So if we are going to count on new domestically produced oil to greatly boost our economy and energy independence in the next 10 years, we better start building and deploying a whole lot more drilling rigs.

The Key to Aftershock Wisdom Investing: The Future Is Not the Past!

The key to correct investing in the future is to recognize that the future will be significantly different from the past. Conventional wisdom says that nothing is fundamentally different about the economy; we've just been going through a rough patch. If we can just be patient and don't do anything rash with our investments, we can count on "natural growth" to eventually return and all will be okay.

Whereas, Aftershock wisdom says that there is no "natural growth," only real growth created by real productivity improvements. We have not had any significant real productivity improvements for many years. Instead, we had the rise and now the decline of multiple bubbles, and therefore the future is not the past, we are in a very different economy than before. In fact, the entire world is in a very different economy than before because we are in a worldwide bubble economy that is popping.

This is different from the past. We have seen bubbles before, such as the Internet bubble, and its demise really wasn't such a big deal, especially on a global level. *But it is different this time.* This time we have not one smallish bubble, but six huge, interdependent bubbles, each dependent on the others, both on their way up and also on their way down. We have never seen so many large and linked bubbles before, and when they finally fall fully, it is not going to be like anything we have seen before—involving rising inflation, rising interest rates, and falling assets across the board.

Certainly, we have had inflation before, such as in the late 1970s and early 1980s, *but it is different this time.* This time, because we have so many large colinked bubbles, high inflation and high interest rates are going to be the final blow to our multibubble economy and the world's bubble economy, as well.

If the Future Is Not the Past, How Will It Be Different This Time? Future Inflation Is the Key

To quickly summarize: This so-called "recovery" is 100 percent fake (see Chapter 1) and is temporarily supporting our multibubble economy (see Chapter 2) due to massive money printing (see Chapter 3) that can't last (see Chapter 4).

Massive money printing eventually causes rising inflation; rising inflation eventually causes rising interest rates; and rising interest rates are not going to be good for maintaining this fake, stimulus-based recovery. Instead, rising inflation and rising interest rates are going to be the final blows that pop the bubbles.

The dollar bubble will pop as a result of inflation spiking up, reducing the buying power of the dollar. There is no permanent way around this coming inflation, only short-term delaying tactics. If somehow massive money printing would never, ever cause rising future inflation, that would be great—in that case, we could forget about paying taxes or even earning money because we could all just print money instead. Clearly, that won't work. Instead, massive money printing will eventually cause rising future inflation.

High inflation will cause high interest rates, putting downward pressure on our asset bubbles. That will make dollar-denominated assets not so appealing, especially to foreign investors, who currently own almost $26 trillion in U.S. assets. When inflation comes, foreign investment will fall, and the dollar bubble will fall. Anyone who deludes himself into thinking foreign investors will stay in the United States because they "have nowhere else to go" is just being silly. Of course they will have other places to go. They will go back to their own countries' assets, such as their own short-term debt, which will be falling as well, but will not be falling as much as our dollar-denominated assets. Even today, most money stays in other countries. It doesn't all come to the United States.

The decline in foreign investment in the United States would not have as much of an impact if there hadn't been so much inflow of foreign capital into our economy earlier. On the way in, that extra money helped pump up our bubbles, and on the way out, the drop in foreign investment will help pop the bubbles as well.

The combination of rising inflation and rising interest rates will pop the huge dollar and government debt bubbles, and will pull down what is left of the already falling real estate, stock, private debt, and consumer spending bubbles. With all our bubbles fully popped, the global Aftershock will begin.

Even if that is not something you can currently let yourself believe is possible, you must at least admit that rising inflation and rising interest rates will certainly not be good for any economic recovery. And once you let yourself see the bubbles, you will realize that, under these conditions, these bubbles cannot last.

Frankly, even without rising future inflation and rising interest rates, these bubbles cannot last. Why? Because they are bubbles! Bubbles don't last forever. What goes up must eventually come down because their rise was not driven by real productivity growth and other fundamental economic drivers. It was driven by speculation and a whole lot of borrowed and printed money.

Despite these facts, CW will try to deny, ignore, and happy-talk our way through an increasingly obvious falling bubble economy. But ask yourself this: how many CW-type analysts and economists predicted or anticipated our current economic situation? This is how CW tries to ignore the change. But, of course, that doesn't stop the reality of the current and future economy.

This enormous resistance by so many sophisticated economists and financial analysts to changing their CW economic outlook, even in the face of overwhelming evidence, is highly unusual in U.S. history. Although there has certainly been cheerleading in the past and blatant ignoring of reality by economists and financial analysts, this current period stands out as an extreme level of resistance to facing facts. CW has become blind as a bat, while insisting its eyes are wide open.

Key to the CW position that nothing too bad will happen next is their belief that inflation poses no threat. Some CW analysts (and even some bears) have gone so far as to say that future *deflation*, not inflation, is the real problem.

The Myth of Deflation Is the Last Refuge of the Deniers

Vital to the CW argument against our analysis is the wrong idea that instead of inflation, we are about to enter into a period of deflation. The idea that deflation is the real threat, not inflation, is the last refuge of the deniers. They want to deny that printing money is a problem. They want to be able to print all the money we need without any consequences, without inflation. So, instead, they say they are worried about deflation.

Let's start with a definition of inflation and then dissect the deflation arguments one at a time. As Nobel Prize–winning economist Milton Friedman famously stated:

Inflation is always and everywhere a monetary phenomenon.

By using the word *monetary*, Friedman meant that inflation is a direct result of increasing the money supply. Increase the money supply, relative to the size of the economy, and you get inflation; decrease the money supply and you get deflation.

Wrong Deflation Argument 1: Some Prices Are Falling

Many people think that if some prices are falling that means we have deflation. This is false. Prices can fall when there is a change in supply and demand: falling demand and/or rising supply naturally reduces prices. That is not deflation. Deflation is caused by a contracting money supply, and inflation is caused by expanding the money supply faster than the economy grows. We have a massively expanding money supply, and we are going to get significant future inflation, not deflation.

Making matters more confusing, there is a difference between a change in the "nominal" price, which is the price paid, and a change in the "real" price, which is the price adjusted for inflation. The nominal price can rise due to inflation, while the real price can fall due to falling demand or rising supply. The fact that some asset values (in real dollars, adjusted for inflation) will fall due to popping bubbles does not mean we have deflation. It means we have falling bubbles.

Wrong Deflation Argument 2: Because Lots of Money Is Being Held in Excess Bank Reserves, It Is Deflationary

Many people think that as long as banks hold printed money in excess reserves, we won't see inflation because the money is not in circulation. This is not true. Excess reserves do not mean that banks are just keeping all the money printed by the Fed. Money in excess reserves does not belong to the banks. Bank reserves are simply funds in client accounts the banks haven't lent out. Excess reserves are just reserves beyond what the banks are legally required to hold.

Money in excess reserves is, in fact, in circulation. Every dollar of excess reserves is in somebody's checking account. The account holders can and do spend it. Why would they sell bonds to the Fed if not to free up cash for purchases? They may be buying stocks, investing in real estate, or for that matter buying a new yacht. It's their money. They can do with it as they please. Have you ever had a bank tell you not to spend money in your account because they're holding it in reserve?

Larger excess reserves are deflationary only in that they postpone the onset of inflation because there is no multiplier effect from bank lending, but it does not prevent inflation from happening.

Wrong Deflation Argument 3: The Fed Can Get Rid of the Extra Printed Money before Serious Inflation Kicks In

There are two reasons why this will not happen. The first problem with this solution is that the economy is showing no signs of growing under its own steam. (Remember, there is no "natural" growth rate; the bubbles have been the growth engine, and without the bubbles, not much growth happens). Pulling money out of a no-growth economy would just make the recession far worse, not better, so that won't work. The second problem is that even if the economy did recover somehow, not only would a contraction of the money supply jeopardize those gains, but the only way the Fed can pull that money out of the economy is by selling $1 to $2 trillion worth of government bonds. Not exactly a winning scenario in an already precarious public debt situation. If they tried to do this by selling the bonds, interest rates would rise. Higher interest rates would have a negative impact on stocks, bonds, real estate, and other assets, which would hurt the economy. So the Fed won't pull the money out to spare us inflation later.

Wrong Deflation Argument 4: Debt Write-Offs and Bankruptcies Reduce the Money Supply

Another common argument for deflation is that when debts cannot be repaid, the resulting write-offs and bankruptcies will effectively decrease the money supply. This argument seems to come from the fact that money is created as debt. But the argument goes one step too far in assuming that when debt is destroyed, that reduces the money supply. A simple thought experiment will show why this is untrue: if you lend me money and I can't repay you, the debt may be wiped out, but the money went wherever I spent it. It's still in circulation. Destroying the debt does not destroy the money.

Wrong Deflation Argument 5: Available Credit Is Declining

A similar argument is that, when we talk about the increase in the money supply, we're not considering that credit effectively functions as money. So if the amount of credit goes down in a struggling economy, the money supply is effectively decreased, too. But decreasing credit doesn't cancel out any money already in the system—it just slows the rate of new money being introduced in the economy, which doesn't matter much if the economy has already been flooded with money. Whenever a purchase is made using credit (say, when you buy a TV with your credit card), sooner or later it ends up in a bank account somewhere. Once it's in a deposit account, it makes no difference where it came from. It's in the economy for good.

Wrong Deflation Argument 6: Demographics Are Changing

Another argument we've heard for deflation is based on demographics. Some have said that as the Baby Boom generation reaches retirement, more people will be saving what money they have, which will make dollars scarcer and therefore more valuable. The problem with this is that, in the twenty-first century, when people save their money, they don't put it under their mattresses. They invest it. It circulates in the economy just like it always has. Even if there were some truth to this idea, there's no way that a little extra penny pinching by the Baby Boomers could offset the massive money printing by the Fed that we've seen so far and will continue to see. Also, remember that we have had no periods of deflation in the United States since the end of the Great Depression when the government began to print more money. Inflation helped pull us out of the Depression. We simply cannot have significant deflation now or in the future when we are massively printing money.

Why We Look at the Monetary Base Instead of M_1 and M_2

When we talk about how money printing by the Federal Reserve is increasing the U.S. money supply, we are talking about the *U.S. monetary base*, not M_1 or M_2. That is because M_1 and M_2 are both impacted by market behavior, while the monetary base is not. The monetary base is the Federal Reserve's balance sheet. It includes the government's money holdings plus those of a few big banks. M_1 is all currency and demand deposits. M_2 is currency, demand deposits, and savings deposits. Because it is possible to have a rise in the monetary base while also having a decline in M_1 or M_2 due to other factors, such as market behavior, the size and growth of the *monetary base* is a more accurate predictor of potential future inflation.

Not Only Will There Be No Contraction of the Money Supply, We Foresee a Lot More Money Printing Ahead

As the economy continues to struggle and markets fall, the Fed will do even *more* money printing, and this will result in even *more* inflation than anyone would expect. The Fed will do even more money printing in the future in order to cover the costs of:

- *Market stabilization.* Like the first rounds of quantitative easing that began in 2009 and continue in 2013, future rounds of money printing will largely come from a need to prop up declining markets and a fragile banking system.
- *Stabilizing foreign currency markets.* The Fed can prop up the market and banking system only to a limited degree, especially as this goes on for a longer period of time. Foreign investors will still get nervous. Hence, the Fed will also need to print money to support the dollar in the foreign exchange markets.
- *Government spending deficit.* Long term, once the Aftershock hits, the Fed will have a very heavy burden of financing the government. We already fund about 40 percent of our spending with debt, and it will be much higher when the Aftershock occurs. The money to buy this debt will increasingly come from additional money printing by the Fed.

Keep in mind that this represents only the base money introduced by the Fed. Any loans created from these reserves will have a *multiplier effect* on that figure. So while we will not have inflation on the level of Zimbabwe or the Weimar Republic, we will certainly have very high inflation, and it will certainly have a very big impact on the future economy.

This Debate Is Really Not about Inflation or Deflation, It's All about Protecting the Status Quo with Denial

Because inflation will devastate the stock, bond, and real estate markets, people want to say it won't happen. If you own a stock, such as Bank of America, you desperately want to believe the problem is deflation, not inflation; otherwise, your investment is about

"I told you the Fed should have tightened."

to be wiped off the planet. For that reason, a lot of people want to believe we will have deflation, not inflation.

Maybe you believe it, too. If so, ask yourself this: if the Fed's buying massive amounts of government bonds with printed money doesn't create inflation, why don't we do more of it? Most economists agree that if we eliminated all taxes tomorrow, including corporate and Social Security taxes, while maintaining all federal government spending, that we would boost the economy right out of the current slump and into a period of enormous growth. All we have to do is borrow that money instead of taxing it. How do we borrow it? By selling bonds to the Federal Reserve. That's exactly what we did in the past with QE1, QE2, and QE3. With the Fed buying the bonds, it won't stress the bond markets. They just buy whatever it takes to fund the government each year. No more. No less.

Since the deflationists strongly assert that massive Federal Reserve purchases of government bonds via QE won't create inflation, then what's the downside? We can just print all the money we want, whenever we want. We can quit paying taxes. In fact, why should anyone work at all? We can all just print money whenever we need it, just like the government. No taxes and lots of shopping would be a great boost to the economy, right?

But we all know in our gut that this is a fraud. We instinctively know that endless money printing is impossible and would eventually create problems. There really is no such thing as Money from Heaven, and having the Fed buy our government bonds with printed money is *not* Money from Heaven. It is the fuel for inflation.

Inflation doesn't start immediately, but that doesn't mean it doesn't happen. Inflation doesn't start at a high level, but that doesn't mean it won't get higher later. That's where we are today— we are far enough along that inflation has started, but it has not gotten to a high level yet. Ask anybody who's lived through an inflationary environment, and they will tell you that low inflation now is no protection from higher inflation later. Low inflation is simply the beginning of high inflation when you are printing massive amounts of money.

Let's also be clear that we have not had deflation in any way since the financial crisis. We have never had a negative Consumer Price Index (CPI), which would be a good indicator of deflation. We have always had a positive CPI. And most honest observers would say that the CPI significantly underestimates the true rate of inflation most consumers are facing.

The current denial of future inflation reminds us of the denial about the real estate bubble before it popped. In 2003, people believed that housing prices would keep going up at 10 percent per year for at least another decade, maybe longer. They were wrong, terribly wrong, but they admitted that only after the bubble popped. Until then, it was all perfectly reasonable and risk free, just like they say all this money printing is now. One of the proponents of believing that real estate was not in a bubble was then Federal Reserve chairman Alan Greenspan (who famously said we had "just a bit of froth on the coasts").

Come to think of it, one of the proponents of the thinking that money printing won't cause future inflation is the current Federal Reserve chairman, Ben Bernanke. It seems that denying economic reality is one of the key job requirements for a Federal Reserve chairman. But denying reality won't change reality as much as Alan or Ben or many others would like to think. It helps people to justify bad investments, but it doesn't turn those bad investments into good investments. As much fun as it is in the short term, denial is not reality. Never has been and never will be.

Why Don't More People See This?

Because they have so much to lose. The bubbles have brought us the greatest flow of easy money in our history. There is nothing more seductive than easy money—it is *much* more fun than hard money; it's absolutely intoxicating.

The Internet bubble was a great example of how people can deny reality when there is so much easy money to be had. Even the most sophisticated investors—venture capitalists and investment bankers—fell victim to the siren song of easy money. Even today, how good is it when you can sell a firm, only a few years after starting it, and with no revenues and no profits, for $1 billion, as was the case when Instagram was sold to Facebook in March 2012. That's pretty good. John D. Rockefeller may have made a lot of money, but he never made so much money so fast as did Instagram.

Real estate has had similar tales. Seaside cottages purchased for $10,000 a few decades ago are now worth over $1 million. San Francisco, Boston, and New York have probably benefited the most from the combined real estate and stock bubbles. But there are lots of incredible tales of fast, big wealth in Los Angeles, Las Vegas, Phoenix, and Florida. The bubbles have been very, very good to us. Even if you weren't lucky enough to get a huge windfall and become a millionaire or billionaire from stocks or real estate, many people also benefited from the businesses that prospered along with this enormous explosion of fast, enormous wealth.

Many of those people worked hard for their money, but they made a whole lot more money because of the bubbles than they would have made otherwise. There was a lot of easy-money icing on top of the hard-money cake.

And finally, many, many more participated in the general increase of easy money in the form of a dartboard stock market that increased more than 1,000 percent no matter where you threw the darts at the stock page, or housing that doubled or tripled in value with little or no improvements. We all gain to some extent from the overall rising bubble economy. And we liked it. Admit it— *easy money is a lot of fun.*

And, we might add, since it is a world bubble economy, there are lots of easy-money millionaires and billionaires around the world, and that has a big impact on Wall Street's thinking as well. They don't want to lose any easy money, whether it comes from the United States or some other country. Fast, big money from China,

Russia, or the Middle East will do just fine to keep them happy. Right now in London, the best homes are selling for over $100 million, which is up from just a few million dollars several decades ago. Many are being bought by foreigners, not the Brits, with fast, big money, from Russia, the Middle East, and elsewhere. It is truly a world bubble economy at this point

Conventional wisdom does not want to officially face any of this—although people who are fooling themselves often know more than they are willing to let on. Instead, most people here and around the world are drawing comfort from the pervasive "groupthink bubble," a term recently coined by savvy *Aftershock* reader David Mulder in Canada, where, by the way, they are deep in denial as well. (Heavily dependent on their exports to the United States, the Canadian economy will be hit especially hard when the U.S. dollar declines and our bubbles pop.)

Interestingly, when the U.S. and world bubbles do begin to burst, most investors will instantly change their minds about any "natural growth" and all the rest of the irrational thinking. Instead, they will instantly and completely understand that they need to get out of the popping bubbles as fast as they possibly can. There will be a stampede to sell, not buy, when these bubbles fall.

Surely, if anyone *really* believed what they say they believe, wouldn't they want to stay in and buy up the so-called "bargains" as prices dropped suddenly? Some will do that, but most will not. At that point, most investors will be *sellers*, not buyers, and CW investing will be no more.

Unfortunately, at that point, a whole lot of their money will have gone to Money Heaven. Until then, most CW investors cannot let themselves see the falling bubble economy and the dangerous Aftershock ahead.

CW Professionals Have to Be Cheerleaders— But You Don't

Most CW financial advisers and analysts are paid to be cheerleaders. They give a buy or a hold recommendation more than 90 percent of the time because they are paid and supported by stock and bond salespeople. They are paid based on selling you on stocks and bonds. They don't get paid for pointing out the bubbles and telling you to stay away. If they did that, they would be out of a job very quickly, and nobody wants to be out of a job, especially in this economy.

But it is important for the rest of us to understand that CW financial analysts and advisers have that bias so we don't count on them to help us figure out what is really occurring or help us prepare for future protection.

Also in this league are many cheerleading money managers who also want to keep their jobs. They can't do that by investing in money market funds or other defensive strategies; they have to invest mostly in stocks, regardless of the risks, and hope the returns will justify their high pay. There are some exceptions to this rule, but generally stocks are the stock-in-trade of money managers. When stocks are in a long-term bull market, being so focused on stocks is fine. But if there is a stock bubble and that bubble is popping and turns into a long-term bear market, that's not so good.

Keep in mind that money managers are investing other people's money. Even if they lose money, as long as they are doing as well (or as poorly) as other stock-oriented money managers, they will likely keep their jobs.

Unlike a money manager who just has to follow the pack for protection, individual investors are risking their own money. If individual investors lose, they lose big—not just their bonuses at work, but money that their families are depending on.

Many CW advisers call individual investors "stupid money," and they call money managers "smart money." At this point we couldn't disagree more. The way we see it, they just have different goals. The people who play with other people's money are working to keep their jobs; the people who invest their own money are working to protect their assets. And the people who are investing their own money are voting with their feet. Even during the rebound of 2011 and early 2012, investors were moving their money out of stock mutual funds. The outflows since the 2008 crash have been enormous, despite the rebound, as Figure 5.5 shows.

Now you might say that means these people are being too cautious and the money managers are right. If the stock market bubble keeps rising, that is correct. But, if the stock market bubble eventually starts popping, reducing your stock market exposure before that occurs is absolutely the right thing to do. (Please see Chapter 6 for more details about investing in stocks.)

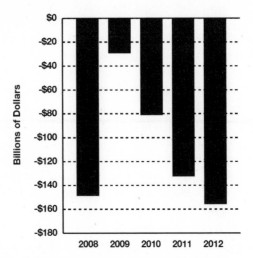

Figure 5.5   Outflows from Domestic Stock Mutual Funds since 2008 Crash

Despite the big rebound in the stock market since the financial crisis of 2008, individual investors remain highly skeptical and have been pulling their money out of stock mutual funds.

Source: Investment Company Institute.

We Give No Easy Pass to the Ostrich Economists

As we have often said, the financial crisis and the Aftershock represent a fundamental failure of the economics profession. Their job is not to be cheerleaders. Their job is to create and support path-breaking new methods of better understanding the economy.

But they don't, and, honestly, they don't even seem very interested. They aren't using their protected, tenured positions as university faculty as a base from which to attack the status quo and advocate uncomfortable but sensible alternatives. Rather, they desperately try to support their privileged station in life by supporting the status quo. Their attacks on the status quo are always muted, and their alternatives are often far less than reasonable. Printing more money and borrowing more money are not reasonable alternative policies in the long term.

It is the job of academics to question the status quo and offer reasonable and sensible alternatives. They don't always do that, but when academics are at their best, that is what they should do. In this task, academic economists have, for the most part, failed miserably. Of course, there are exceptions, but compared to financial analysts and money managers who have an obvious economic reason to support the status quo, there are far too few academics who are willing to seriously question and, most importantly, create good alternatives to the status quo economic policies.

What if We Are Wrong and the Past 10 Years Were Like the 1970s and Maybe the Next Big Stock Boom Is Right Around the Corner?

That's actually a good question. Investors do tend to get more pessimistic when markets have been doing poorly, as they have in the past 10 years. The same sentiment occurred at the end of the 1970s. Many investors thought that the market was entering a period of longer-term problems. None predicted an Aftershock-type situation, but few saw the enormous gains to be had in the 1980s and 1990s.

The difference is that we were just entering the stock, bond, and real estate bubbles at that point. There was also significant real growth in China and in Europe. Japan had troubles in the 1990s but was buoyed by the booming bubbles in the United States. All of these factors are not in existence going forward. Real growth in China will be hard to find once its massive construction bubble pops. Europe is already showing signs that its longer-term growth prospects are very limited. Japan is no longer growing off our bubbles since they are popping and will pop further. Real economic growth will be hard to find.

So maybe we could just find new bubbles to replace the old ones? Well, that is exactly what is happening. We are using the government debt and dollar bubbles to prop up the old bubbles. Will that last for another 20 years and keep the stock market moving up for another 20 years? The problem is that the government debt and dollar bubbles are best at maintaining old bubbles and not creating new ones. The reason is that if we powered up those bubbles to the point where they would create new bubbles, they would scare investors here and around the world. Tripling our money supply again and boosting our deficit to $3 trillion just to put the stock market into hyperdrive would quickly backfire because it would scare investors away.

So even if they won't take us back to the good old days of the 1980s and 1990s, maybe the government debt and dollar bubbles can at least help us keep our gains for another 20 years? If we only had a government debt bubble, it's possible we could keep it going for another 10 years or so. But to help maintain the government debt bubble, we have had to create a dollar bubble. And that makes long-term viability not possible. If the government debt bubble could be maintained without money printing, then maybe we could make it another 10 years before it explodes in an Aftershock. Unfortunately, though, the money printing behind the dollar bubble has lit a fuse on the rest of the bubble economy, and that's why we can't keep maintaining the bubbles for another 20 years.

However, as we said before, it can maintain them for another two to four years. But that could be a very rocky road. Maintain doesn't mean a Dow of 12,000. The stock market could easily fall 30 percent or more while being maintained by the government debt and dollar bubbles.

Again, if we were willing to borrow a whole lot more and print a whole lot more, we could keep such declines from happening and even get the market growing rapidly again, but we won't. As we said, it could backfire pretty quickly. So even though government borrowing and printing will maintain the stock and bond bubbles, that doesn't mean they will be maintained at a high level.

Maybe we're not in a bubble at all? Maybe what we are seeing is real growth? If you still have your doubts about that, please go back to Chapters 1 through 4.

It's Time to Leave CW Behind and Create an Actively Managed Aftershock Portfolio

The goal of the wise Aftershock investor is not perfect timing or even maximum short-term profits, but *reasonable returns with limited volatility* and, most importantly, doing it without big exposure to a major downturn in stocks or bonds. It sounds simple, but implementing it is not so simple, yet that is exactly what most investors need to do.

Chapter 14 provides more details about creating your Aftershock investment portfolio. For now, the take-home message is that your old CW portfolio is not going to save you from the Market Cliff and Aftershock. From this point forward, you need an *actively managed* Aftershock portfolio.

Even if there is no Aftershock, you still have to change your CW portfolio. That's because this is a new investment environment and the old ways will no longer protect you. Our advice about what to do instead of the usual CW investing is contained in the rest of this book, with separate chapters on stocks, bonds, real estate, insurance, and more.

The bottom line is, regardless of whether you believe we will have a full Aftershock or maybe something less dramatic, given the coming rising inflation and coming rising interest rates, if you have a conventional wisdom investment portfolio (and most people do), you essentially have two options:

Change It or Lose It.

PART

II

AFTERSHOCK INVESTING

CHAPTER 6

Taking Stock of Stocks

FACING THE FUTURE OF STOCKS, MUTUAL FUNDS, AND INDEX FUNDS

We know what you want. You want us to tell you exactly what stocks to buy and sell, and exactly when to buy and sell them. You want us to lay out a detailed road map that will guide you to and through the coming Aftershock, with clear signs and signals you can easily follow that will bring you maximum profits today and still provide all the protection you will need later. You want to know the right percentages of your portfolio to invest in various stock sectors. And you wouldn't mind knowing the specific stocks we recommend within each sector, depending on your age, wealth, and risk tolerance.

In short, you want us to give you exactly what you used to be able to get from any experienced investment adviser or financial advice book—back before all this mess started. You want your stock investing to be easy, low risk, and of course, profitable.

We understand what you want and we sincerely wish we could give every bit of that to you. But in this new era of fake recoveries, massive money printing, and the looming threat of future inflation, rising interest rates, and the coming multibubble crash and Aftershock, what you want us to give you is no longer possible. Everything has changed.

Instead, you have to adjust to the fact that no one can tell you exactly what to do or how to correctly time every buy and sell. Instead of giving you the advice you want, we will do our best to give you the advice we believe you need, the advice that best fits the new reality.

Naturally, you won't like it too much. It's hard to let go of what you want, especially when stocks have been so very good to us for so long. It would be great if the love affair would last forever.

Unfortunately, it won't.

Stocks: A Love Story

Over the course of half a century, the American investor has fallen deeply in love with stocks. Stocks occupy the heart of most investment portfolios and are at the heart of what has made so many Americans so much money over so many decades, especially in the 1980s and 1990s. And what's not to love? The stock market, as measured by the Dow Jones Industrial Average from 1980 to 2000, rose an astounding 1,000 percent. Not 100 percent, but *1,000 percent.* That's pretty darn good. It's especially good when you consider that the economy, as measured by gross domestic product (GDP), grew only 260 percent during that same time period. That's a whole lot less than 1,000 percent.

By contrast, in the prior period from 1928 to 1982, a time of huge growth of the U.S. economy, the Dow grew a more reasonable 300 percent in 54 years. And yet, in just 20 years (1980–2000), the Dow shot up more than 1,000 percent. That is truly extraordinary!

It is also the quintessential definition of a bubble.

Like most bubbles, the stock market bubble originally started to rise for good, fundamental reasons: the U.S. economy was growing and so were company earnings. Investors began to fall in love with the profits from stocks, and the more stocks went up, the deeper they fell in love, which meant they were willing to pay more and more for them. Big institutional investors, who manage pensions, endowments, and life insurance funds, fell in love with buying stocks, too. And not just American investors were smitten; increasing numbers of foreign investors were joining the love-fest as well, helping to push up U.S. stock prices faster than company earnings rose or the overall U.S. economy grew. Thus, the stock market bubble was born in the mid-1980s.

But even love is not enough to keep a bubble going forever. Given enough time, economic gravity does eventually kick in and bubbles pop. Prior to fully popping, bubbles sometimes just sag for a while, then pick up a little and sag again. But a full pop will eventually come because all bubbles, by definition, do pop. The only way to avoid a full pop is to not be a bubble in the first place.

Knowing that there is a stock market bubble does not mean we have to exit it immediately because it is not going to pop today. But it is essential that you be aware that it is a bubble (see Chapter 2 for details), and you must understand that bubbles eventually pop.

We don't know exactly when this bubble will pop, and we don't know exactly how it will move up and down prior to popping fully. We do know, however, that the stock market bubble is currently being artificially boosted by massive money printing (see Figure 6.1). Even back in 2010, when we were writing our 2011 *Aftershock*, Second Edition, we wrote that "In the short term, more massive money printing could continue to support the stock market and could even push it higher in 2011 and beyond . . . continued massive money printing could potentially push the Dow back to its 2007 all-hihg high of 14,164 or higher." And of course, that is just what happened.

We also know that massive money printing will eventually cause significant rising inflation (the Fed's own analysis says so), and that high inflation and interest rates will eventually pop all the bubbles. Even without the bubbles, high inflation and interest rates would

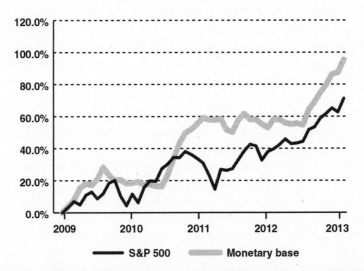

Figure 6.1   S&P 500 Rises with the Fed's Money Printing, mid-2009 to mid-2013

Stocks have been rising in nearly lockstep with the rising money supply.

Source: Bloomberg and the Federal Reserve.

put downward pressure on any economy, and it will be especially negative for a vulnerable bubble economy.

We also know that before the bubbles pop, the stock market will become increasingly dangerous. So if you choose to stay in this artificially supported bubble a while longer, you will need to *actively manage* your portfolio.

Active management in this new investment environment is not like the active management of years ago. It used to be that the term *active management* meant a lot of moving in and out of stocks to gain maximum profits. Now when we say active management, we mean being *aggressively defensive* in a changing market to minimize risk.

Even the meaning of the word *risk* has changed. Our focus now is no longer about managing individual company risk, but managing the general risk of the overall stock market. Unlike individual company risk, overall market risk cannot be managed by diversifying *within* the stock market. Market risk can be reduced only by diversifying *among markets*. In other words, the issue is less about which stocks you should buy or sell and more about whether you should be in the stock market at all. And if so, how much of your portfolio should contain stocks and how will you manage that risk, while also making some profit?

We won't window-dress it—this kind of active management is not easy. It's true that profits can be made in any market, but that is a lot harder to do in some markets than in others. In this market, there are big risks to staying in stocks, and it's not clear exactly how much upside is left, although there could be some. Since 2000 there has been little upside (overall, the S&P has barely risen in the past decade when adjusted for inflation) and there has been a huge amount of volatility. For Nasdaq stocks, the past decade has been even worse, with a loss of about a third.

The short-term future is hard to predict, but if you time it right and get out before the stock bubble pops, you could also lock in some larger gains. Even if you decide to move entirely or heavily out of the stock market, or move to a more defensive stock position, you will still need to actively manage your portfolio to protect yourself and still make reasonable returns.

To understand our view of stocks and how to actively manage an investment portfolio containing stocks, you need to understand the conventional wisdom (CW) view of stocks. To understand the CW view of stocks, it's essential to understand the recent history of stocks. You don't need to know how stock markets were formed and other ancient

Irving Fisher: Stock Market Cheerleader
of the Great Depression

Yes, stock market cheerleading didn't just start recently; it's been around for a while. It has simply gained an enormous number of practitioners recently with the massive boom in the stock market since the 1980s. One of the most memorable people to take up the cheerleading profession was Irving Fisher. The reason he's such an iconic figure is that he started with one of the earlier great stock market bubbles—the 1920s. Of course, that was a mere pimple compared to our current bubble, but there are similarities.

The other characteristic that makes Fisher so iconic is that he was not part of Wall Street. He didn't earn his money on the Street and no one paid him to cheerlead. He was as pure a cheerleader as you can get. He actually believed it! And he had a lot of credibility. Fisher was one of the most renowned economists from one of the most renowned universities in the nation: Yale.

He not only had good credentials. He actually did good economic work. He was one of the most outstanding and most respected economists of the time. His two books, *The Rate of Interest* and *The Theory of Interest*, both were important contributions to our current understanding of interest and capital.

However, Fisher was not so great at predicting the Great Depression. In fact, he infamously said, just three days before the 1929 crash, "*Stock prices have reached what looks like a permanently high plateau.*"

Of course, no one at the time thought that statement would later become infamous; they just thought Fisher was a very smart economist who made very smart observations that were right. That quote was reflective of a great deal of stock market cheerleading Mr. Fisher did in the late 1920s. We know now that his very smart observations turned out to be absolutely wrong, and he himself lost quite a bit of money because of it. Just getting popular support for your economic predictions doesn't make them *right*—it just makes them *comfortable*. The stock market collapsed and did not become fully vibrant again for decades, and the economy sank into the Great Depression.

So Irving Fisher was one of those really smart economists with great credentials whom everyone wanted to believe was right, but wasn't. And he won't be the last incredibly smart economist or financial analyst with good credentials who is a market cheerleader. Irving Fisher serves as a wonderful cautionary tale to today's financial analysts and economists who keep cheerleading. However, it is a cautionary tale that is largely ignored today but will come back to haunt the cheerleaders later when they lose both their historical respect and their jobs.

history, but you do need to understand the more recent history upon which current Conventional Wisdom (and our love for stocks) is based.

How Stocks Became the Heart of Most Investment Portfolios

Stocks were not always the popular investment they have been for the past several decades. Before stocks became the darlings of the investment community, bonds had a more favored status. And before bonds, it was gold. As each asset class proved its reliability over time, it became more popular. Only when stocks began growing across the board for decades at a time did they become impossible to ignore for all but the most risk-averse investors.

Originally, stocks were primarily valued for the dividend payments that came with them. Rather than hoping to benefit from rising share prices, investors looked at stocks essentially as bonds with greater yields—payments could be variable, of course, but investors paid close attention to earnings and gravitated toward blue-chip stocks with a consistent record of dividend payments.

It was only in the 1920s that many investors began to see the value in buying stocks with the intention of earning capital gains by selling them later at a higher price. At that point, the stock market became more speculative in nature and trading activity increased. This sent stock prices soaring. In a six-year span, the Dow Jones Industrial Average would quadruple in value, but it would take only a few days for everything to come crashing down in October 1929. Although it's worth noting that even after the crash ended the great speculation of the 1920s, it took several years for the stock market to fall during the Depression to its historic low point in 1932.

After the market crash and the Depression, stocks were naturally very unpopular. New Deal reforms, in particular the establishment of the Securities and Exchange Commission, sought to curb the unethical and manipulative behavior that had been rampant among publicly traded companies. But it wasn't until the 1950s that stocks regained popularity among the general public.

Part of the current success of the stock market was due to the work of Merrill Lynch, who systematically established a retail network that helped make people feel comfortable with stocks for the first time since the Great Depression. Because of Mr. Lynch, average American investors began to routinely add some stocks to their bond portfolios. It was a landmark shift.

By the 1960s, the stock market was booming again, though that boom turned into a mini-bust in the next decade due to recession and particularly high inflation (the natural enemy of the stock market).

Like Throwing Darts: It Used to Be Easy to Pick Winning Stocks

A stock is a certificate indicating that you own some small portion of a company. When you buy stock from a company, you are paying for part of everything owned by that company. If the company makes a profit in the future, the value of your stock goes up. As partial owners of the company, stockholders have the power to vote on decisions that may impact the future of the company. The more shares you own in a company, the more decision-making power you have.

Various types of stocks, mutual funds, and index funds are bought and sold on various stock markets around the world. Some readers may need or want more background on stocks, and some may not. So, in our attempt to keep the flow of the book moving, we have put some background material on stocks in Appendix A. Financial books can get a bit dull at times and we want to avoid that.

As we mentioned earlier, for most of the past few decades, an investor could make money in the stock market just by throwing darts at a dartboard and watching his portfolio grow. And in today's era of 24-hour stock market analysis on TV and the Internet, there's a temptation to divorce stocks as a commodity from the companies whose ownership they represent. Now we buy and sell stocks not just based on company earnings, but also based on speculation about what other people will speculate on. We want to buy what's hot.

Whenever investors are willing to pay more for something than its inherent value justifies—particularly when that investment is fueled by debt—we have an asset bubble. But how do we assign an accurate, nonbubble value to a stock? It really comes down to company earnings. But how to translate earnings into a share price can be tricky. We'll look at some of the traditional ways and then at the ways we think are more reflective of a company's value.

In Theory, When You Buy Stocks You Are Buying Future Earnings

Earnings, fundamentally, are what you are buying when you buy a stock. You're usually not buying assets; you're buying all of the company's future earnings. Not just next year's earnings but *all* its future earnings—forever. But how do you put a value on something so long term and something so unknowable? Well, that's the trick. It is a bet you are making. You, of course, hope that bet is more than just a guess. At the very least, you want it to be an educated guess.

Before we can tell you about how we look at stocks, you have to understand the Conventional Wisdom approach to valuing stocks. Again, you have to know CW before you can understand any deviation.

Discounted Cash Flow Models

When you buy a stock, you are buying the company's future earnings. The question analysts face is how to model that. One of the most commonly used methods to calculate the value of those earnings is a discounted cash flow (DCF) model (it actually uses the free cash flow instead of profits, but the concept is the same). Although this is a very simple model and high-powered financial analysts use more sophisticated models to calculate a company's value, it contains the key elements of many valuation models and serves to quickly illustrate what is involved in such a model.

Essentially, a DCF model attempts to capitalize all of a company's future earnings and thus calculate the current value of the company and its stock price. Of course, that's not as simple as just adding up the future earnings of the company. Those earnings have to be "discounted" to their current value. That discount is determined based on a number of factors, including the cost of capital, the uncertainty of the earnings, and the uncertainty of the stock market valuation. That discount rate is then applied to the company's future earnings.

However, since you can't add up the earnings of a company forever (how long is forever?), a typical DCF model only adds up the earnings for, say, five years in the future. To capture the "forever" part of the company's value, a "terminal value" is calculated. Much of the value of a company in a DCF model is in the terminal value. Needless to say, this model isn't perfect. What it does is try to put numbers behind all the intangible issues of uncertainty in earnings and in valuing the company's earnings forever. It also illustrates just how tricky it can be to calculate the correct value of a stock and how much is always left to the judgment of the financial analyst.

Price-to-Earnings Ratio

One of the most commonly used methods to value earnings is to determine a price-to-earnings ratio (P/E ratio or just P/E). This is basically a measure of how many years' worth of earnings you are willing to pay for the company's stock. For example, a P/E of 10 to 1 (often shortened to just 10 by financial writers) means you are willing to pay 10 times the company's current annual earnings for the stock. So if the company's annual earnings (not revenues) are $10 million, the company is worth $100 million at a P/E of 10. If you want to calculate the price of a share of stock, you just use the earnings per share. So if the earnings per share is $10 and the P/E is 10, a share of stock is worth $100.

There is no magic rule as to how many years' worth of earnings investors should pay for a stock. For S&P 500 stocks the P/E has varied from 8 in 1980 to 22 in 2000. Generally, P/Es are higher for companies with higher growth.

Although the ratio is simple, what goes into determining the correct ratio can be very complex. One of the key issues to consider is the cost of capital. You're paying now for earnings coming later. Those earnings in the future are not worth as much as the same amount of cash now (the time value of money).

Also, there is uncertainty regarding those earnings. What if the company's earnings decline quite a bit in the next few years? What if it goes out of business? What if revenues grow but earnings decline? Lots of things can happen to a company's earnings over a period of 10 or 20 years. Hence, the more years' worth of earnings you are willing to pay, the greater your risk because the likelihood of bad things happening to a company's earnings are much greater over a 20-year period than a 10-year period.

Finally, what if the stock market values those earnings less in the next few years? Your company may have exactly the earnings you hoped for, but the market values them less and, hence, your stock is worth less.

Valuing uncertain future earnings in an uncertain stock market is a very tricky game. That's part of the reason why valuations can vary so much over time. There's no certainty in the calculations.

Most important, partly because of all this uncertainty, psychology plays a huge role. Some people may see fewer risks in a company's future than others. Some people may see fewer risks in the future economy than others. Who knows who's right and what the right P/E should be.

However, if the economy slows, expect P/Es to decline. Some of that decline may have been anticipated, but lately, stock market analysts have been none too good at predicting economic slowdowns. Hence, the P/Es fall only when the economy has proven to be in a slowdown. That also means that P/Es could fall a lot if the economy slows down a lot.

Of course, in a down economy, not just P/Es are falling, but the actual earnings are often falling as well. This will cause further damage to a stock's price. In addition, earnings can fall substantially if interest rates rise substantially. These are two key vulnerabilities that the stock market faces in the future as we near the Aftershock. We will talk more about these issues later in the chapter.

It's easy to see how psychology can enter the stock valuation game. A lot of uncertainty and judgment are a key part of valuing stocks. In addition, if bubble psychology enters the game, it often doesn't matter what the "correct" P/E should be. All that matters is that stocks have been going up in price and investors want to get on board that rising boat. Earnings valuation and analysis is needed only to make investors feel good about their decision to jump on the bubble boat.

To make matters even worse, earnings themselves are not always easy to define, and therefore the correct P/E is not a certainty. Hence, different people look at the history of P/Es differently. Yale economist Robert Shiller, the person who helped create the Case/Shiller Home Price Index and did great work in tracking real historical home prices, has also done a good job in tracking historical P/Es. His historical chart of P/Es is presented in Figure 6.2. Shiller developed a more accurate measure of P/E by adjusting for cyclical differences. This is the ratio of the stock price to the *moving average of the previous 10-years' earning*, adjusted for inflation (CPI). This is a better way to look at market trends and stock evaluation.

Many people will have different views of historical P/Es, just as they have different views of historical home prices. However, we think Dr. Shiller has done the best job at giving us a good idea of what historical P/Es have been.

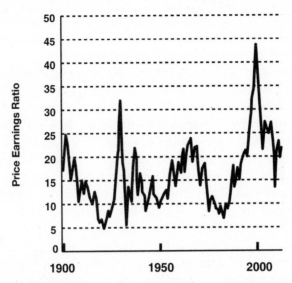

Figure 6.2   Historical Price-to-Earnings Ratios (Based on Cyclically Adjusted P/E Ratio)

The high points were right before the declines of 1929 and 2000. The current level is higher than at any time since 1900 other than in 1929, 2000, and 2008.

Source: Robert Shiller, Yale University.

More Ways to Value Stocks

Although the P/E is the most common method for valuing stocks, there are other methods for valuing a company that currently doesn't have earnings but could have in the future, or whose assets have value beyond their earnings (possibly due to mismanagement of the company's assets). We should also say that there are a multitude of methods used to value companies, some of which are proprietary, and many of which are much more complex than those discussed in this book. What we are trying to give you is a basic overview of how stocks are valued, as a background to understand Conventional Wisdom and why it is wrong, not a course in equity valuation and analysis.

- *Price-to-revenue ratio.* If a company doesn't have earnings due to mismanagement or an economic downturn, or for a variety of reasons the company's earnings are not a good measure of the company's future or potential health, a different measure of value could be used, which is the price-to-revenue ratio. In this valuation method the investor simply looks at the price of the stock relative to its revenues to determine its value. The clear risk in this analysis is that by ignoring earnings you could be getting yourself into an investment that ultimately doesn't pay off. Even very large companies and investors have made big mistakes relying on such analysis to make investments. It is also much easier to get a bubble valuation when you ignore earnings.

- *Book value or liquidation value.* Sometimes a company mismanages its assets. Maybe it's an older retail chain that isn't very good at retailing anymore but owns a lot of good retail real estate. Maybe it's an oil company that is not well managed and is just riding on the earnings from oil and gas wells drilled many years ago. In this case, valuing the company at its liquidation value makes sense. A liquidation value is the value of the company's assets, not its earnings or revenues. This may help an investor see what may be the hidden value in a mismanaged company. A comparison of the company's stock price to its liquidation or "book value" is also one way to measure how the market views the quality of a company's management and its assets. Currently, many large banks are valued below book value, indicating that many investors think the bank is overvaluing its assets and is possibly managing what assets it has very poorly.

- *Private-company valuation.* Private companies are usually valued at a significant discount to public companies. This is largely because they are less liquid (harder to sell) than public companies. You can sell a share of public company stock very easily. Not so with a private company. This is often referred to as the marketability or liquidity discount. However, today a big part of the reason that private companies are valued significantly less is that they are not participating in the public stock market bubble.

  Compared to public companies, private-company valuations don't usually vary that much over time, unless they happen to be in a hot industry, such as social media. In fact, they usually trade for about 4 to 6 times earnings. That means that private buyers are willing to pay about 4 to 6 years of profits to buy a company. That actually makes sense, given all the uncertainties in any company's future earnings. But notice how much lower that is than public company stocks, which often have valuations of 15 to 20 times annual earnings. A normal marketability discount might be 20 to 30 percent. But the actual discount for being private is much higher, which is a partial indication of a bubble stock market.

In addition, many private companies are bought with borrowed money based on paying back that loan from the company's earnings. Hence, many people buying a company don't want to buy a company that will take more than four to six years to pay off its loans. They don't plan to flip the company. They plan to make money from it, and they want to make money from it as soon as possible. This type of valuation makes a lot more fundamental sense than a bubble valuation.

Benjamin Graham

No discussion about stock valuation would be complete without some mention of the bible of stock valuation, Benjamin Graham's classic book, *Security Analysis*. Published in 1934, this landmark book on stock valuation is what Warren Buffett most often refers to when speaking about his own views on company valuation and "value investing." His book is an excellent explanation of good rules for Conventional Wisdom investing that have worked in the past. Graham's book offers investors three guiding principles.

First, always invest with a margin of safety by buying at a discount to a stock's "intrinsic value." That way, if the market value falls a bit, you are still ahead. Second, expect market volatility and find ways to profit from it. Options for doing this include dollar-cost averaging and diversification. And, third, know your investing style: actively involved and willing to research and learn on your own over time or more passively involved and in need of professional assistance and lower risk.

Conventional Wisdom on Stocks

The overriding mantra of the recent stock market CW cheerleader is that stocks are always poised for growth, while gold is at its peak and ready for a fall. Never mind that since 2000 exactly the opposite has been true. The goal of the stock market cheerleader is to *sell stocks*, not to do proper historical analysis. Of course, as we always say, CW faith in more growth ahead is grounded in history— at least the part of history they like best (i.e., the rising bubbles). CW says the future will be like the good past. Yes, the CW cheerleader would agree that the recent past has not been kind to stocks, but if you look farther back in history, the performance in stocks has been quite good. On this, the cheerleaders are correct. Just like real estate, stocks have been a good buy over the long term, especially if we define the long term as since 1950. If we ignore the Great Depression and the long, slow recovery of the market during World War II, stocks look pretty good historically.

If you look at the Warren Buffett chart on stocks since 1965 that we presented in Chapter 5, it looks even better. So if the future is like the past, especially those golden years of 1980 to 2000, when the stock market was up over 1,000 percent, the future is pretty bright. It's also easier to overlook the past 10 years and assume that this is more like the 1970s—just a prelude to another stock market explosion of 1,000 percent or more.

CW Stock Cheerleading Is Based More on Salesmanship than Rigorous Analysis

However, none of this analysis looks at the fundamentals. In fact, it really isn't even analysis. It's just saying that the good part of the past will inevitably continue and the bad part will inevitably give way to the good part. As we said earlier, there are fundamental economic reasons why the future will be different from the past, especially the good parts of the past. Actually, if you go back over the past 200 years of financial and economic history, it's easy to see that big change is the real pattern of financial history—not just endless and enormous growth in the stock market as far as the eye can see.

That type of analysis is not analysis—it's just salesmanship. And even hard-nosed stock market analysts are primarily employed by

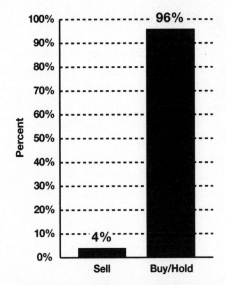

Figure 6.3   Stock Analysts' Buy/Sell Recommendations, November 2011

Very few analysts recommend selling stocks. Mostly, they suggest buying or holding.

Source: Fact Set Research Systems.

firms that all started as stock and bond sales firms and which to this day are heavily driven by the sales of various stock-and bond-related securities. So it's no surprise that when the financial analysts employed by these firms are asked to rate stocks, they usually rate them as a buy or a hold. In fact, research on analysts' opinions shows that they rate stocks as buy or holds over 95 percent of the time, as indicated in Figure 6.3.

This seems a whole lot less like analysis and a whole lot more like salesmanship. And that salesmanship mentality pervades Wall Street and the financial press. In one way or another, the livelihoods of all these people often depend, in one way or another, on good sales of stocks and bonds. We're not trying to be critical—it's just the truth. Everybody has to make money. But that means it's not the best environment for hard-nosed and objective analysis. Ask someone who knows and has tried to do objective analysis, like Mike Mayo, who recently wrote *Exile on Wall Street* (see sidebar) about his work analyzing the banking industry. The financial press doesn't always like someone who challenges the prevailing CW on Wall Street, and neither does Wall Street.

CW Analysis Makes Key Assumptions

Many financial analysts would say in protest that they are doing proper analysis and not cheerleading. They are applying the valuation methods just discussed in one form or another, and those methods, although improved, haven't fundamentally changed during the stock market bubble. That's true, but as we pointed out in that discussion, assumptions of future economic conditions and company earnings are absolutely fundamental to that analysis. And the current analysis depends on two key assumptions, which we discussed in Chapter 5: (1) the assumption of a natural growth rate and (2) the assumption that we are not in a multibubble economy.

Mike Mayo: The Courageous Stock Analyst

Mike Mayo is no stranger to controversy. A stock analyst for 25 years, Mayo has worked for some of the world's largest financial firms, including Deutsche Bank, Credit Suisse, and Lehman Brothers. His frank analysis has led to some shaky tenures and in some cases his departure. "Eventually, when I left [Lehman Brothers]," Mayo says, "I was literally escorted out of the office." In late 2011, he wrote *Exile on Wall Street*, a book detailing the fundamental problems with the financial industry.

In 1999, while working at Credit Suisse First Boston, Mayo made waves by writing a report advising the sale of all bank stocks, citing lowered standards for loan procedures across the board. The response was less than welcoming. He was skewered by the financial community and mocked on cable news programs. He recounts in his book: "One trader . . . printed out my photo and stuck it to her bulletin board with the word 'WANTED' scribbled over it."

Clearly, Mayo had touched a nerve, but his analysis was prescient. In 2007, Mayo was one of the few analysts who saw the impending crisis in the financial sector, predicting that the crisis could cost as much as $400 billion, "a number that was much higher than anyone else's estimate to that point, though one that still turned out to be too low."

Mayo argues that the culture of the financial industry gives analysts, ratings agencies, and regulators little incentive to provide investors with honest assessments. "Less than 5 percent of stock ratings on Wall Street are a negative rating," says Mayo. "Any first-year business school student can tell you that not 95 percent of stocks are worth buying."

Today, Mayo continues to send ripples through the financial community. In May 2012, now working at CLSA, he downgraded his rating of JPMorgan Chase, widely considered the industry's sturdiest firm, to the industry's only negative rating. Just before this move, he downgraded Bank of America, and then later he issued a warning about Morgan Stanley's reputation after it mismanaged Facebook's IPO.

Clearly, Mike Mayo has never been afraid of calling it like it is, even at great personal risk. And for that we give him an ABE Award for Intellectual Courage.

Stock analysts and cheerleaders naturally assume (almost unconsciously) that there is a natural economic growth rate. That means an economic growth rate that always goes up no matter what, and that means a stock market that always goes up. We discussed earlier why there is no such thing as a natural economic growth rate—there is simply no theoretical or historical basis for a natural growth rate in any country at any time. All economic growth is basically derived from productivity improvements, and those happen only when people make changes to improve their productivity. Even during periods of high-productivity growth, like the twentieth century, the growth rates can change dramatically because productivity improvements are not being made all the time. Just look at China over the past century or even the United States over the past century. It's hardly been one solid straight line of growth.

The second assumption is harder to refute since we are still living in a multibubble economy and it is very hard for people to see bubbles until they pop—especially people who don't want to see them. We made the case for the multibubble economy quite a while ago in *America's Bubble Economy* in 2006, but don't expect the cheerleaders to see it. It's simply not in their stock and bond salesperson's interest.

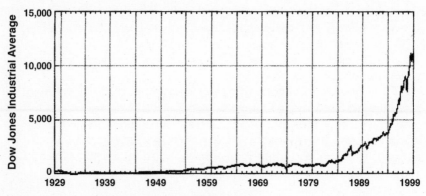

Figure 6.4   Growth of the Dow, 1928–1999

The stock market had modest but reasonable growth until the 1980s and 1990s, when growth exploded.

Source: Bloomberg.

Why Conventional Wisdom Is Wrong Now

Big asset price growth that is not firmly based on real fundamental economic drivers adds up to a bubble. Research by the eminent economist Milton Friedman showed that over a longer period of time, company earnings don't outpace growth in GDP. That's because any excess company earnings above economic growth are eliminated.

As we mentioned in Chapter 2, if you look at a longer-term historical perspective, the stock market grew 300 percent from 1928 to 1980—a period of more than 50 years of massive economic growth and population growth—whereas in just 20 short years, from 1980 to 2000, it grew more than *1,000 percent.* That's a bubble.

We think you will agree that Figure 6.4 even *looks* like a bubble. Why else would there be so much growth in the stock market so quickly, compared to the past? And economic growth was stronger in the past, not weaker.

Also, it's not just the rocket rise of stocks; it's the whole rising multibubble U.S. economy and the rising multibubble world economy that makes an even greater case for calling this a stock market bubble. We discussed this in Chapter 2 and in more detail in *America's Bubble Economy* and *Aftershock,* Second Edition, so we won't go over it again here. Suffice it to say that Aftershock wisdom calls this a stock market bubble. And as you already know, bubbles do eventually pop.

Normal Valuation Methods Are Being Replaced by Bubble Valuation

As discussed earlier, the normal valuation methods are highly subject to economic and financial assumptions that are changing and are about to change even more. What matters now in stock market valuations is bubble-think and the ability of various economists and financial analysts to make people feel more comfortable believing that bubble valuations are real valuations.

Investor attitudes are key to stock market valuations today. However, investor attitudes can and will change. Bubble blindness, after all, is only a temporary condition. All bubble blindness has a cure: *time.* Over time, it becomes increasingly obvious that we really are in a multibubble worldwide economy and there is no "natural" economic growth rate to save us. Over time, it will also become increasingly obvious that the government cannot borrow enormous amounts of money that is enabled by enormous amounts of money printing without creating inflation.

Most important, bubble blindness is quickly cured by others who lose their blindness. If only 20 percent of the investing public loses their blindness, that is enough to pop the bubbles. As with all bubbles, only a few investors will get out the door before this bubble pops. Most investors will stay blind until the bubbles pop and their money suddenly goes to Money Heaven.

So, bubble blindness is always temporary. The only question is whether it is cured before the bubbles pop or it is cured when the bubbles pop.

Stocks Will Fall in Four Stages

Not all investors will run and stay out of the stock market at the first signs of trouble. That's why the stock market will not fall all at once but will decline in stages. Here is our best approximation of how that will happen.

Stage 1: The Recent Past and Now

During the global financial crisis of late 2008, stock markets around the world fell 40 percent or more. Since then, massive money printing by the Fed and massive borrowing by the U.S. government have been helping to boost and support the stock market.

In early March 2013, the Dow returned to its high of 2007 (14,164) and has even grown a bit higher since. Although this is a big bounce off the bottom in 2008, the massive government stimulus has not been enough to push the market too much higher than the previous 2007 highs. That's because it is easier to create a rebound than it is to push a sagging bubble higher than a rebound, without real fundamental growth.

But the fact that stock investors are generally still trusting current stock valuations doesn't mean those valuations are worthy of that trust.

Stage 2: The Short-Term Future

If you are worrying about exiting stocks at just the right time, please don't because you already missed the boat. As we said in Chapter 4, the perfect time to exit the market and move into gold was in 1999. So if you are still in the market, the question is less about perfect timing and more about preservation of capital.

Stocks won't likely fall dramatically in the immediate future. In the recent past, it seems that even very negative news does not always create as big a drop as one might expect. When stocks do start to fall longer term, prices will not drop in a straight line. In the short term, each time stocks fall a bit, there are some investors who see bargains rather than a falling bubble, and they begin to buy those "bargains," which prevents a deeper fall.

In Stage 2 U.S. stocks still have appeal for both foreign and domestic investors. Remember, these people are in love with stocks, and it will take some time to give that up.

Stage 3: Medium-Term Future

However, over time, as inflation and interest rates rise, the bloom of love will begin to wilt. Certainly, rising inflation and rising interest rates will not be good for companies or their stocks (or for any of the other bubbles). That's because massive stimulus is not the same thing as massive growth. And, increasingly, the stimulus will have less of an impact, over shorter and shorter periods. "Green shoots," if any, will turn brown faster and faster. Without a real recovery, there will be lots of stock market oscillations.

Stage 4: The Market Cliff and Aftershock

Even if the Fed were to stop all money printing today (and they certainly are not), we have already increased the money supply threefold since March 2009. That is more than enough to give us future inflation and rising interest rates which will damage the future economy and the stock market. However, high inflation and high interest rates are not going to occur overnight. It will happen over time. So the more time that goes by, the greater the risk to stocks.

However, time is not the only risk factor. There are a number of other potential triggers that could push things along sooner. Among these possibilities are further problems with the European debt crisis, an economic downturn in China, or trouble with the emerging markets (see Chapter 4).

Because so much of any bubble is driven by investor psychology (both on the way up and on the way down), when it finally bursts, it can pop very, very quickly.

Before the Aftershock, the federal government can and will delay the crash as long as they can with more money printing. But as we've said, eventually this crash-delaying medicine becomes a crash-inducing poison, and there will be little the Fed or anyone else can do without making things worse.

Right now, the Fed can put more money into the system with very few short-term consequences because any potential inflation will lag at least by a couple of years behind any new money printing. But over time, inflation anxiety will rise among CW investors when they see more financial analysts mentioning inflation fears and when more people are asking why we need to print more money. At that point, when more people are aware of inflation risks, the lag time behind any new money printing will get shorter and shorter, inflation will rise faster and faster, and investors will naturally become increasingly concerned. Once enough investors, particularly foreign investors who now own so many dollar-denominated assets, get anxious enough to begin to exit stocks, the stock bubble will suddenly burst.

What's a Savvy Aftershock Investor to Do?

Clearly, being 100 percent out of all stocks *before* significant inflation and the Aftershock hit is essential. However, we are not there yet. That means there is still time before inflation and interest rates rise high enough to kick off the coming Market Cliff, multibubble pop, and the Aftershock that will follow. Before that occurs, some

" A TEMPORARY SOLUTION WOULD BE TO WHITE OUT THIS PART OF THE CHART. "

stocks will hold up better than others. So in the shorter term, it is still okay to own some stocks—as long as they are part of a *well-diversified, Aftershock-based, actively managed portfolio* (see Chapter 14).

As we say throughout this book, Conventional Wisdom will no longer protect you. So the first thing every stock investor must face is the fact that this is a bubble and it is going to pop. Once you have a firm grasp of that, the next logical questions are what to do about it and when?

The Case for Active Management

In a rising bubble economy or in a growing nonbubble economy, successful investing means picking stocks that are going up or about to, and then hanging on to those stocks until you are ready for some profit taking. However, that kind of buy-and-hold or set-it-and-forget-it investing, based on the old ways of valuing stocks, doesn't work too well in a falling bubble—even if that bubble's fall has been temporarily slowed and boosted by massive government stimulus.

Instead, if you are going to own any stocks between now and the Aftershock, then your portfolio requires *active management.* The word *management* seems pretty straightforward. It means you have to make some good decisions and execute those decisions correctly. That is tricky enough. But it gets even more challenging because you also need "active" management, meaning you have to *keep* making correct decisions and keep executing those decisions correctly, again and again, as the economy and the investment environment evolve over time.

For the next year, stocks will continue to be driven by more money printing in the form of quantitative easing (QE). So far, we've had three big rounds of money printing: QE1, QE2, and currently QE3, which is really QE3 and QE3.5 because it started at $40 billion per month in 2012 and then more than doubled to $85 billion per month.

When the Fed prints money, stocks generally go up. However, QE will work for only so long to support the market. Eventually, it will have less and less impact on stock values because more people will see QE as just a temporary fix. Hence, QE-driven stock prices will only last so long, and in the future playing the QE trade by buying when more QE is announced will likely not work as well as it did in the past. The decreasing impact of money printing on the stock market will also ultimately lead to a long-term decline in stock prices.

Again, if this were not an already stalled and sagging bubble, we would expect stocks to continue to rise, regardless of QE or no QE. That isn't the case. This is a falling bubble headed for a big bubble pop when we hit the Market Cliff (see Chapter 4).

Prior to the Market Cliff, you can still play the market if you want to, but please don't push your luck for too long (get out well before others do), and please see Chapter 14 for more details about how to create and actively manage a dynamic Aftershock portfolio.

Bye-Bye Bonds

WHY BONDS ARE GETTING RISKIER AND WHEN TO GET OUT

Why do investors buy bonds? To radically oversimplify, the main appeal of bonds is that they are not stocks. Investors buy bonds to preserve capital (stocks are riskier) and to earn some fixed income (stocks are far less reliable). If the stock market were a jackrabbit, full of excitement and profit potential, bonds would be your steadfast turtle—slow, reliable, and safe.

Financial advisers tell us to have a greater ratio of bonds to stocks as we get older. While a younger person's portfolio might be 30 to 40 percent bonds, older investors usually go for 60 percent or more bonds, especially as they near retirement. Because the profit potential for bonds is limited, there is a broad assumption that their risk potential is limited as well. Under normal conditions, this is usually true; bonds are generally less risky than stocks.

But not always.

Recently, while stocks have been doing well, bonds have begun to decline as interest rates have risen slightly. In May 2013, bonds had a big drop. Is this the end of the long bull bond market? Probably. Interest rates have been at historical lows for a long time and can't go much lower.

Are investors worried? Yes, but not too worried. Bonds have been very good for a very long time. In general, Conventional Wisdom (CW) says stick with bonds; they were good to us before and they will remain good to us in the future. The new Aftershock investing wisdom says some bonds may be okay for now, but you better keep your eyes open and get ready to get out as the economy continues to evolve and interest rates rise.

Just as we explained in the previous chapter on stocks, it is not necessary to give up on bonds immediately. However, please do not fool yourself into thinking bonds will provide you with lasting safety. As with stocks, owning bonds requires *active portfolio management* based on a clear and correct macroeconomic view of what is occurring and will happen next.

Remember: "Past performance does not predict future results."

How Do Bonds Make Money? "Total Return" Is the Key

A bond is basically a loan. Bonds are fixed-income securities issued by private or public entities in exchange for your lending them money. But unlike a typical loan you might make to a friend or a bank might make to you, a bond can also be bought and sold for a profit or a loss on the bond market. This makes bonds more than just a loan; a bond is also a security that can be traded.

Based on the type of borrower, there are several types of bonds. The most common of these are:

- *United States Treasuries,* issued by the federal government. These come in many varieties, based on maturity dates (short, medium, or long term) and other features, such as inflation protection (Treasury inflation-protected securities or TIPS).
- *Municipal bonds,* issued by states and local government.
- *Corporate bonds,* issued by private companies.
- *Mortgage-backed securities,* issued by government-sponsored agencies, such as Fannie Mae (Federal National Mortgage Association), as well as by private corporations.
- *Savings bonds,* issued by the federal government.
- *Floating-rate notes,* change as an interest rate index changes. With some corporate bonds, the coupon changes, while with TIPS, the principal changes.

Bonds earn money two ways. Over time, the issuer of the bond pays the bondholder a set percentage of interest on the loan, called the *coupon.* Interestingly, it's called the coupon because, decades ago, bonds were issued on actual paper and interest was paid when investors literally clipped coupons off their paper bonds and took them to the bank to receive each interest payment. Now we use electronically issued bonds and interest payments, but the old "coupon" name remains.

In addition to the coupon, at any point the bondholder may choose to sell the bond on the bond market for a potential *capital gain* (or loss). Together, the net of the coupon (the interest rate) plus the capital gain (or loss) equals a bond's *total return*.

Your bond's total return is what really matters, not simply its coupon.

As we mentioned in the previous chapter on stocks, some of our readers may need or want more background on bonds and some may not. To keep the book from becoming too boring, we have put some additional background material on bonds in Appendix A. This chapter will focus on how bonds make money and how to avoid losing money on bonds as we approach the Aftershock.

"THANK GOODNESS WE INVESTED IN LONG TERM BONDS."

Your Bond's Total Return Is Always Changing

As mentioned before, a bond's total return is the sum of the capital gain and the coupon. Because bonds are traded on the bond market and their prices continuously change, the bond's effective or current yield also changes, regardless of its original coupon.

For example, if you buy a 10-year $1,000 bond with a 5 percent coupon for $1,200, you are no longer getting a 5 percent yield from it. You will still get the same fixed 5 percent coupon of $25 twice per year. But because you paid $1,200 for the bond, not $1,000, this coupon *effectively* represents a 4.2 percent annual yield. Therefore, its effective or current yield is 4.2 percent.

But wait a second. You also have to consider that when the bond matures, you will not get your $1,200 back. You will get $1,000, which was the original price of the bond. That's a $200 capital loss to take into account, which is why it's a good idea to calculate a bond's *yield to maturity*. Yield to maturity spreads the discount or premium paid for a bond across the length of time you own it.

For example, if you bought this 10-year $1,000 bond two years after it was issued, spreading that $200 loss over the time you own it gives you a yield to maturity of only 2.25 percent. You may be getting $25 every six months, but when the bond matures, you are effectively losing half of that yield (getting 2.1 percent instead of 5 percent) because of that $200 loss on the premium price. Of course, this is the case only if you paid a premium for the bond. If you paid a discount for the bond (meaning you paid less than $1,000 for a $1,000 bond), then the current yield and yield to maturity *add* to the value of your bond.

Your total return (the coupon plus the capital gain) is the *real value* of your bond at any given time, whether you sell it or not. It may be tempting to think that your fixed-rate bond is just plodding along, earning you a steady stream of income, and it is. *But bonds are much more than their coupon value.*

Every minute that the bond market is open, the total return value of your bond is changing. In addition, your options for putting your money into other investments are also changing.

All these factors must be considered when you decide if owning bonds is in your best interest. If you look only at the bond's coupon interest rate, you are missing the bigger picture of the bond's total return. And as we will see shortly, missing the bigger picture can lose you a lot of money very, very quickly.

Higher Risk, Higher Yields

Bonds may be less risky than stocks because, unlike stocks, they pay interest and also guarantee the return of principal, but they are hardly risk free. The level of perceived risk affects how much interest bond issuers are willing to pay when a bond is first issued. After a bond is issued, any changes in the level of risk will impact how much investors are willing to pay for that bond on the bond market. These risk factors include changes in interest rates, changes in creditworthiness, and the passage of time.

Interest Rate Risk

The bond market is ultra-sensitive to changes, even very small changes, in interest rates. Depending on current interest rates, bonds may trade at a premium or at a discount to their par or face value (i.e., the principal for which it was originally purchased and will be paid at maturity). If interest rates have gone up since a bond has been issued, the bond will trade at a discount to make up for the lower coupon payments, compared to the currently higher rates one can get on newly issued bonds. However, if interest rates have gone down since the bond was issued, that bond will trade at a premium because of its higher coupon, compared to current interest rates.

In general, the longer the bond has to maturity or the lower the coupon, the more price sensitivity that bond has to yield changes. The degree of this price sensitivity is measured in terms of something called *duration*. The greater a bond's duration, the more sensitive the price of the bond is to interest rate changes. For example, a bond with a duration of two will move 2 percent in price for every 1 percent change in yield. A bond with a duration of four will move 4 percent for every 1 percent in price change in yield, and so on. Clearly, as time passes and interest rates rise, the prices of bonds with the highest duration will fall the fastest.

In every market, what investors *believe* may happen in the future impacts how they value or discount any asset. In the case of bonds, if investors foresee a decline in interest rates in the future, they will want to buy bonds now in order to sell them at a profit later. However, if investors believe that interest rates may rise in the future, they will not be too eager to buy lower interest rate bonds now unless they can get them cheaply. When interest rates rise more and more, demand for already existing bonds will decline more and more, and bond prices will fall more and more.

This is why investor beliefs about the future direction of interest rate changes make a difference in the current market value of bonds. Just as we discussed in the previous chapter on stocks, *investor psychology matters.*

Credit Risk

In addition to being ultra-sensitive to interest rate changes, bond values are also responsive to changes in perceived credit risk. As with any loan, higher perceived risk of the creditor comes with higher rewards to the lender (meaning higher interest rates), while lower perceived risk loans come with smaller rewards (lower interest rates). Thus, the safest bonds tend to have the lowest yields,

Just a Small Rise in Interest Rates Means a Sharp Fall in Bond Prices

Think U.S. Treasury bonds are a safe investment? Sure, the U.S. Treasury may not default on bonds in the next couple of years, but bonds can still lose a lot of value when inflation goes up and forces interest rates to rise. To give you some idea of how much a Treasury bond can lose with relatively small interest rate increases, we offer you the following example. Let's assume you just bought a 10-year Treasury bond that is earning 3 percent. If the interest rate rises from 3 percent to just 4 percent, your bond loses a whopping 12 percent of its value. Table 7.1 shows what happens if interest rates go even higher.

Table 7.1   Interest Rates Up, Bond Values Down

Interest Rate	Lost Bond Value
5%	18% lost
6%	25% lost
7%	31% lost
10%	46% lost
15%	63% lost

and riskier bonds from the least creditworthy companies, or junk bonds, come with the highest yields.

Under normal conditions, credit risk typically does not radically change from the time a bond is issued until the time of its maturity, but that is not always the case. A once creditworthy bond issuer can become not so creditworthy over time. That is the credit risk. Even without a big change in creditworthiness, this risk does change somewhat over time.

If investors feel that the creditworthiness of the bond issuer has gone down since the bond was first issued—meaning the borrower has for some reason become less likely to pay the coupon or return the principal—then bondholders are more likely to want to get rid of these bonds, and their market prices will decline.

However, when investors feel confident in the bond issuer, they are willing to pay more for a bond that appears to be at lower risk than for a bond that seems to be at higher risk. Of course, the lower risk also means a lower coupon.

The degree of credit risk is not a permanent feature of a bond. Just like interest rates, creditworthiness changes over time and investor psychology plays an important role. Because the coupon is higher for the higher-risk bond, investors may want to take a bet on them, hoping the bond issuer's poor public image may improve down the road. When investors feel less confident about the future, they may feel less eager to own even currently high-rated bonds if investors become concerned about future credit risk.

Time Risk

All risk, including interest rate risk and credit risk, increases over time. The longer the maturity date, the greater the odds of either interest rates going up or the bond issuer's creditworthiness going down. So the greater the amount of time to maturity, the greater the risk, and therefore the higher the interest rate paid. By tying up your principal for a longer time, you are making a bigger sacrifice by not having your money available for other purposes (the time value of money), and you are taking on greater interest rate and credit risk. So, generally speaking, long-term bonds come with higher coupons than medium-term bonds, which come with higher coupons than short-term bonds.

The Bond Ladder

One traditional way to protect yourself from fluctuating interest rates is by creating a *bond ladder*. This is done by buying a variety of bonds with staggered maturity dates, so that you have bonds maturing at least every year, with the longest bonds maturing at later dates. Bond ladders can be as short as 30 days to 6 months or as long as 30 days to 30 years. As you get some of your principal back each year, you can reassess the current financial circumstances and reinvest accordingly. If interest rates rise, you won't be hurt as badly as if you had all one kind of bond, and if interest rates fall, at least you will have some portion of your bond portfolio that will benefit.

This is a great plan—under normal conditions. But, as we keep saying, these are not normal conditions. We aren't saying you should abandon the bond ladder strategy entirely now, but please proceed with caution and take note of the caveats raised in this chapter, especially with longer-term bonds.

But it doesn't always work that way, particularly if interest rates are expected to go down, not up. In that case, long-term bonds may come with lower coupons than short-term bonds. A long-term bond that does not come with a higher yield than a short-term bond can be a losing proposition for the bondholder unless you feel confident that interest rates will fall.

However, if interest rates rise—as we know they will when inflation increases—then long-term bonds are a very bad bet because the future interest rates will likely be much higher than what these long-term bonds currently pay, making the market value of the long-term bonds fall.

Conventional Wisdom on Bonds: The Safety of the Recent Past Means We Can Count on More Safety Ahead

Almost all Conventional Wisdom–type thinking usually has a good historical basis. So to understand CW we need to look at recent history. Only by understanding CW can we understand the Aftershock view on bonds and why CW is wrong.

Like stocks, we don't need to go back to the beginning of the bond market; we just need to take a brief look at the more recent history of bonds because that's what CW focuses on. So if we look back at the beginning of the modern bond market in the late 1800s and early 1900s, we see that bonds dominated the investment landscape. Stocks were not very important. As we discussed in the previous chapter, stocks were considered too risky, even for institutional pension funds.

Eventually, as we moved into the 1960s, stocks became more acceptable, but bonds maintained their position as a much less risky and more stable alternative to stocks. Bonds were the way to reduce risk in a stock portfolio.

In general, investors have considered bonds to be among the safest of all investments, based on three comforting reasons:

1. *Bonds issued by private entities are backed by the assets of the bond issuer,* so even if they become less creditworthy or go into bankruptcy, as a creditor, you have the right to collect on this debt. Bonds are safer than stocks in this situation because bondholders get paid before shareholders.
2. *The bond issuer guarantees repayment of the principal.* No stock issuer can make that claim.
3. *Bonds issued by public entities are backed by state and federal governments.* These entities have the ability to raise taxes to make good on their payments.

Given these nice safety features, over the years investors have gotten very used to thinking of many bonds as nearly risk free. But the evolution of the bond market entered a new era, beginning in the early 1980s, which together worked to greatly heat up the bond market.

The first big change was that the previously very high interest rates of the early 1980s were about to significantly decline. Falling interest rates naturally made bonds a particularly good investment. Remember what we said earlier about the importance of looking at the *total return* of the bond, not just its coupon rate. As interest rates fell, bonds were showing excellent capital gains. As you can see from Figure 7.1, this bullish bond market (due to falling interest rates) continued through 2012.

The second big change was closely tied to the first. Due to falling interest rates, beginning in the 1980s the amount of outstanding debt has exploded, as Figure 7.2 indicates. This included all forms

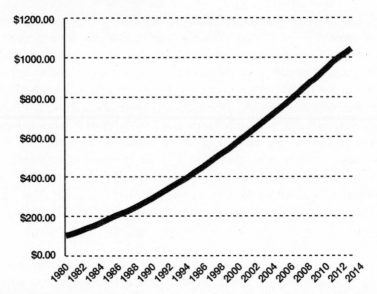

Figure 7.1   Falling Interest Rates Pumped Up Bond Prices from 1980 through 2012

The rising yield on constant-maturity 30-year U.S. government Treasury bonds shows that the bond market has been in a strong bull market since 1980.

Source: Bloomberg.

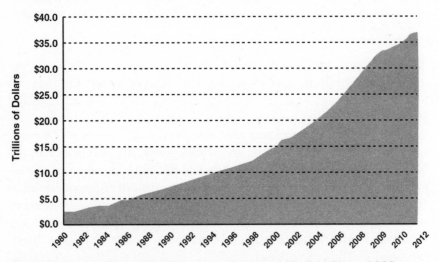

Figure 7.2   Growth in the Size of the U.S. Bond Market Since 1980

The size of the bond market, including U.S. Treasuries, municipal bonds, mortgage-backed bonds, corporate debt, and federal agency securities, has exploded since 1980.

Source: Securities Industry and Financial Markets Association.

of debt—government, corporate, mortgage, and consumer debt. Looser government regulation made it possible for the banking sector to issue more debt, and the federal government was issuing enormous numbers of bonds to run large budget deficits.

Consumer debt and corporate borrowing also took off like rockets, often backed by bonds, such as mortgage bonds. And this wasn't just a U.S. phenomenon; borrowing was rising rapidly all around the world. There was a massive worldwide increase in debt and exposure to debt.

Understandably, the long bull bond market has generally made bonds very appealing to investors.

Why Conventional Wisdom on Bonds Is Wrong Now

Conventional Wisdom on investing in bonds is wrong because it relies on two key assumptions that, unfortunately, are dead wrong:

1. The recent past is a good reason to trust the near future.
2. If all else fails, the federal government will somehow save us (as it did for the mortgage bond market).

Let's tackle each of these wrong assumptions one at a time.

Wrong CW Assumption 1: The Last Few Decades Were Good to Bonds, So the Future Will Be, Too

First of all, and most importantly, the future is not the past! It never was and it never will be. *Markets always evolve.* There is never a question of *if* a market will evolve; it is always only a question of *when.*

The bond market has enjoyed an amazing run, beginning in the 1980s. As great as it has been, what justification or evidence do we have right now to believe that somehow that great run will never end? Interest rates have been ridiculously low, but more recently have started to rise. Is it reasonable from here to expect interest rates to fall even lower? Logic tells us that interest rates are far more likely to eventually rise than to fall even further.

You don't have to buy our macroeconomic point of view to see this eventually happening. As a general rule, interest rates tend to run about 2 to 3 percent above the inflation rate. That is certainly not the case today. Interest rates are very low, relative to inflation, and some interest rates have actually gone so low that they were for a while in negative territory. For example, back in June 2012, the Swiss two-year bond had a coupon of negative 0.5 percent. That means investors who buy this bond are not only willing to make no profit on the bond, they are also willing to lose money, just for the safety of "parking" capital in what they view as a safe haven.

With current interest rates so atypically low and even occasionally negative, the odds are that interest rates will eventually rise, or not fall much further, in the future. You don't have to believe in our Aftershock point of view to see that the bond bull run may be winding down.

If we add in the Aftershock point of view—that massive money printing will cause inflation and rising interest rates—then falling bond prices are inevitable as interest rates rise.

Not only bonds will suffer, but rising interest rates will eventually make all our bubbles pop. Not just America's bubble economy, but the world's bubble economy, particularly the world's giant debt bubble. The bursting of the massive world debt bubble will be absolutely explosive. We saw a small preview of what's to come with the mortgage debt–fueled financial meltdown in 2008. But remember, mortgage debt is only a small part of the world's overall debt, so when the worldwide debt bubble bursts, it's going to be a lot bigger than that little taste we got before.

Remember, you don't need too much of an increase in interest rates to get a *big drop in bonds.* Even a small increase pushes bond values down (see sidebar and Table 7.1). Therefore, a big rise in future inflation and interest rates will create a massive downside for bonds.

Wrong CW Assumption 2: If All Else Fails, the Federal Government Will Somehow Save Us

This will be true, right up until the minute it is no longer true. Certainly, the federal government will do all it can to protect bondholders, if for no other reason than as soon as it stops protecting bondholders, it can no longer issue any more bonds because no investors will be willing to buy those bonds.

Governments around the world have been and will continue to do all they can to save their bond markets. Since the financial crisis of 2008, the U.S. government, through its massive borrowing and money-printing powers, has been able to step in and essentially take over much of the mortgage debt market. In Europe the same thing is happening, with a combination of increased borrowing and some money printing being used to stabilize the government debt situation for Greece, Spain, and Italy.

Many people think that because the U.S. government was able to take over the mortgage market, and European governments have been able to keep the European debt situation from melting down, at least so far, that means we don't have to worry, there isn't a much larger debt problem. But the massive debt problem is still there; it just can't be as easily seen. And if it can't be easily seen, you can bet that CW won't see it. The last thing CW wants to see is problems.

What can be easily seen is that bonds have performed very well over the past few decades, and even before then they were certainly quite safe. Yes, there were some problems in 2008, but according to CW, they were solved. Hence, bonds still seem safe and their past performance has been amazing. So, needless to say, CW is very happy with bonds, even with the more recent drop in May 2013. History proves that CW is right. Right?

But what if the underlying conditions of the past change in the future? What if that massive increase in debt is actually undermining the ability of governments and people to pay off these bonds? And most importantly, what if the world's bubble economy pops and inflation and interest rates rise substantially?

Rising Interest Rates Will Make Bonds Drop Like a Rock in the Aftershock

Rising interest rates would be bad for any economy, but they will be especially bad for a multibubble economy already in decline. High interest rates will be bad for stocks, real estate, and businesses. And high interest rates will be especially bad for the bonds.

Remember, even a small rise in interest rates means a big drop for bonds (look again at Table 7.1).

High interest rates are going to be especially bad for the government debt bubble. We never actually pay back any of the principal of our public debt, only the interest payments, and we make these interest-only payments by borrowing more money. Therefore, each time interest rates rise, the government has to borrow again and again at the new, higher interest rate, adding exponentially to the public debt.

As inflation and interest rates rise and the government debt spikes ever upward, investor psychology will turn increasingly negative. It is hard to believe now, but eventually investors won't want to buy any of our debt. At that point, we will continue to make our interest-only payments with more printed money, but soon that will not work either because more money printing will push inflation higher and higher and interest rates higher and higher, too. At some point, massive money printing will have to end and our interest-only payments will not be made, the U.S. government will be in default on its debt, and the huge government debt bubble will pop.

As of this writing in mid-2013, Standard & Poor's (S&P) rates the United States at AA+, while Fitch and Moody's still maintains its AAA credit rating for the United States. But that could change with the next big federal budget showdown. Also, inflation and interest rates are low. But later, when inflation and interest rates rise enough to force an end to massive money printing, and when the government can no longer make its interest payments on the debt, U.S. government bonds will drop to XXX credit score very quickly, just like the mortgage market crash, because investor psychology will change very quickly.

Don't Be Overly Impressed by Credit Ratings

While credit ratings can be a good measure of a bond issuer's creditworthiness at the moment, these ratings are not necessarily good indicators of true future risk. That is because the ratings agencies generally are assuming the continuation of a stable economy and do not foresee any major changes ahead. They are not predicting significant future inflation and rising interest rates, let alone a worldwide, multibubble burst. Once that happens, credit ratings in general are not going to mean very much.

Keep in mind that credit ratings have really been tested only during relatively good and stable economic conditions. And the few occasions when hard times have come, these ratings systems have not fared particularly well. Case in point: Standard & Poor's, Fitch, and Moody's all gave Lehman Brothers an A rating—right up until just before Lehman collapsed. So much for the value of credit ratings!

Why Aren't Bond Investors More Worried?

Actually, with the recent drop in bonds in May 2013, investors *are* getting worried.

But not that worried. Investors have some comforting reasons for not being too concerned about bonds (yet). First, as explained earlier, recent history has been very good for bonds. That is hard to ignore, especially when you want that good recent history to continue.

In addition, investors draw comfort from the many nice safety features of bonds, such as the guaranteed return of the original principal, which other investments generally do not have. And, of course, bond investors draw deep comfort from their faith that the federal government can always print more money and buy more bonds, keeping the demand for bonds strong.

But even more than these reasons for their comfort with bonds, investors' unwavering confidence in bonds comes from an even deeper and more powerful source: the *psychology of denial*. It is natural to want good things to last forever; that's just human nature. It is also human nature to not want to face certain facts that might threaten the current good status quo until those facts absolutely have to be faced. However, we actually often quietly know more than we want to openly face. We lie to ourselves, but to a certain extent we sort of already know that it is a lie.

In the case of bonds, most investors actually already know on some level the very thing that they don't want to face. Most of them know that quantitative easing (QE) causes inflation, that rising inflation causes rising interest rates, and that rising interest rates cause bonds to fall. Because they would rather not face these facts, they are highly motivated to believe that whatever the current level of money printing we are now doing is just the right amount. Like Goldilocks with her favorite bowl of porridge, the amount of QE is always "just right"—not too hot, not too cold, not too little, not too much. Each time more massive money printing occurs, CW investors and analysts declare it is just the right amount. No matter what is happening, it is all "doable," it is all just fine because *the government will not let us fail*.

Denial is what will keep the party going in the stock market and the bond market right up until the moment when the denial suddenly evaporates and everyone wants out. *That is how you know it is denial*. If investors don't already know on some level that things are not as wonderful as they seem, why is it so easy for them to change their minds on a moment's notice and head for the door?

Clearly, deep down, investors are more skittish than they let on, even perhaps to themselves. But when the time comes, they generally don't take very long to figure out that they all want out. (This denial stage is the first of the six psychological stages of dealing with the coming Aftershock, described in more detail in our 2011 book *Aftershock*, Second Edition).

Bonds Will Fall in Four Stages

Not all investors will run out and stay out of the bond market at the first signs of trouble. That's why the bond market will not fall all at once, but will decline in stages leading up to the Aftershock, before the biggest crash. Here is our best approximation of how that will happen.

Bill Gross: King of Bonds

Bill Gross is the founder and co-chief investment officer of PIMCO, an investment firm based in Los Angeles (Newport Beach). He manages the largest bond fund in the world, the PIMCO Total Return Fund, with over $1.4 *trillion* in assets. That's also the largest mutual fund or exchange-traded fund in the world. So, needless to say, when Bill Gross speaks about bonds, people listen. He can literally move the markets. Of course, since he has a vested interest in what he is saying, you have to keep in mind he may want to move the markets in whatever direction benefits him. But, even with that caveat, he is well worth listening to, as he is one of the best of the big bond fund managers.

One pronouncement he made in the spring of 2011 was most interesting. He said he was moving out of U.S. Treasuries. That's a bold statement for a big bond manager. He said he thought the risks were increasing and it was time to move.

As it turned out, it was not time to move. His fund suffered and missed out on the big bond rally caused in part by the downgrade of U.S. bonds by S&P. Yes, the logic of the bond market is pretty screwy right now, but that's the way it is when so many people are increasingly afraid of stocks. His fundamental instincts about problems with Treasuries were right, but his timing was off. It serves as a good lesson about Aftershock investing. Even if you can see a bubble as clear as day, that doesn't mean it is immediately going to pop. It will pop; it just may not pop tomorrow or even next year.

Stage 1: The Recent Past and Now

As you may have noticed, during the global financial crisis of late 2008, while stock markets around the world were falling 40 percent and more, the bond markets remained generally unfazed. If anything, bonds benefited to a certain extent from the crisis because investors viewed bonds as a safe haven as they fled from stocks. This just provided more evidence to the CW cheerleaders that bonds are very low risk. But the fact that the bond market is currently trusting bonds, which is keeping interest rates low, doesn't mean bonds actually are worthy of that investor trust. Lots of things can temporarily sell at the "wrong" price until investors figure it out. At that point, investors' views of trustworthiness can change very quickly.

Stage 2: The Short-Term Future

As long as the United States is still viewed as a safe haven, especially compared to Europe, and as long as massive money printing by the Federal Reserve keeps working to keep interest rates low, bonds will do okay. But bonds will become increasingly vulnerable over time. Clearly, any future rise in interest rates will hurt bonds, so the big question is what will happen next for interest rates? How much lower can they go?

With U.S. interest rates already so low, it is hard to see them going much lower, although they could temporarily. Interest rates could even fall below zero, but that clearly would not be sustainable. (An interest rate below zero means that the bondholder is guaranteed to lose money over time. Even if investors were willing to put up with that for a while, they certainly don't want that over the longer term.)

It is much more likely that interest rates will rise, not fall, over time. In the short term (2014), interest rates will not likely rise too dramatically. But remember, any rise in interest rates will have a negative impact on bond prices. Please go back and take another look at Table 7.1 if you need any further convincing about how fast bond values drop as interest rates rise. Even a small rise in interest rates will hurt bonds. The saving grace for bonds in the short term is that whenever stocks take a significant dip, investors typically like to move temporarily into bonds in a flight to safety. This will help keep up demand for bonds, even if interest rates start to creep up a bit.

Stage 3: The Medium-Term Future

As time goes on, interest rates will creep up even further. What will make interest rates rise further? Well, by now you know all too well what we are about to say: Massive money printing will lead to rising inflation, and rising inflation will eventually bring us rising interest rates. This is not something we can get out of by pretending it isn't there. Even if the Fed were to stop all money printing today (and they already said clearly that they will not), we have already increased the money supply threefold since March 2009. That is more than enough to give us plenty of future inflation and rising interest rates.

High inflation and high interest rates are not going to occur overnight. It will happen over time. The more time that goes by, the greater the risk to bonds. Rising interest rates will clearly make bonds fall more and more.

As money printing and other manipulations begin to backfire, inflation and interest rates will rise, and bond prices will decline much further. But not every bond will crash in value overnight. Bonds from weaker issuers—the ones with higher interest rates that some investors thought would pay off big—fail first, as those companies can no longer secure cheap debt to prop up their earnings and are forced to default.

Stage 4: The Market Cliff and Aftershock

Leading up to and during the Aftershock, many companies will be forced to sell off their assets, but with so many going on the market at the same time, they will have little value, and hordes of corporate bondholders will line up for their many pieces of a very small pie.

Bankruptcies, decreased lending, and a mass exodus of foreign investment will lead to a collapse in the stock market, and suddenly even the most rock-solid companies will start to look like another Lehman Brothers. While a stock market holiday may be declared (see Chapter 4), there will be no need to declare a bond holiday because the bond market will effectively shut itself down.

The federal government can, and will, ease the pain of this for as long as it can with more money printing. But as we've said, eventually this medicine becomes the poison, and there will be little the Fed or anyone else can do without just making things worse. Right now, the Fed can put money into the system with very few short-term consequences, as any potential inflation will lag at least by a couple of years behind QE. But once inflation gets going (in the 5 to 10 percent range), the lag time behind any new money printing will become shorter and shorter, until eventually the economy responds almost instantly to any additional money printing by the Fed by raising prices.

This is truly being stuck between a rock and a hard place for the federal government. With tax revenues dropping due to high unemployment and expenses skyrocketing due not just to inflation but to bailouts and covering guarantees on pensions, insurance, and other debt obligations, the government has no choice but to go deeper and deeper into debt. But with inflation at exorbitant levels, no one wants to put their money into Treasury debt without significantly higher interest rates. Traditionally, here is where the Treasury could turn to the Fed to print money and finance its debt, but with any increase in the money supply leading to near-instant inflation—not to mention terrifying investors everywhere—that "solution" becomes self-defeating.

Treasury debt can't be paid. Guarantees can't be covered. Expenditures are out of control. When the federal government can no longer borrow money, there's no longer any need to worry about its credit rating. They'll probably call it something like "repudiating payment," but make no mistake: this is where the most rock-solid of debtors, the U.S. government, goes into default. Not all government obligations will be repudiated, but it's likely that most outstanding bonds will cease to be paid. Cases of hardship will be given priority, but then that's not a position that most investors will want to be in.

In the Aftershock, the government safety nets for bonds of all kinds will fail because the government will not have the money to cover them. We will not be able to print money forever due to the rising inflation. Once we can no longer print money, the government will no longer be able to make its interest payments on the federal debt, and the government debt bubble will pop. Needless to say, at that point, nearly all dollar-denominated bonds and other assets will crash.

What's a Savvy Aftershock Investor to Do?

Clearly, just as for stocks, being *100 percent out of all bonds* before the Aftershock hits is essential. If U.S. Treasuries are in trouble, no bond of any kind will be safe. However, remember that we are not there yet. That means there is still time before inflation moves up high enough and interest rates rise high enough to kick off the coming multibubble pop and the Aftershock that will follow. Before that occurs, some bonds will hold up better than others. So in the shorter term, it is still okay to own some bonds, *but only if they are part of a well-diversified, Aftershock-based, actively managed portfolio* that includes a variety of asset types, such as stocks, bonds, gold, foreign currencies, and more (see Chapter 14).

Remember, as we have said in every chapter of this book, buy-and-hold investing is over. Completely over! If you stick with a conventional buy-and-hold portfolio, you will eventually experience *buy-and-lose.*

What, Me Worry? How Dangerous Are Your Bonds?

Many investors make the mistake of thinking that if interest rates go up, they can still get some benefit from holding on to their bonds because at least they are earning *some* interest on the bond, and earning *some* interest is better than no interest at all, even if they aren't getting the highest possible interest rate.

But there is much more to the story than that. The problem is not merely that you will earn a lower interest rate. The problem is that the *value* of your money tied up in the bond will be falling due to rising inflation. For example, if you are holding on to a 2 percent bond because you think that earning 2 percent is better than earning zero percent, and if inflation is 12 percent, then you are losing 10 percent per year. If inflation is 22 percent, you are losing 20 percent per year.

Even if you don't believe inflation will go that high, you are already losing money today because inflation is already more than the 2 percent you are getting on your bond. And if interest rates rise, as they likely will even if we don't have an Aftershock, your bond is only going to drop in value. So a low-percent bond is *not* better than no bond at all because if you have no bond at all, you have that money available to invest in something that keeps up with inflation—or, even better, earns you a profit.

How to Temporarily Own Bonds in an Actively Managed Aftershock Portfolio

Let's start with what *not* to own. First, we know that weaker bonds will be the first to crash. This includes less creditworthy *corporate bonds, municipal bonds* that are not government insured, and *high-yield bonds.* Don't be lured in by their higher coupon rates. The very real risks are not worth the potential rewards.

The next big red flag is all *long-term bonds*, which are more sensitive to interest rate changes than short-term bonds. Interest rates are probably already as low as they can realistically go. This is due to the artificial demand for bonds created by the huge number of government bonds purchased by the Fed in recent years via QE (money printing). Any increase in interest rates is going to hurt long-term bonds the most, so sticking with shorter-term bonds works to limit risk and can ease the pain when interest rates do rise.

So with these caveats, what does that leave us?

Generally speaking, we want to stick with the lowest-risk, government-backed, short-term bonds for the sake of capital preservation. The point here is not to chase high interest rates, but to maintain wealth in a well-diversified, actively managed portfolio between now and the Aftershock. In the short term, before the Aftershock, bonds to consider are:

1. Mortgage-backed securities
2. Short-term T-bills and Treasury notes
3. TIPS

Mortgage-Backed Securities

We said that real estate would be the first area hit and that many mortgages would go under, which will be bad for mortgage-backed securities. However, federally sponsored mortgage-backed bonds are federally guaranteed, and while that guarantee won't mean much down the road in the Aftershock, it will be helpful before the federal government is forced into default on its debt. That is still off in the future and there will be plenty of warning signs well before that happens, so in the meantime, government-sponsored

Which Is Better, Buying Individual Bonds or Bond Funds?

Whether you're in the market for newly issued or secondhand bonds, the most common way to purchase bonds is through a broker. Just like with stocks, you can use a full-service broker or discount broker, depending on how much help you need in choosing bonds. If you use a full-service broker, be sure that you understand how the commission is charged. It is often included in the price of the bond, meaning that you won't receive that part back when your principal is returned. You can also buy U.S. savings bonds from your local bank.

However, individual bonds are harder to sell. You will take a discount when you sell them. For some types of bonds, like smaller-entity municipal bonds, you may have to take a substantial discount of up to 5 percent or more to sell them. Hence, we recommend buying bonds using exchange-traded funds (ETFs) or mutual funds. ETFs and mutual funds are a convenient way to buy and sell bonds and are as liquid as buying and selling a stock. You will get the market value of the bonds whenever you sell, just like selling a bond, but with less of a discount because the ETF or mutual fund is more liquid. But, unlike a bond ETF or mutual fund, if you hold a bond to maturity and it doesn't default, you will get your entire principal back, but you will be paid with less valuable dollars, depending on the level of inflation. Even if you hold to maturity, you're not getting paid more with a bond than with a bond fund, it's just that the true market value is hidden.

mortgage-backed securities can actually be a good option for capital preservation *in the short term.*

Short-Term T-Bills and Shorter-Term Government Bonds

T-bills are very short term and pay very low rates, but they are far less risky than higher-paying corporate or municipal bonds. Short-term government bonds (two to five years) pay a bit better and also are more reliable than the riskier, higher-paying bonds.

While the Fed cannot print money forever, it can keep it up long enough to make these investments very safe from credit risk in the shorter term. They may still lose some value from inflation, but because these mature faster than shorter-term bonds, that helps to limit the negative impact. Also, because they roll over so frequently, you can repurchase them at the new higher interest rates.

TIPS

TIPS will be among the most resilient bonds prior to the Aftershock. Since the principal is indexed to the CPI, their value will go up as inflation rises, both in principal and in market value. Even if the yield is very low, these bonds can hold up very well and for significantly longer than other types of bonds.

Recently, TIPS have taken somewhat of a hit (as of mid-2013), especially shorter-term TIPS (one to five years), such as the ETF called STPZ. Short term TIPS have fallen because inflation expectations have fallen. However we still favor TIPS for the longer term because inflation will surely rise. (Remember, money printing causes inflation—no way around that.)

But even the longer-term TIPS will eventually be a bad idea when we hit the Market Cliff and Aftershock. Inflation will rise higher than TIPS will be adjusted. And given that the CPI may significantly understate the true rate of inflation, you will be losing some purchasing power. Also, when the government eventually does default on its debt, adjustable-rate loans, such as TIPS, will be among the first to be repudiated. So it's important to keep an eye on the situation and get out of TIPS before it is too late. In other words, even TIPS require active investment management.

The Bottom Line for Bonds

Bonds have been very safe and reliable investments for many, many decades, and in the past several years they have been especially good investments during the bull bond market. But bond values are entirely dependent on interest rates and therefore any rise in interest rates will have a negative impact on bonds.

You needn't buy our entire Aftershock point of view to realize that interest rates cannot go much lower and there are many forces that can push rates higher in the future, even if not as high as we believe interest rates will eventually go due to high future inflation.

Therefore, it makes sense not to continue to count on bonds to be the safest and most reliable portion of your investment portfolio. That does not mean you must get out of all your bonds today. It means that if you are going to own bonds, you should no longer consider them a long-term buy-and-hold investment.

As with stocks, we will have more details in Chapter 14 about how to own a variety of bonds in an actively managed Aftershock portfolio in each stage of the falling bubble economy.

8

Getting Real about Real Estate

One of the nice, short-term consequences of the current fake economic recovery is a temporary uptick in real estate in some areas. That's good news if you are a seller and even if you aren't a seller, it just feels good to see your home's value rise a bit.

However, please don't get lulled into thinking this is a full-on real estate rebound. It isn't. If this was truly a real estate recovery, we would not have about half of all home sales now done in cash, according to a 2013 Marketwatch report. Most people need a mortgage to buy a home and they just aren't getting them. That doesn't bode well for a real housing recovery. So while home prices may continue to rise in some areas, this is not part of a longer-term trend that will restore home prices to previous highs and higher.

We view the latest real estate upturn as part of the larger fake recovery because home prices are not being driven up by real fundamental drivers, such as rising incomes. Instead, some home prices are going up a bit due to the temporary fake recovery, created by:

- Continued massive money printing, which boosts the stock market and indirectly the real estate market.
- Artificially low mortgage rates (due to massive money printing).
- Earlier bank bailouts made it possible for there to be little recognition of how so many loans went bad.
- Massive increase in Federal Housing Administration (FHA) loans, which used to be less than 5 percent before the boom and now account for almost one third of all mortgages, again

absorbing much of the risk. These are low down payment and government guaranteed loans.

All of the above means that, by definition, the current uptick in real estate is being artificially produced and therefore it is not sustainable. Without adequate job growth and rising incomes we cannot expect significant rises in home prices or for any rises to continue for very long—unless it continues to be artificially created. Like the artificially created fake recovery, the upturn in real estate cannot be counted on. It will fall with the rest of the bubble economy.

Real Estate Is Still a Bubble

Our first book, *America's Bubble Economy*, warned in 2006 that home prices were rising much faster than incomes—a clear sign of a bubble. We knew real estate was a bubble because home prices in some areas had risen as much as 100 percent from 2000 to 2006, while incomes were up only about 2 percent in the same time period. That is about as classic a real estate bubble as you can get.

We also warned in 2006 that the real estate was only one of six large colinked bubbles, and it was likely to be the one to pop first, putting downward pressure on the rest.

So when the real estate bubble began to burst in 2007 and helped bring on the global financial crisis in 2008, a lot of people were taken by surprise, but we were not among them. It had to happen that way because the real estate bubble was the easiest of the six to pop (Chapter 2 reviews all the bubbles).

But, unfortunately, few people saw it coming and even when the real estate bubble began to pop, most people still did not see it as part of the beginning of the end of America's multibubble economy.

At first, when the financial crisis hit in 2008, the Conventional Wisdom (CW) "experts" said it was nothing more than a subprime mortgage problem, but soon the subprime mortgage problems spread to non-subprime mortgages and then to real estate in general, as prices began to fall. No subprime mortgage problem could have done that if we didn't already have a big fat, vulnerable real estate bubble.

Even after it was clear to most people that we had a real estate bubble on the way down, the CW experts *still* told us not to worry; real estate recovery, they promised, was imminent. So far, that has not happened. Instead, the falling real estate bubble has been very painful since 2008. Disappearing equity has put as many as 25 percent of U.S. mortgages underwater. And not just in California, Nevada, and Florida. The problem has been very widespread.

Now, six years after the real estate bubble first began to fall, we are still not out of the woods. In fact, according to a Case-Shiller survey, 26 percent of the homes in the top 20 U.S. cities are still below peak values. Even worse, in 25 of the top 30 metropolitan areas, more than 25 percent of home mortgages were underwater in the first quarter of 2013, according to Zillow. That is more than one out of every five mortgages in the United States. It's an improvement from last year, when the number was closer to one in every four mortgages. But in spite of some improvements, 13 million U.S. mortgages are still underwater.

And here is the bigger problem: *this bubble is not done falling*.

It's true that some real estate prices are moving up right now, and it's true that all real estate is unique to your particular location and situation. But, in general, home values have not returned to previous highs, and although prices have recently stabilized or picked up in some areas, in other areas that is not the case. More importantly, because the recent gains in home values are tied to the rise of the stock market, which in turn is tied to the Fed's massive money printing, we don't view the current uptick in home prices in some areas as a sign of a *real* real estate recovery.

Instead, we see it as a falling real estate bubble that is not falling in a straight line down but will fall again in the future—just as will stocks, bonds, and the overall bubble economy.

This is not a comforting thought for real estate owners, but avoiding reality will not help. If you own property of any kind, you have two choices: see the real estate bubble before it's too late to protect your equity, or see it later, after the value of your property falls further and there are far fewer willing and able potential buyers.

We are not saying that you must panic and sell all real estate now; we are saying that you must *face reality* now, so you can make your own wise decisions about what to do and when to do it.

What Really Drives Real Estate Prices?

It's easy to think that real estate prices should always go up over time. But there are real fundamental economic drivers behind rising real estate prices, and without those fundamental drivers, the only way to push up prices is by inflating a bubble.

What fundamental economic drivers moved real estate prices up in the past, and what changed to create an overblown real estate bubble?

Centuries ago, most people lived on farms, with more or less everything they needed within close proximity, even if a great deal of labor was required to keep it going. This arrangement changed dramatically in the nineteenth and twentieth centuries, with three fundamental economic drivers giving us a period of long, sustained growth in real estate prices that continued nearly uninterrupted for generations:

1. *Population growth.* The amount of land on this earth does not increase. So when population grows rapidly as it did in the nineteenth and twentieth centuries, it is a simple matter of supply and demand for real estate. Demand goes up, supply stays about the same, and therefore prices rise.
2. *Urban migration.* Increases in population and changes in the economy led to the growth of cities as people moved away from farms and competed for living space in relatively small areas. Again, the forces of supply and demand made real estate prices rise.
3. *Wage increases.* Technology and economic changes led to improvements in productivity, and massive productivity growth drove a corresponding growth in people's incomes, giving them more money to spend on their homes. That was more good news for real estate prices.

All three of these fundamental economic drivers contributed to each other and contributed tremendously to the rise of real estate prices over more than a century. Adding to this feedback loop was the increasing popularity of vacation homes. As cities became more and more congested, people sought refuge in quieter, faraway places. Vacation houses were cheap, but over time more and more people with more and more money were chasing the more desirable vacation spots, which, of course, just drove real estate prices up even more.

After the Fundamental Drivers of Real Estate Began to Slow, the Bubble Started to Rise

Beginning in the early 1970s, those three key factors of population growth, urban migration, and wage increases all started to slow down substantially after more than 100 years of high growth. Nonetheless, real estate prices continued to climb. The late 1970s and early 1980s were a time of relatively high inflation, so at first the price increases in real estate did not reflect much change in real value, just higher prices due to a cheapening dollar (inflation).

It is important to also note that income growth—a strong fundamental driver of nonbubble real estate prices—did not increase much during this time. In fact, since the late 1970s, real wage growth has been rising slowly for more than a generation. So the primary driver of rising real estate prices in the 1970s was inflation, certainly not income.

Then, in the early 1980s, things changed. As inflation declined, real estate prices began to take off due to something else: *low interest rates and a booming economy.* During the high inflation of the late 1970s and early 1980s, mortgage rates had been as high as 18 percent, so when interest rates fell, the cost of borrowing money decreased a lot. And not only real estate got a big shot in the arm from this. Lower interest rates and easy credit for consumers in the 1980s helped launch the beginnings of our rising multibubble economy, of which the real estate bubble was just one.

The beauty of all this cheap, easy credit was that lots of money was available to make all kinds of purchases, real estate included, with a lovely perk: Instead of spending one's *own* limited and hard-earned cash, home buyers and consumers got to play with the bank's money. And, my goodness, is other people's money a whole lot easier to spend!

Naturally, as more and more people bought homes and other properties, real estate prices went up and up. This created a bubble-inflating feedback loop: when home prices went up, people were then able to refinance their mortgages and pull out some of the increased equity in their homes—making it possible to go shopping for *even more stuff,* including more real estate, not to mention all sorts of other bubble economy goodies, from new cars to vacations to home improvement projects and more.

Cheap loans, easy credit, and rising real estate values became a wonderful win-win for the banks and consumers. Soon the banks and other lenders were aggressively seeking more and more mortgage buyers, especially mortgage refinancing, which began to grow rapidly. In fact, by the early 2000s, homeowners were routinely using their rising home equity like personal ATMs, withdrawing essentially "free" money that helped pump up the rest of the rising bubble economy.

"We sold our two-bedroom in the village at a great price and bought the Virgin Islands."

Without the low interest rates, the easy access to credit, and the overall rising bubble economy, real estate prices would not have risen much over the past three decades, because during that time we had nearly no growth in real wages (adjusted for inflation).

In other words, it has been almost all pure bubble growth.

Why Conventional Wisdom about Real Estate Is Wrong

Conventional Wisdom says that, despite the recent downturn, rising real estate prices are bound to return, even if that takes a while. And prior to its happening, home values will certainly not fall too much lower. The worst is behind us. It is just a matter of time before we get back on track to the assumed "natural growth" of real estate values—just like we've had for more than 100 years.

Conventional Wisdom not only believes we will "get back on track" soon, they also believe that the main problem that caused the real estate drop and financial crisis in 2008 was a lot of subprime mortgages going bad, and that it was not due to any other problems.

Now that we have begun to solve those subprime-related problems, CW expects to see real estate gradually recover. They acknowledge that the economy faces some temporary headwinds that are keeping the real estate rebound from happening sooner. But, in time, demand will pick up and all will be well again.

CW Believes Low Interest Rates are Here to Stay

One reason CW feels so very confident in ever-rising real estate is that they fully believe that *low interest rates will last forever*. Low interest rates are what helped make home buying so affordable, and low interest rates will continue forever, ensuring that real estate remains the fabulous investment that it has already proven itself to be for so many, many years.

CW sees no fatal future flaw in this logic—primarily because they desperately do not want to see it. They don't want to face the fact that future inflation is coming and interest rates will rise. They want to see low interest rates forever.

Over the long haul of time, real estate has been a great investment, not just for a few decades but for many generations. More recently, especially between 2001 and 2006, real estate profits had become enormous, morphing into a supercharged investment. Not only could you earn a cool 10 to 15 percent or more (in some cases even 25 percent) per year in increasing equity; you could *leverage* that investment with other people's money at super low interest rates.

It used to be that only the big players, like hedge funds and big real estate developers, had easy access to leverage, and they used it well to create massive profits. It was rare for average American consumers to get access to so much leverage, and now they, too, were using it to create huge returns. And, of course, the bigger real estate investors were using leverage, too. Why spend $100,000 to earn a 10 percent return equaling $10,000 when you can put down just $10,000, borrow the other $90,000, and earn 100 percent equaling $10,000. Wow, what a bonanza!

The profits from leveraged real estate investments were absolutely astronomical, and CW absolutely does not want that to ever end, so we understand their reluctance to face facts.

But Conventional Wisdom on real estate is wrong because it is making four big mistakes:

1. The idea that there is a "natural" growth rate for real estate (or for any asset) that guarantees continued growth is just plain wrong. In fact, we have had many periods of slow growth, no growth, and even negative growth in real estate prices. Growth will not automatically return simply due to the passage of time. Something has to actually *cause* more growth, such as rising incomes creating rising demand.

2. The idea that, because the amount of land on Earth is limited, real estate prices will always rise is also wrong. What matters far more is "land use," not limited land (see sidebar).

3. Low interest rates, easy access to credit, and the overall rising bubble economy helped create the rising real estate bubble. The striking contrast between low income growth (in inflation-adjusted dollars) compared to dramatically rising home prices from 2000 to 2006 conclusively confirms that real estate has been a bubble that CW did not see coming.

4. CW is wrongly assuming that the current rise in some home prices means that real estate will soon return to previous bubble highs. CW is not recognizing that this is part of the temporary fake recovery being artificially created by the government's massive money printing and borrowing. When the fake recovery ends, the real estate bubble—and all the bubbles—will fall further.

Land Use Impacts Prices

Will Rogers once said, "Buy land. They ain't making any more of the stuff."

Two centuries earlier, Thomas Robert Malthus predicted that population growth with a fixed supply of land would inevitably lead to starvation.

We now know he was wrong. After Malthus made that prediction, farms in Great Britain became much more productive, and improved sea travel made importing food much easier. These changes in *land use* turned out to be far more important to the price of land than the fact that land was limited.

Some might argue that technological developments with that kind of impact are all in the past, but we say it's not that hard to imagine making better use of our land in the near future than we do now. The recent innovation of urban vertical farming may prove to be an example. Because expanding *land use* creates greater supply, future improvements in land use would generally mean lower land prices, not higher.

The government also impacts land use and therefore land prices. Farm subsidies make farmland more valuable. Restricting the use of some land to discourage development or offering tax advantages for undeveloped land also limits land use, pushing up land prices.

However, building new highways or easing zoning restrictions makes land more accessible (increasing land use), which lowers land prices.

So many things, beyond the finite size of the Earth, impact real estate prices. *Land use* is far more important than most people realize.

Rising Interest Rates Will Pop the Rest of the Real Estate Bubble

The biggest flaw with Conventional Wisdom on real estate is the idea that interest rates always will stay low, as they have for decades. Instead, we will have rising interest rates. Rising inflation (due to massive money printing to support the falling bubbles) will drive interest rates up significantly, and without an endless supply of low interest rates, the whole CW argument—not to mention the bubble itself—falls apart.

As interest rates rise and mortgages become more expensive, we can kiss what is left of the real estate bubble good-bye. On the way up, this bubble was fueled by low interest rates and easy lending, allowing people to buy houses they would not be able to afford under normal conditions. But with higher mortgage rates, more money will go toward the buyer's interest payments, leaving less money available to pay for the property. When people cannot afford something, they buy less of it and prices go down. Figure 8.1 shows how even relatively small rises in mortgage rates can cause significant drops in home prices.

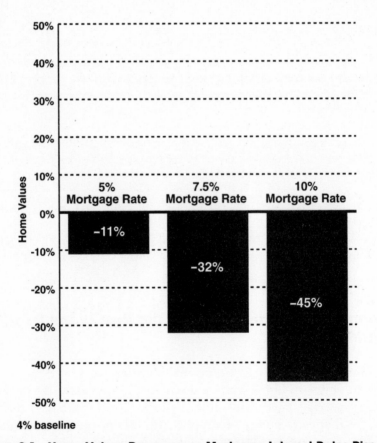

Figure 8.1   Home Values Decrease as Mortgage Interest Rates Rise

This chart assumes the current mortgage rate is 4 percent. An increase to 5 percent would force home prices down 11 percent to maintain the same monthly payment.

Source: Aftershock Publishing.

Remember, at the same time that mortgage rates rise, employment will also fall further, so there will be fewer potential buyers. Fewer buyers means even more inventory for sale. Increasing supply and falling demand means falling home prices and a big real estate bubble pop.

How Can the Experts Be So Blind?

We certainly do not blame people for believing that real estate prices should always generally go up. That is what most of us have seen, and it is an awfully nice idea to believe in. Aside from occasional dips due to recessions and one depression, home prices have generally risen, not only since most of us were born, but since our parents and even our grandparents and great grandparents were born. So we don't blame homeowners for having faith that real estate will eventually rise again and will generally keep rising forever.

But we do blame the so-called "experts" (investment analysts, economists, government officials, etc.) who should have known better. By looking at the facts rationally, it was not all that hard for us to describe the rising real estate bubble in our first book, written in 2005 and published in 2006. Nor was it so terribly hard for us to predict that the real estate bubble would be the first of our six big colinked bubbles to blow, putting downward pressure on the others. This took insight and analysis, but mostly it took a *willingness* to see it. Without a willingness to see it, the *correct* macroeconomic view is a lot harder to see.

The correct macroeconomic view is that real estate prices *do not* just go up automatically and endlessly without cause. There are real economic forces that push real estate prices up, and if those forces are absent and if real estate goes up anyway, then we have a rising bubble. But bubbles do not rise forever. Eventually, bubbles pop. It is as simple (and as painful) as that.

The popping real estate bubble is an excellent example of what all the other falling bubbles will look like when their time finally comes. At first, we maintain complete bubble blindness for as long as possible, until the rising bubble begins to level off and fall a bit. Then begins the excuse making, aimed at rationalizing what is assumed to be just a temporary downturn.

Next, when things don't dramatically improve, there is more minimizing of the facts and more happy talk about the good old days soon returning. The denial-fest continues and the cheerleading carries on, right up until the moment of the final pop. At that point, it all seems so obvious and the "experts" pretend they have been expecting it all along.

It is only a distant memory now, but prior to 2007, rarely did the media even mention the term *real estate bubble.* Now, of course, it is a household phrase.

What's a Savvy Aftershock Investor to Do?

If you want to spare yourself any further losses from the falling real estate bubble, the first thing you must do is be willing to face facts, without influence by the CW cheerleaders who want you to believe we are on the verge of a lasting recovery. While falling prices may have stabilized or even risen a bit in your area, there is no credible reason to believe that there will be a big rebound to previous real estate values in the near future. Instead, prices will eventually fall even further. This bubble has not fully popped.

Between now and then, real estate owners have a choice: see the falling bubble before it's too late to protect what is left of your equity, or see it later, after everyone else sees it, too, leaving very few buyers to whom to sell your property. At that point, you will either have to sell at a significant loss or hold on to the property for many, many years.

Unlike stocks or bonds, real estate is more than just an investment; it is often an important part of our personal lives. We may live and raise our families in these properties, or perhaps our parents did. We may have built businesses under some of these roofs. So there is often more to making real estate decisions than just a consideration of finances. You may also need to think about sentimental value, school districts, distance to work, and a variety of other issues. In a book, we can't really help you much with that.

However, we can help you analyze the future prospects for real estate and your current options. Our advice depends on the type of real estate you own, so now we will discuss the following:

- Your primary home
- Vacation properties
- Income-producing rental properties
- Commercial real estate
- Farmland

Your Primary Home—Keep It or Sell It?

Everyone has to live someplace. If you decide to keep your current home, be sure that you understand that you will not be able to sell it 5 years from now without taking a big loss compared to what you could have sold it for earlier or today. Its price may remain stable or even go up a little in the next couple of years, even for 5 years, but in the 5- to 10-year range (and possibly sooner), the next big drop is coming.

Once real estate prices begin to drop again (likely in the 5- to 10-year range), you should think of your mortgage payment as if it were rent because, as with rent, you are not going to get it back later. Even though paying a mortgage does have some advantages over paying rent, the basic point here is that you are *no longer building equity*; you are simply paying for a place to live. Therefore, ask yourself, "Is this someplace I would like to live for the next several years at my current mortgage payment, without building equity and without the ability to leave unless I take a big equity loss?" If your answer is yes, you might as well stay. If the answer is no, you will do better to sell now or in the next couple of years, and find a rental so you will have the flexibility to move later if you wish, without a big equity loss.

But it's really not that simple, is it? You may have children in a school district you like or a good job nearby, and a suitable rental in your area may be hard to find. Maybe this house was your parents' home, or maybe you just love the place and want to spend the rest of your life there. We understand there are many good non-financial reasons for keeping your current home. (All three coauthors of this book own their homes and don't plan to sell, each for different reasons.)

But whether you decide to stay or to sell, here are some important points to keep in mind:

- *All mortgages should be fixed-rate loans, not adjustable rate.* As inflation rises, you will pay back fixed-rate loans with cheaper and cheaper dollars as the value of the dollar falls, while adjustable-rate loans will become increasingly more expensive. If you currently have an adjustable-rate mortgage that you don't intend to pay off in the next two years, now would be a good time to refinance to a low *fixed-rate* loan.

- *Don't make more than your minimum payment.* Inflation will allow you to pay off your loan later with cheaper dollars. Accelerating your payments means you are paying off your loan with more expensive dollars. No point in doing that.
- *Avoid an adjustable-rate home equity line of credit (HELOC) for more than short-term loans.* If your HELOC loan is at an adjustable rate, your payments will get increasingly larger as inflation and interest rates rise. If you have a fixed-rate HELOC loan, your monthly payments will remain the same. So if you have an adjustable-rate HELOC loan, either pay it off in the next couple of years or refinance it as soon as you can to a low fixed-rate loan.
- *Don't exaggerate the value of the mortgage interest tax benefit.* Since the amount of interest paid declines as you pay down your loan, the tax benefit also decreases over time. More important, the gain of that tax benefit will be entirely erased by the loss of your home's value as real estate continues to fall, before and during the Aftershock.
- *If you decide to sell, don't stubbornly hold out for your top price.* Lower your asking price sooner rather than later so you can find a willing and able buyer while there are more of them still around (see sidebar). There is no panic now, and you can still hold off for a while if you wish, but selling sooner is better than waiting too long.

Your Pool of Potential Buyers Is Not Infinite

It is easy to assume that whenever we want to sell something, there will always be a buyer. If you are considering selling your home or other real estate in the future, here's a new way to think about it. Your pool of potential buyers for your property is not infinite. At any given moment, there is only a finite number of people who might want to buy your property, and as the bubbles continue to fall, that pool of potential buyers will shrink.

While it is true that you only need to find one buyer to sell your property, the smaller your pool of potential buyers, the less likely you are to find that person. As time goes on, your pool will shrink each time someone figures out that this "recovery" is not real. Your pool shrinks when they can't get credit or they don't have the down payment.

Your pool will shrink each time someone climbs out of the pool because they don't want to risk more price drops later. And, eventually, as inflation and interest rates go up, your pool will shrink each time someone gets kicked out of the pool by higher mortgage rates and stricter credit terms. The longer you wait to sell, the smaller your pool of potential buyers will become. Eventually, the only way to get someone to jump back into the pool is to drastically lower your asking price, which, if you need to sell, you will eventually do.

So if you are thinking of selling, you can either go fishing in your pool now, while it is still stocked with potential buyers, luring them in with a reasonable selling price, or you can wait too long to go fishing or not make the bait attractive enough, and never catch a buyer.

What if I Am "Underwater" on My Mortgage?

Depending on your circumstances, you may qualify for one of the new programs now available to help homeowners refinance if their mortgages are greater than their homes are currently worth, especially if you can't make your payments. The web site www.making-homeaffordable.gov has information about government programs.

If you don't qualify for any government help and you are behind on your payments, you may be able to fight foreclosure and eviction on technical grounds. This could involve spending some money on legal services, but it may be worth doing because sometimes homeowners discover that their loan documents were not properly created or procedures were not properly followed by the lender, which makes it very difficult for a bank to foreclose.

Even without a technicality like that, it takes a lot of time for foreclosures to finalize. According to RealtyTrac, as of March 2013, the national average is 477 days. In New York, the average time is 1,049 days, and in Florida, the average time period is now 893 days. Banks are not enthusiastic to foreclose because it forces them to try to sell the real estate and take a loss. So you may be able to negotiate with the bank to give you a new and better arrangement, perhaps making smaller, fixed payments over time.

Failing that, you may have to walk away from the property, but only when eviction is imminent. If you do that, the bank may be able to get a deficiency judgment against you, which varies from state to state. In a deficiency judgment, the lender can come after you for any losses they sustained in the foreclosure proceedings. Of course, this may not matter much if you don't have any assets to be seized. Not paying your mortgage will certainly damage your credit score, but during the Aftershock lots of previously creditworthy people will have poor credit scores, and there won't be much credit available anyway.

If fighting foreclosure or walking away is not for you, another option is to try to get the bank or lender to agree to a "short sale." It's called a short sale because the property is sold for less than the loan, and the lender forgives the difference. Banks won't always agree to this, but if they think the only other option is foreclosure, they may consider it the cheaper of the two losses. If you do a short sale, keep in mind that the amount of debt that has been forgiven is typically counted as *taxable income* when you file your federal and state tax returns.

Should I Keep Paying My Underwater Mortgage?

There are two schools of thought on this. Some people decide to stop making payments on an underwater mortgage and do one of the options described in the previous section so they can get away from their bad investment and stop throwing good money after bad. Others decide to stay in their homes and keep making their payments. If you can make your payments without hardship, and if you have a low, *fixed-rate* loan (or can get one), you will find that rising inflation over the next 5 to 10 years will eat away your mortgage payment. This assumes that your income will go up more or less with inflation, while your mortgage payment stays the same, making it relatively easy to pay off your home, despite its being underwater now.

But remember, you may not be able to count on uninterrupted income for the life of your mortgage, so having a cash cushion is important. (Also, having a diversified Aftershock portfolio of other investments that keep pace with or outpace rising inflation is important, too.)

Won't Inflation Push Up the Price of My Home?

Yes, inflation will make the *nominal price* in dollars rise. But high interest rates and the crashing real estate bubble will make the

> ## The Reality of Real Estate
>
> The reality of real estate, if the Aftershock happens, is that you won't need to worry quite so much about the decision you make today. Many people will simply stop paying their mortgages because foreclosures will be slow and difficult to enforce. It already takes a long time today, and it will get much longer then. To the extent the bank moves to foreclose, it will likely be quite willing to simply work out a rental arrangement at a very low rental rate. They can't sell the house since there are few buyers and almost no mortgage money to be found with reasonable terms. The upside to all of this is that the cost of housing will be very low—and that will be an important plus in the Aftershock when money is tight. Like all real estate, there will be differences depending on where you live, but the same large macroeconomic factors will affect all real estate and it will be surprising just how much effect it has, even on high-end real estate.

real value of homes (in inflation-adjusted dollars) go down. For example, it won't really matter if your home is worth twice as many dollars as it used to be if it costs four times as many dollars to buy groceries or fill up your car. Furthermore, when the real estate bubble fully pops, expect it to happen very quickly. Inflation may push up prices over time, but the crash could easily devastate the value of your real estate nearly overnight.

Is Now a Good Time to Buy?

We think the Fed will keep interest rates low, but they have already jumped up a bit and could go higher sooner than later.

In general, we say *stay away* from buying real estate now. This bubble is still popping and prices will only fall lower later. Don't let the cheerleaders talk you into seeing bargains where there really aren't any. Premature real estate "bargains" are the false mirages of the bubble blind.

However, there are two exceptions to our general Don't Buy rule:

1. If you want or need to buy a primary residence (not investment property), then this could be a good time to buy, while mortgage interest rates are still very low. We think that the

Fed will continue to keep interest rates low, but interest rates jumped up a bit in mid-2013 and they could go higher sooner rather than later. So buying now might make sense if you are buying with a mortgage. But only do this if you are prepared to either sell the property in the next few years or hold on for at least 10 years; otherwise, you will take a big hit later when you have to sell it at a loss or walk away. And, of course, take out only a *fixed-rate* loan, no adjustable-rate debt.

2. If you can buy a property below current market value and resell it quickly to a willing and able buyer for a profit, then this could be a good time to buy. The danger is that you will get stuck holding the property for too long, prices will drop again, and your potential profit will evaporate. If you never flipped a property before, now is not the time to start your learning curve. If you are a seasoned flipper, it would be wise to tighten up your criteria for what you identify as a "good deal."

What about Reverse Mortgages?

A reverse mortgage is a special type of home loan that lets you convert the equity in your home into cash, usually in the form of monthly payments to you. Unlike a home equity loan or traditional mortgage, a reverse mortgage provides you with money that you never have to repay and it allows you to keep your home for as long as you live. Because older people tend to have untapped home equity at the same time that they may have reduced income, a reverse mortgage may make sense for some people *in a normal economy*.

The key phrase, of course is "in a normal economy." The potential trouble with reverse mortgages begins where the normal economy ends.

The majority of reverse mortgages are insured by the Federal Housing Administration (FHA) through its Home Equity Conversion Mortgage program. Borrowers pay for this insurance with an "upfront" premium at the start of the loan and with additional monthly payment to the FHA. Insurance fees vary depending on the type of the reverse mortgage.

This insurance benefits both the lender and the borrower. If the lender or bank later becomes unable to pay the borrower, the FHA would continue to make the payments to the borrower on their reverse mortgage, drawing out of a fund set up for this purpose. This government fund is also available to make up any potential losses to lenders if there is a decline in property values.

Like other government funds, such as the FDIC insurance fund, this FHA mortgage fund is not infinite. Under normal conditions, there is ample money in the fund to cover occasional losses, which protects both borrowers and lenders. In the unusual event that this FHA fund runs out of money, the federal government would step in and cover any additional needs—even if the only way they could do that was by printing more money to cover it. So under normal economic conditions and even under difficult economic conditions, reverse mortgage borrowers are generally safe.

However, from an Aftershock point of view, once all the bubbles fully pop—including the real estate bubble—we don't expect the government to be able to fully meet all of its many obligations. This will not happen overnight. At first, when these various federal insurance funds (FHA, FDIC, etc.) begin to run low due to so many claims, the government will add new money to these funds through more money printing. But in the later stages, when the government can no longer print more money (due to it causing even more inflation), the government will not be able to bail out so many funds, banks, institutions, and even states through continued money printing.

Once the government no longer can cover all the losses of all mortgage lenders and borrowers in full, they will likely make partial payments to those who are insured for as long as they can, and when that becomes impossible they will likely switch to some hardship-only payments. At some point, even that may become impossible for a period of time, prior to a real economic recovery.

Right now, it's hard to imagine a time when the government will be unable to borrow or print more money. But eventually, when the dollar bubble (massive money printing) and the government debt bubble (massive borrowing) burst, the rest of the bubbles that are now supported by money printing and borrowing (such as the stock and real estate bubbles) will fall.

Even if you don't believe we are headed for the Aftershock, given that the Fed has already increased the US monetary base by *more than 300 percent* since 2008, we will certainly have high future inflation. That means whatever amount you receive as your reverse mortgage monthly payment will buy a lot less in the future than it would today. And even if your reverse mortgage contract contains an inflation rider, it will not likely cover you up the peak inflation rate we will eventually face in the future.

We continue to believe that reverse mortgages may make sense for some people in some situations, depending on your age and many other factors. However, in general, we do not give a blanket endorsement to all reverse mortgages because the future longer term risks, in our opinion, are real.

If you decide to get a reverse mortgage, please make sure that your contract clearly states that you are not responsible for making up the difference if there is a future drop in the value of your home. And most importantly, make sure to include both yourself and your spouse's name on the new deed in case one of you passes before the other. Otherwise, the company can take your home as soon as the lone person on the deed dies, leaving your spouse homeless and with no more payments.

Also keep in mind that a reverse mortgage reduces the total value of your estate. By selling some or all of your home equity in exchange for an up-front or monthly payment, there will be less left later to bequeath.

However, when the real estate bubble fully falls, your equity will also disappear, so getting some money out of your house now and still being able to live in it may not be such a bad idea. It really comes down to what you will do with the money (live on it or invest it), whether you can get an upfront lump sum, and whether you have the confidence and experience to handle the potential investment risks? That's a lot of "ifs" and chances are a reverse mortgage is not such a great idea for most people.

Vacation Properties

While vacation home prices have picked up in some areas, they will later drop hard in the Aftershock. As we have already seen in the first phase of the real estate bubble pop, vacation properties lose value even faster than primary residences. They are a discretionary purchase that is not needed in the same way that one's primary home is needed. The market value of these less needed homes will be devastated in the Aftershock, and before then they will drop in stages as the other bubbles fall.

So unless you have strong sentimental or other reasons for keeping it, selling all second homes and vacation properties as soon as possible is a good idea. Don't wait for more evidence that the real estate market is not recovering. By then, the pool of potential buyers will be even smaller than it is now and you will likely have to sell for a lot less than you could sell for today.

In the shorter term, the value of some vacation properties in certain areas of the country may be somewhat protected, especially at the higher end of the market where some potential real estate buyers may be temporarily buoyed by the stock market bubble. In the longer term, however, all real estate will fall.

If you want to sell now but have been unable to get a buyer, lower your asking price if necessary to make the sale. Remember, if you don't lower your price now, you will only have to lower it even more later.

Please cheer up! There will be many wonderful second homes and vacation properties available for pennies on the dollar during the Aftershock—but only for those who were savvy enough to protect and grow their assets now so they have money available to buy those bargains later.

Income-Producing Residential Rental Properties

Right now, it may seem like owning rental property is a good idea. In some areas of the country, demand for residential rentals has gone up as the real estate bubble has come down. More people are renting because they have lost their homes to foreclosure or have put off buying, either because they are waiting to see if real estate falls further or they cannot get a loan. In the short term, this higher demand for rentals has led to higher rents in some areas, and will likely continue for a while longer.

However, in the longer term, these higher rents will not last. Future rents will decline because:

- Rents always eventually track real estate values. As real estate falls further, rents will eventually fall, too.
- Later, as unemployment climbs, rents will fall because a growing number of renters will lose their jobs and will stop paying rent altogether. Renters are usually the first to get hit in a downturn. In the Aftershock, the courts will be too backed

up for a quick eviction and your renters will simply squat in your property without paying anything, perhaps for years.

• When enough people are squatting without paying rent, those who do still pay rent will not be willing to pay too much.

If you are willing to own these properties after they no longer produce significant rental income, then there is no reason to worry about any of this. Maybe you will use it for other purposes by then (perhaps as future rent-free homes for your friends and relatives who didn't read our books).

But if you don't want to hold on to rental properties when they no longer bring you income, then you will at some point want to sell these while you still can.

It is hard to let go of income-producing real estate while the money is still coming in, especially if you count on that income. So it's understandable that you would want to put off selling for as long as possible. However, the longer you wait to sell, the harder it may be to find a buyer who is willing and able to pay your asking price. And if you wait too long to sell, you may not be able to find a buyer at all. Our ideas about timing your exit from income-producing real estate are offered later in this chapter.

Income-Producing Commercial Real Estate

As the bubbles fall, commercial real estate will decline for the same reasons that residential real estate will decline: rising supply (because more properties will be up for sale) and falling demand (because there will be fewer willing and able buyers). Right now and in the near-term future, commercial real estate values are not dropping significantly, if at all. Some have dropped a lot but have more recently rebounded. When to sell is a tricky decision, but clearly selling while there are still potential buyers who think we are in or on the verge of an economic recovery is a lot better than trying to sell when your potential buyers are less enthusiastic about buying because they see real estate prices falling. As we keep saying, if you wait until there is a lot of proof that there is no recovery, there will be far fewer potential buyers.

In the long term, commercial real estate values will decline substantially in the Aftershock because unemployment will rise, consumer spending will drop, and demand for rental space will fall dramatically. Retail, wholesale, warehouse, and office space will simply not be needed at current levels.

We don't have to be 100 percent right about this for you to be 100 percent out of luck. Even a 20 percent drop in your occupancy rate could kill your profits.

We agree with Conventional Wisdom that *medical* commercial real estate is different—but not that different. Medical commercial real estate will take longer to fall in value but will not be immune. Some medical practices will be more Aftershock-proof, but many will not, particularly discretionary practices, such as cosmetic surgery and medically supervised weight loss centers, as well as high-end boutique practices in general. Even basic medical and dental practices will sustain a big income loss and will seek lower-cost leases in order to stay in business. At first, you may see only a slight decline in medical real estate values, and then as the bubble economy falls further and pops, a faster exit of high-end medical practices and then other medical practices, as they can no longer pay their leases.

We also don't recommend that you count on government programs, such as "Section 8" housing payments, to hold up forever. Even if they continue, they will not keep pace with rising inflation, and in time your costs will outstrip your income on these rentals.

Farmland

Of all real estate, we like farmland the best. But it is still real estate and will still be affected by all the same forces, although with some buffering.

There are two very separate types of farmland: income-producing farms and non-income-producing farms. Our advice depends greatly on which one of these you have.

For farmland that is non-income-producing, the value of the land will fall with the rest of the real estate bubble. Most family farms that are currently being used for residential homes and perhaps family recreation (hunting, fishing, etc.) should be considered as any residential property, rather than a "farm." If the farmland does not have a house or other usable structures, and it is not being used for raising crops or animals, it is essentially raw land that will rapidly fall in value as the bubbles pop.

However, if you have farmland that is producing an income, either from crops or livestock, then you have more than just a piece of real estate—you have a business. In valuing that business, the general trend of falling land values is only one consideration. A larger consideration is the current and future business income, plus the value of the equipment the business may own.

Over the past few years, farmland prices have gone up significantly in some areas, creating what some are calling a farmland bubble. While prices may have gotten overheated in some states, we don't view it as a traditional bubble because farmland that is productive will continue to be in demand, and therefore it will hold up better in the Aftershock.

In the shorter term, the huge rise we've seen in farmland prices recently (see Figure 8.2) is a setup for a farmland bubble pop or at least a correction as we head into the Aftershock. During the Aftershock, farmland will still hold up better than other land.

As inflation rises, the price of agricultural commodities in the United States will increase as well, so if you own farmland that produces food, your gross income should rise with inflation—which is much better than most businesses will do as inflation rises. More importantly, as the dollar falls, exports of agricultural goods will increase and real prices (adjusted for inflation) will rise. However, your

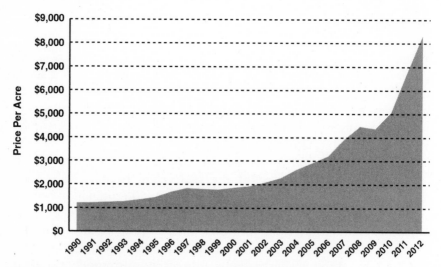

Figure 8.2 Farmland Prices Up Dramatically Since 1990

Iowa Statewide Farmland Values prices are up significantly since 1990, looking a lot like a bubble, and will likely see a downward correction in the next few years.

Source: Mike Duffy, Iowa State University.

expenses will also go up, at the same time that government agricultural financial support declines and credit becomes increasingly tight.

With real estate values down during the Aftershock, farmland will sell mostly on a cash basis, based almost entirely on the value of the agricultural business. For owners of farmland and those looking into it, the land value itself will be far less important than the value of the commodities produced on the land.

Timing Your Exits Out of Real Estate

Regardless of the type of real estate you may wish to sell, our general advice for exiting is the same:

Sooner Is Better than Later.

Unlike stocks and bonds, you cannot unload real estate at the click of a mouse. It takes time to sell real estate, so you have to plan ahead. Remember that evaporating pool of potential buyers we described earlier. The longer you wait to sell, the more potential buyers will figure out that real estate prices are not going back up and are continuing to go down.

Also, the longer you wait to sell, the higher mortgage rates will rise, which will have a very negative impact on real estate prices (see Figure 8.1). As mortgage interest rates rise, buyers with a set monthly payment for real estate can only afford cheaper and cheaper purchases.

Now that you have read this chapter, you know that the combination of falling demand and rising mortgage rates will push real estate prices down dramatically in the longer term. However, in the shorter term, most people don't know this yet. Therefore, while the economy is still relatively strong, the sooner you begin the process of trying to sell your real estate, the more likely it is that you will be able to find a willing and able buyer.

If you already know that you want to sell your primary home or vacation home, put it up for sale as soon as you can. If you are still thinking about it, don't think about it for too long.

What Can I Do to Make My Property Sell Faster?

Depending on location, we sometimes hear people complain that they can't sell their homes or other real estate as fast as they would like. Here are some potential solutions for upping the odds of attracting a buyer more quickly:

- *Engage a real estate agent who will do more than just take their commission.* Get recommendations from friends or from good customer reviews on the Internet for an agent who is willing to work hard to help sell your property. The right agent can make the difference between selling quickly or stalling out. If your home has been on the market for more than a few months, consider taking it off the market for a while and trying a new agent.
- *Make your property stand out from the pack.* You can distinguish your place from others for sale by offering something extra or unusual that gets you noticed. For example, throw in a flat-screen TV in the living room. Or offer to include a paid vacation, cruise, or one-year membership to the local pool or country club for the buyer and their family. For higher-end homes, we've seen sellers include a brand new car in the driveway or a six-pack of tickets to the Super Bowl. Don't laugh—sometimes this works.
- *The number one fix for a property that isn't selling: lower your price.* Nobody likes to hear this but it works extremely well. Find out what similar places are selling for in your area and cut it by 5 to 10 percent. As time goes on, you will likely lower your price anyway, along with all the other sellers. By doing it before the other sellers, you increase your odds of finding a buyer before the other sellers.

Exiting Out of Income-Producing Real Estate Is Trickier

In an ideal world, you would naturally want to continue to collect your income for as long as you could and then sell your property later when it is no longer producing a profit. The problem with this plan is that by the time the property stops being profitable, the value of the property will have fallen significantly. So each month that you continue to earn income on your real estate, you are one month closer to the time when you cannot sell your property without taking a loss.

How do you time your exit out of something that brings ongoing income now but will fall in value later? On one hand, you want to wait as long as you can so you can keep getting that income; on the other hand, you want to sell before the price declines enough to wipe out the gain for that income. If we knew exactly how much the selling price would fall and we knew the rate of the fall over time, we could create a formula to figure out the golden moment when it makes the most sense to sell, in a way that will maximize both your income and your selling price.

Unfortunately, we don't have that level of precision when predicting the rate of decline of various real estate prices in each local area. So the first thing you must do when deciding when to exit your income-producing real estate is to come to grips with the fact that it is nearly impossible to time this perfectly. Therefore, you are either going to be a bit too early or a bit too late. No one wants to be way too early, but a bit too early is clearly better than a bit too late. The closer we get to the Aftershock, the faster real estate prices will fall. Given that we expect to see inflation and interest rates begin to rise significantly in the next couple of years, selling before that occurs would be ideal—or just as it begins to occur is okay, too.

Once you make the decision to sell, don't make the mistake of holding out too long for a high price. If you can't get a buyer within a reasonable amount of time (a few months, not years), lower your asking price if necessary to make the sale. As we mentioned earlier, if you don't lower your price now, you will only have to lower it even more later.

What about Investing in REITs?

A real estate investment trust (REIT) is essentially a holding company that invests in real estate, and investors can buy shares of a REIT just like a stock or mutual fund. Obviously, if we're advising against owning real estate, REITs would not be at the top of our list of safe investments. However, for savvy investors who want to put a small portion of their portfolio in REITs in the short term, there still may be some good opportunities for growth. However, the same caveat applies here as it does to any other real estate investment: it's better to get out too early than too late. REITs are interest rate sensitive and will not do well in a rising interest rate environment.

The High Cost of Doing Nothing

Many people find that owning real estate makes them feel comfortable and safe. This is understandable. Owning your own home feels, well, like home. Change, especially when it involves leaving home or losing income, takes courage. Remember that good decision making helped you acquire the real estate you have today, and good decision making will also help you create your future during this unusual time. If you choose not to sell your real estate now or soon, while you can get the most for it, that's perfectly fine as long as you are fully aware of what you are doing and its consequences. Over the next several years, your real estate equity is going to Money Heaven and it's not coming back.

Please also know that the biggest cost of hanging on to falling real estate is not just the loss of your current equity; it is the much bigger *opportunity costs* of losing wealth when you could have been protecting and growing your money elsewhere.

CHAPTER

Future Threats to the Safety Nets

THE FUTURE OF WHOLE LIFE INSURANCE AND ANNUITIES

Why do people buy whole life insurance and annuities? Our faith in these products is so solid that the question seems almost silly. We buy them for protection, of course! If bonds are considered safer than stocks, then insurance and annuities are supposed to be even safer than bonds. The universal assumption is that these policies *always pay out*. These are the bedrock safety instruments that allow even the most anxious investors to sleep soundly at night. Like the old Prudential ad that calmly reassures us: you can always count on "The Rock."

Where did this "rock solid" mentality come from? Like most of our ideas about money and investing, it came from the past. Today, people don't worry too much about the safety of their money in banks, but before the Federal Deposit Insurance Corporation (FDIC) was established so that the government insured depositors' money, banks were not always so safe. If you lived in New York or Chicago, you might have access to some very reputable financial institutions. But if you lived in more remote parts of the country, the pickings were slim. If you had a nest egg to protect, keeping it under your mattress or burying gold in your backyard may have seemed like a better option than risking it at the bank.

Enter whole life insurance and annuities. These could be bought from a national company with a solid reputation. An annuity could provide investors with the income they needed for the remainder of their lives. And with whole life insurance, the policyholder had reliable savings that could be borrowed against when necessary, not to mention the protection for his or her heirs. For many people, this made whole life insurance and annuities more attractive options than a savings account at a potentially less reliable local bank. Why take a risk when you could own a piece of The Rock?

But this long history of comfort that people have derived from owning whole life insurance and annuities has kept most of us from thinking about the deeper and riskier realities of these policies. That is because . . .

All Insurance and Annuities Are Essentially Investments in Bonds

When you pay your premiums to an insurance or annuity company, they are not just stashing that cash under a mattress; these companies are *investing* it. Therefore, whether you know it or not, *you* are investing it. When you buy an annuity, whole life insurance, or long-term care insurance, you are directly exposed to the investments that these companies own.

What do these companies invest in? For many years, they invested primarily in long-term corporate bonds. One of the main reasons that insurance and annuity companies have the reputation for being so very safe is that traditionally they invested almost exclusively in safe, highly rated bonds. By pooling the policies of their clients into what is called a general account, insurance companies typically invest in a highly diversified portfolio of bonds, providing protection against default and related risks in the bond market.

In the past few decades, insurance companies have also begun investing in some stocks, and more recently they have been providing permanent financing to commercial real estate development, and even to some large-scale residential real estate projects.

If you have a whole life insurance policy, it is easy to think of it like car insurance—something you can count on if an unfortunate event occurs. But, really, your whole life insurance policy is an investment, with bonds making up the biggest piece of your company's investment pie. If (or we should say when) the value of these investments declines, the insurance company will face some real challenges.

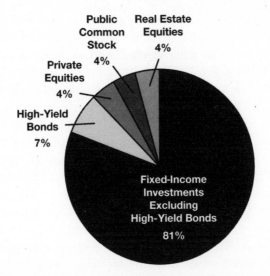

Figure 9.1 Bonds Make Up the Lion's Share of Most Insurance Companies' Investments

Most insurance companies, such as Northwestern Mutual, are heavily invested in bonds, making them especially vulnerable to rising interest rates.

Source: www.northwesternmutual.com.

As a good example of how bonds make up the lion's share of most insurance company portfolios, we looked at the investments held by Northwestern Mutual (see Figure 9.1). We chose Northwestern because it is such a highly rated and well-managed company. Interestingly, they invest in almost no government bonds due to their lower coupon rates. They prefer mostly long-term corporate bonds, which carry a higher risk and therefore offer higher yields.

Conventional Wisdom on Whole Life Insurance and Annuities: Perfectly Safe and Worth Every Penny!

Based on past performance, today's Conventional Wisdom tells us these policies are rock solid and safe. The top insurance companies in the United States have high ratings based on their historical reliability and creditworthiness. Many of these companies have been in business since before the Great Depression, and they have weathered every recession, every market fall, and every inflationary period along the way. This certainly inspires the full and long-term confidence of investors who want to hold on to their policies for 20 or 30 years or more.

The insurance industry's primary rating agency, A. M. Best, analyzes and grades insurance companies regarding their creditworthiness, debt, overall financial strength, and other factors. Like a report card, they rate each insurance company from A++ for those considered the most superior, to F for those in liquidation (see Table 9.1).

As an additional way of spreading out and limiting risk, insurance companies may also use reinsurance. Many insurance companies also have very large reserves and are well capitalized, further adding to their strength. This type of strength is part of what A. M. Best is looking at when determining its insurance company ratings.

Adding to the overall sense of security, each state maintains a fund (funded primarily by an insurance policy premium tax) standing ready to cover insurance policyholders in the event that an individual insurance company happens to fail. And, if necessary, even the federal government could potentially step in to bail out insurance companies, as it did with AIG.

All This Provides a Deep Sense of Safety, but That Comfort Comes at a Premium Price

With the support of seemingly rock-solid credit ratings and the potential for government backup if necessary, it is understandable that insurance and annuities provide a deep sense of safety. Not

Table 9.1   A. M. Best Rating Scale for Overall Financial Strength

Secure	Vulnerable
A++, A+ (Superior)	B, B2 (Fair)
A, A– (Excellent)	C++, C+ (Marginal)
B++, B+ (Good)	C, C– (Weak)
	D (Poor)
	E (Under Regulatory Supervision)
	F (In Liquidation)
	S (Suspended)

Source: www.ambest.com.

surprisingly, that comes at a price. Here is a brief description of these policies and the relatively higher premiums you must pay in order to feel safe.

Whole Life Insurance

There are two general types of life insurance: term and whole life. Term life insurance provides your beneficiary a set payout amount in the event of your death if it occurs within a limited "term" of time. When that time period is up, your term policy ends. If you want to buy another one at that point, the new term policy will likely be at a higher premium because of your greater age. And if you have also developed a medical problem since you bought the first policy, you may not be able to buy another policy or you may have to pay a much higher price.

In the case of whole life insurance, you are buying a combination of what you would get with a term life insurance policy except that, rather than terminating after a set number of years, it lasts your "whole" life. In addition, whole life insurance acts as a forced savings account. Whole life insurance gives some people the peace of mind that comes from feeling that they are guaranteed coverage for life, and it provides a tax-free death benefit to the beneficiaries. It also often provides for the payment of a certain amount of money later, under certain conditions or at specific times. Most policies also usually allow loans to be made against the policy. A third type of insurance, called universal life, is a hybrid of both term and whole life.

Whole life insurance policies (and to a lesser extent, universal life) are significantly more expensive than term life insurance. You are paying for the feeling of safety of lifetime coverage, whether you need it or not, and the feeling of safety that you have a forced savings account (even though you could earn more by investing it on your own). Whole life insurance is much more of an investment than term life insurance and, accordingly, it costs more.

Annuities

An annuity is a contract between you and an insurance company, in which you give them either a one-time or series of payments in exchange for a guarantee of periodic payments to you, beginning now or in the future. Annuities are popular in retirement plans because earnings are usually tax deferred. When withdrawals are later taken, the gains are taxed as ordinary income, not capital gains.

There are three types of annuities: fixed, indexed, and variable. In all three cases, the annuity is basically an investment in some type of asset (typically bonds, but also stocks), plus the addition of insurance that provides some minimum payout in the event that your investment falls below a set amount. A fixed annuity is essentially the purchase of a fixed-interest-rate bond with the addition of bond insurance, plus perhaps some life insurance. An indexed annuity pays based on changes in an index, such as the Standard & Poor's (S&P) 500, and provides insurance that earnings will not fall below some specified minimum, regardless of index performance. A variable annuity pays based on the performance of a variety of investment options, each with different levels of risk and return, similar to a variety of mutual funds. It also provides insurance that earnings will not fall below some specified minimum.

Buying an investment plus some insurance for that investment costs more than simply buying the investment directly, so whenever you hear the word *annuity*, it really means investment and *insurance* because that is the extra feature you are buying. Annuities can be complicated and come in many varieties, but the bottom line is that annuities are essentially investments with some level of insurance protecting those investments.

Many annuities are heavily invested in bonds. In the case of a fixed annuity, this is especially ironic because you are buying a bond and you are insuring your bond investment with some insurance that itself is an investment in bonds. The annuity uses the safety of one set of bonds (the bonds the insurance company owns) to insure the safety of another set of bonds (the bonds you own in your annuity).

Like all forms of insurance, your bond insurance is limited. It generally covers a relatively narrow range of conditions, such as only a certain change in interest rates. It does not cover you under all conditions. In the past few decades, that has not been a problem. Bonds have done very well as interest rates have dropped since the early 1980s. And even if interest rates rise a bit in the future, your annuity is still safe because that narrow range of change would still be covered by your bond insurance. As long as conditions do not significantly change, all is well for annuities.

Just as with whole life insurance, when you buy an annuity, you are buying a level of comfort. Rather than simply buying the investment directly at a lower price, you are buying an investment plus some investment insurance. You are paying a premium in order to feel safe.

Long-Term Care and Disability Insurance

Long-term care (LTC) insurance covers some of the costs of health care that are needed over an extended period, such as in old age, in particular, nursing home care. The younger you are when you buy LTC insurance, the cheaper the payments will be, but the longer you will probably have to make payments before you need it.

There are three basic types of LTC insurance: indemnity, expense-incurred, or cash policies. Indemnity plans pay a fixed daily rate regardless of what you spend on care. Expense-incurred policies reimburse you for actual expenses, up to a fixed amount. Cash-based policies pay you a fixed amount even if you incur no expenses (for example, if a relative provides your care). For an additional cost, your LTC insurance may also provide a limited inflation rider, a return-of-payment rider in case you don't use it, and simple or compound interest earned on your payments.

Like whole life and annuities, buying long-term care insurance is purchasing a feeling of safety.

Annuity Buyer Beware: If It Sounds Too Good to Be True, It Probably Is

Salespeople want to sell, so we often have to look at what they are trying to sell us with some logical skepticism. No annuity company can really pay you 6 or 7 percent when Treasuries are paying only 2 percent and corporate bonds are at 4 to 5 percent. So if you are being offered what seems like a high interest rate, it's probably not really true.

A common advertising technique is to blur the lines between the actual yield (what you get each year) and high-percentage income riders (which potentially allow you to earn more in the future, but only under certain conditions). By combining these two into one percentage rate, the deal sounds a lot better than it actually is.

(continued)

Another pitfall to watch out for: endless fees! Mortality fees, expense fees, income rider fees, death benefit rider fees, mutual fund expense fees, and management fees can add up and whittle your small percentage yield down to something even smaller. Read your contract closely because there are many ways the annuity company could end up paying you less than you may have originally thought.

Some people bought annuities back when interest rates were much higher than they are today. If you already have an annuity that is paying 6 percent or more, great! But if your neighbor has an older annuity with a great rate and you want that, too, don't believe you can get the same rate today. You can't.

Are Any of These Policies a Good Deal?

Conventional Wisdom says absolutely yes! Their track records in the past have ranged from okay to great, in large part because their main underlying investment—bonds—have done so well, especially since the early 1980s. All that profit has helped insurance companies grow, adding to their "rock-solid" image.

In addition to their investments growing, selling whole life and other insurance products has been quite profitable for these companies. With the sale of a whole life insurance policy, the company gets a customer for life. Even when that customer eventually dies and they pay the death benefit, most of that payout will come from the policyholder's own premium payment. And even if the payments don't fully cover it, whatever difference they have to make up will almost always be only a fraction of the total income the company made by investing their customer's money over the life of the policy. In the case of annuities, the companies also do well, selling bonds plus bond insurance. So, naturally, these companies push pretty hard to sell whole life insurance and annuities.

But are they a good deal for you?

While not fantastic investments, these policies have been okay investments (and even good investments) in the past, depending on your age, income, family situation, and goals at the time. And they are still okay investments now. These policies are generally very safe under the current conditions. And even in a deeper recession, there would be little reason for concern.

The question is will these policies continue to be okay going forward, as the economy continues to evolve and we approach the coming Aftershock?

Why Conventional Wisdom Is Wrong: Facing the Real 800-Pound Gorilla in the Room

Do you remember that old television commercial with the very large gorilla sitting next to an average-looking American, perhaps on an airplane or in an open convertible, begging his bewildered human companion to consider the many must-have benefits of buying an annuity?

"You could have guaranteed income for life!!" pleaded the giant primate, as the person stared off anxiously into the unknown.

"But, hey, what do I know? I'm just the 800-pound gorilla in the room."

Clever ad. However, the *real* 800-pound gorilla in the room is actually a multitrillion-dollar monkey on our backs, in the form of the ballooning U.S. money supply (more than $3 trillion, as of mid-2013) and massive federal debt (nearly $16 trillion and continuing to rise rapidly). By this point in the book we probably don't have to remind you that we believe this massive money printing by the Fed will eventually cause significant rising inflation, rising inflation will cause rising interest rates, and rising interest rates will help pop what is left of our already falling bubbles—especially the dollar and the government debt bubbles—and bring on the coming Aftershock.

Conventional wisdom (CW) on insurance is wrong because CW is making the usual mistake of assuming that inflation and interest rates will never rise significantly. As we said in the previous chapter on real estate, CW imagines low interest rates for as far as the eye can see.

How Will Rising Inflation and Rising Interest Rates Impact My Insurance or Annuity Policies?

One of the biggest misconceptions about whole life insurance, annuities, long-term care insurance, and the like, is that these are just insurance policies, and therefore they are somehow separate and protected from the dangers of the markets. But that is false. These instruments are *investments* and they must be analyzed and managed as such, as these markets evolve.

The safety of whole life insurance, annuities, and the like is directly tied to the safety of bonds and, to a lesser extent, the safety of stocks and real estate. This is not just our point of view. Even the credit rating agencies know this is true. Why else would the safety of these instruments be assessed and graded *using similar indicators to ones used to assess the safety of bonds?*

So far, the rating agency we mentioned earlier, A. M. Best, has had a good track record for rating the stability of insurance companies. But just like the other rating agencies, such as Moody's and S&P, they have never really faced an Aftershock-type situation in the markets, and their ratings do not reflect how a given company might hold up under the enormous pressures of multiple collapsing asset bubbles. Even under minimal stress, ratings have not always been so accurate. As you may recall from Chapter 5, bonds from the global financial services firm Lehman Brothers had a very high rating from both Moody's and S&P until a few days before it went bankrupt in 2008.

Since insurance companies are so heavily dependent on bonds, what happens to bonds when inflation and interest rates rise (see Chapter 5) will happen to insurance and annuities as well. Rising inflation will mean rising interest rates. Rising interest rates will mean falling bond values (see Table 9.2)

Insurance companies are making a big bet on interest rates not going up. Because insurance and annuity companies are so heavily invested in bonds, rising interest rates (and falling bonds) will decrease the value of their investments. In a rising interest rate

Table 9.2   Interest Rates Up, Bond Values Down

Interest Rate	Lost Bond Value
5%	18% lost
6%	25% lost
7%	31% lost
10%	46% lost
15%	63% lost

environment, whole life insurance has a bit of a buffer. As their bond investments begin to fall, whole life insurance companies can still pay out for a while, dipping into their large reserves. But as inflation and interest rates continue to rise, whole life policies will be worth less and less.

Annuities have less of an initial buffer than whole life insurance. They are basically just bond investments with some added bond insurance. At first, when interest rates start to go up and bond values fall, the bond insurance will kick in. But it will only cover a small rise in interest rates, after which your annuity's value falls. As pointed out earlier, that bond insurance is itself mostly just bonds. So don't count on its holding up when interest rates rise and bonds fall. Also, many annuities have market adjustment clauses that adjust the cash value of an annuity if you take it out early.

Your Insurance Company Need Not Go Bankrupt for Your Policy to Be Worth Much Less in the Aftershock

Please understand that the value of an insurance company's assets does not have to fall to zero in order for the company to no longer be able to pay full value on your insurance policy or annuity. There is a fairly sensitive balance between inflow and outflow in these companies. If their bond investments fall, this balance will be undone and they won't have the resource to pay you as promised. Remember, they don't have a big pile of money stashed away somewhere; the money you have been paying them all these years is invested in bonds, stocks, and even real estate. A significant drop in those assets will have a big impact.

Please also don't make the mistake of thinking that your insurance or annuity company is "too big to fail" or has been around so long that it is "too *safe* to fail." *Whatever is the fate of bonds is the fate of insurance and annuity companies.* Please see Chapter 7 for details about the fate of bonds in the Aftershock. Rising interest rates will decimate bonds. Most insurance companies invest mostly in bonds.

And even if your company can somehow escape all of this and is fully functional and can continue to pay on your policy in full, you still have another very big problem: *With rising inflation the value of that payout will be worth far less.*

The bottom line: There will simply be no way to come out ahead on your whole life insurance or annuity policies when serious inflation and interest rates rise.

What About the State and Federal Governments—Won't They Protect Us?

For a while, yes, they will. In the early stages, when only one or two insurance companies are in trouble, the state tax funds that we mentioned earlier will protect policyholders within that state. The problem will come later when many more companies need help or even go under. Quite quickly, state funds will get tapped out.

At that point, the federal government will surely step in to bail out insurance companies. But that will quickly become too large a task. Hence, as it becomes more difficult to bail out the entire insurance company, the government will focus on helping policyholders. They won't have the money to pay insurance plans in full, but they will be able to make hardship payments that are means tested. If you have few assets or little income, you will likely qualify for some type of hardship payment from the government. The payments are low because at the same time that the insurance industry will need big backup by the government, many banks and other government-insured entities will clearly need backup, too.

And, even worse, just at the time when the government will be so badly needed for backup in so many financial industries, the government itself will be in financial trouble as well. They will continue to print money for as long as they can (more borrowing at this point will be impossible), but eventually the money printing will have to end due to the rising inflation that it will cause. At first they can ignore rising inflation, and will. But after a while people will adjust wages and prices for inflation more quickly, and the government will find less and less positive impact from printing more money.

Eventually, with borrowing and money printing over and income tax revenue declining, the federal government simply will not have the money necessary to cover your insurance or annuity policy. They will do all that they can, for as long as they can. But there will be a limit. Not every need will be fulfilled.

What's a Savvy Aftershock Investor to Do?

The first step, as always, is to face reality. No matter how much you may want to believe in the safety and comfort of these policies, how can you believe in them if you also believe that massive money printing will cause future inflation and that rising inflation will cause rising interest rates? If you believe our macroeconomic point of view—even if only partially—then how can you continue to trust that bonds will do well over the next 20 years? And if bonds don't do well, how can your policies be worth what you thought they would be worth?

This isn't rocket science, as they say. It's just a matter of logic. So let's be logical and figure out what to do about your whole life insurance and annuities. Remember that the Aftershock is likely still a couple of years away, so there is no need to panic and nothing has to be done immediately.

Life Insurance

If you want to protect your financial dependents during your income-producing years, then term life insurance is preferable over whole life insurance. Whole life costs more, and when the Aftershock hits, your whole life policy will be worth a lot less than it's worth today.

If you have whole life insurance, now is a good time to explore your options for cashing out of it. Learning about exit options is a very important first step to protecting yourself. As you see more evidence that we are right (such as rising inflation and falling asset values), you can make your move to cash out then, hopefully before interest rates climb too high. Or, if you are already fully on board with our Aftershock point of view, you could consider cashing out now and investing elsewhere (see Chapter 14).

Another option is to borrow against the cash value of the policy. Often, this money never has to be paid back and is simply subtracted from the death benefit. If you invest wisely, this is not much of a penalty. Borrowing might be difficult with certain policies, and it is valuable only if the proceeds are properly invested and not consumed.

If cashing out of or borrowing against your whole life insurance policy now seems a bit rash, there is no significant harm in waiting a while longer until you see more evidence that we are right. Keep an eye on interest rates. When you see interest rates on 10-year bonds climb to 4 to 5 percent, it's time to strongly consider getting out, if you haven't already.

For those looking to buy new life insurance policies, term life insurance is the way to go. Term life insurance makes sense for young and middle-aged people with dependents. Disaster could strike at any time, and it's important to make sure loved ones will be provided for.

Term life insurance will help replace your income should you happen to die while you are still a breadwinner, so the timing of the policy is important. If you get it for too short a term, the risk is that you may not be able to get it again because you may have developed a medical problem that will push up the cost of term insurance beyond your reach. Longer-term plans solve those problems. They are more affected by inflation, but the premiums you pay don't go up with inflation either, so you aren't losing money, just losing the value of your coverage. Hence, you may want to increase coverage over time as inflation is rising. However, that may not always be possible.

Annuities

If you have a good-paying annuity (3 percent or better), hang on to it for now. If you have something less than that, there is no reason to panic. Just as with whole life insurance, you can wait to see more evidence that we are right before considering to sell it.

To cash out of an annuity, there is usually a sliding scale of penalties that decreases over time. You should find out what these are. Pulling out before you turn 59½ can also lead to penalties from the IRS. We hesitate to suggest taking penalties of any kind, but at a certain point it may be better to take a relatively smaller penalty than to lose most of your investment later.

If you have reached the age when you can make withdrawals without a penalty now, you may want to consider doing that sooner rather than later. Regardless of your age, as we get closer to the Aftershock and you feel increasingly confident that we are right, you should move faster out of all bond-based insurances, such as annuities. The inflation and interest rate protections they offer will very quickly be overwhelmed by high inflation and high interest rates after the bubble economy fully pops. Again, no need to panic now, but exiting before that happens is wise.

Long-Term Care Insurance and Disability Insurance

Long-term care insurance will also not fare well as inflation and interest rates rise. Since long-term care insurance is generally bought while the policyholder is relatively young, these policies have an investment component (although less so than whole life insurance) that will not be reliable when asset values are falling. Even now, these policies can be challenging for some insurance companies. Many companies have already pulled out of the long-term care insurance business because they cannot make enough money on their bonds to keep up with the rapidly rising costs of nursing homes and other health care expenses. In the Aftershock, this kind of insurance will all but disappear.

In many cases, long-term care insurance is not worth buying or keeping. However, if you already have long-term care insurance and you are in poor health now, or in your 70s or 80s and think you might need long-term health care in the next few years, then it makes sense to hold on to your policy.

But if you are in your 60s or younger, and in good health, the odds are that you will not need long-term health care for at least another 20 years, if ever. Most people will not need long-term care, even when they are older. For example, only one out of four people will go to a nursing home, and the average age of admission is 83, so it could be many decades before you would need this policy. And given the coming Aftershock, by that time you will not be able to count on it anyway.

Disability insurance is highly vulnerable to inflation. Although many policies do have some inflation adjustments, they often have limits on the amount of adjustment. If you are still in your working years and hold an individual disability policy, it makes sense to continue it for now. But when the bubbles pop and the Aftershock begins, these policies are going to become less reliable as the assets of insurance companies crash in value and state and federal governments are stretched very thin, trying to cover so many needs. So continue paying your premiums on the policy while all is still relatively well, but discontinue your payments as we near the Aftershock.

One important difference between long-term care insurance and disability insurance is that disability insurance is often provided as a benefit from an employer and is not bought individually, so even though the benefit will be worth less in a period of high inflation, at least you aren't paying for it.

Other Types of Insurance that Are Not Investment Dependent: Health, Auto, and Home Insurance

Not all types of insurance are dependent on the performance of investments. Health, auto, and home insurance, for example, are much more dependent on premiums and not very dependent on the performance of the company's assets. When the values of bonds fall, your health, home, and auto insurance will still be fine. Premiums will continue to go up, but it won't be because of poor performance in the bond markets.

Because of this, we mostly agree with Conventional Wisdom on these types of insurance. Insurance policies that are not investment dependent are good to have, and you should have them. But we do have a few suggestions that we think are worth noting.

First, when possible, choose the higher-deductible policies because they generally cost much less than the lower-deductible plans. Unless you are a frequent claimant of insurance, high deductibles usually make more sense in the long term and can pay for themselves in just a few years.

Second, on your homeowner's insurance, make sure you are not overpaying because the land value shot up during the rising real estate bubble. You only need to insure the dwelling, not the land (it usually survives a fire and is hard to steal). You should check your insurance to make sure the dwelling value seems appropriate. If not, you should get the dwelling reevaluated and/or get a second insurance company bid to confirm you have the right value.

Finally, if your employer provides your health insurance and you have some choices, take the best deal you can get. But if you must buy your own health insurance, shop around. There are a lot of choices and a wide range of costs. Choose a plan that best matches your best guess of your future health needs.

When to Exit Your Investment-Dependent Insurance Policies

In keeping with the three stages we described in the chapters on stocks and bonds, it is reasonable to expect insurance policies that are dependent on the performance of stocks and bonds to follow the same fate at each stage.

Stage 1: The Recent Past and Now

Just as bonds did okay during the global financial crisis of late 2008, so did most insurance companies.

Stage 2: The Short-Term Future

As long as interest rates remain low, all is well. In the short term, interest rates will not likely rise too dramatically. But remember, even just a small rise in interest rates will have an early negative impact on bonds. You should learn how to exit your bond-dependent insurance policies so when the time comes you know what to do. It may be too early to exit, but you should be increasingly ready to pull the trigger.

Please do not exit too soon. We are not saying to get out now, especially if you are earning anything over 3 percent. In the short term, you are better off staying put.

Stage 3: The Medium-Term Future

As interest rates rise and bond prices begin to decline, you should exit bond-based insurance and annuities. High inflation and high interest rates are not going to happen overnight. It will take time. The more time that goes by, the greater the risk to bonds.

Stage 4: The Market Cliff and Aftershock

In the Aftershock, the government safety nets for insurance policies of all kinds will fail because the government will not have the money to cover all the demands on it. Some policyholders may continue to get some help, based on need, but that will be limited.

Getting out of your investment-dependent insurance policies *before* all this occurs is obviously a good idea. It is never too early to at least look into your various options for exiting, including finding out the face value of your policies, the options for borrowing against it, and the penalties (and tax consequences) for early withdrawal.

Your Best "Insurance" Is an Actively Managed Aftershock Portfolio

In deciding how to handle your whole life insurance, annuities, and other insurance policies, first, be aware of the risks; second, be ready to make a move; and third, build an actively managed Aftershock portfolio.

Money that you can rescue from these bond-based policies (that will be so badly impacted later by rising interest rates) can be better protected by investing in assets that can withstand and even profit from the economic changes ahead. You may choose to do this all at once and as soon as possible, or you can do it incrementally, perhaps making small regular purchases, just as you would if you were paying for an insurance policy.

The key to correct investing before and during the Aftershock is to diversify across a range of asset classes, not just within an asset class, and most importantly to *actively manage* those investments. That means not just setting it up once and walking away. Active management means making changes to your portfolio that are in step with the evolving economy. (More details about building an actively managed Aftershock portfolio are offered in Chapter 14.)

CHAPTER 10

Gold

THE ONCE AND FUTURE KING

W hy do investors buy gold? Or should we ask, why do so *few* investors want to buy gold now and why will so many more investors want to pile into gold later in the Aftershock?

Right now, the idea that gold is a good long-term investment is controversial and prickly. Even though gold prices have risen dramatically over the past decade or so, people still generally don't like it. Gold may be favored by some unconventional investors, but, by far, most Americans do not currently own gold and they have no interest in doing so. Recently, even non-American investors have lost some enthusiasm. With the price of gold either flat or falling since its peak at the end of August 2011, the King's crown has temporarily lost some of its glow.

What is currently tarnishing this precious metal? Here are some key reasons that gold has dropped, especially since September 2012:

- Inflation and inflation expectations are still low. Massive money printing has not yet created significant inflation (see Chapter 3 for details about lag factors), and expectations for future inflation have declined. Both have lowered the demand for investment gold. However, physical gold demand still seems good, especially in China and India. There might even be a physical shortage. In any case, when inflation does begin to rise, both investment and physical gold will certainly benefit.

- The stock market has temporarily returned to its previous highs, mostly due to massive money printing (see Chapter 6), making stocks more attractive and gold less attractive. Later, as we approach and go over the Market Cliff, investors will rush out of stocks and pile into gold in a flight to safety and huge profit. For now, stocks are still looking more attractive.

- The dollar seems strong, given the problems in other economies, particularly Europe and Asia. A strong dollar makes gold less appealing—again, only for now.

- The current fake recovery, created by massive money printing by the Fed (see Chapter 1), is making investors feel more optimistic about the overall U.S. economy and therefore less interested in owning an asset that is essentially seen as a bet against the dollar. This will likely continue as long as the fake recovery continues.

- Some market intervention is likely occurring. Gold is seen as a barometer of the public's confidence in the economy and the actions of its central bank. Sharply rising gold prices indicate that public confidence is low, and therefore the government's motivation to depress the price of gold should not be underestimated. The spot price of gold is likely being influenced by various interventions in the futures market. When large amounts of gold futures are suddenly sold, people get nervous and start selling gold and gold exchange-traded funds (which are backed by physical gold), so more physical gold becomes available.

    This may explain what occurred in April 2013 when gold suddenly fell sharply. Particularly worrisome is how much gold moved in price in the overnight markets due to a large sale of gold. Typically, a large investor wouldn't want to make such big volume moves. These are red flags that manipulation may be occurring (see Appendix B for more details). We remain very wary of whatever made gold drop in spring 2013.

All of the above helps explain why gold has temporarily lost some of its luster after its long rise over many years, yet even with these strong negatives and recent price drop, gold is still up more than 300 percent since 2001 (see Figure 10.1).

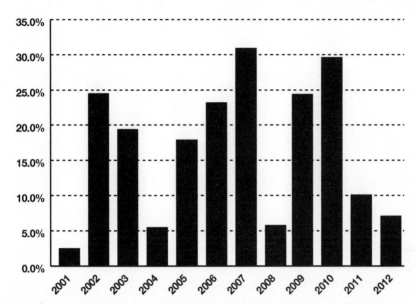

Figure 10.1   Gold Has Increased about 300 Percent Since 2001

Even with the recent drop in gold prices, gold rose every year from 2001 to 2012, for a total rise of more than 300 percent.

Source: Bloomberg.

There is also good reason to believe that while demand for paper gold (gold futures) fell sharply in the third quarter of 2013, demand for physical gold is quite strong (see Figure 10.2). In fact, there could even be a bit of a physical gold shortage.

Meanwhile, non-Western central banks (such as China, Hong Kong, Singapore, India, and others) have been increasing their holdings of gold at a very rapid pace, going from 6,300 tons in early 2009 to more than 8,200 tons at the end of Q1 2013, according to Sprott Asset Management. And many investors outside the United States have continued to buy physical gold.

Nonetheless, most Americans have been pretty uninterested in investing in gold. Traditionally, Conventional Wisdom (CW) portfolios are generally loaded with stocks, bonds, and perhaps real estate. The idea of adding a significant amount of gold to the mix seems unnecessary, even silly to most financial advisers and the famous investors they revere, like Warren Buffett and others.

This is what we meant earlier in the book when we said that Aftershock investing is so uncomfortable. It just doesn't *feel* right

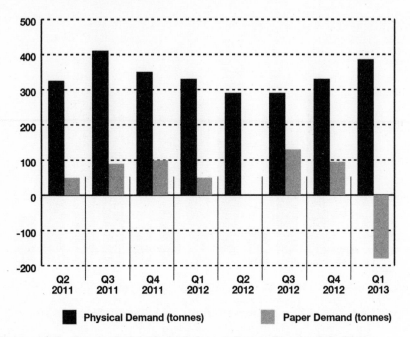

Figure 10.2   Paper Gold (Gold Futures) Down, Physical Gold Up

Physical gold buyers continue to increase their holdings, while demand for paper gold (gold futures) has fallen.

Source: World Gold Council.

compared to the comfort of conventional investing, and you won't find strong mainstream support for it, and it is hard—*very hard*—to go against Conventional Wisdom.

In our first book *America's Bubble Economy*, which we wrote in 2005, it really was not that hard to see all the bubbles (stocks, real estate, etc.) rising and then beginning to fall. Based on this same macroeconomic view, it is also not that difficult to see that gold will likely become the biggest, most profitable bubble of our lifetime. And there are multiple ways that you, or anyone at any level of wealth, can benefit immensely from that rising bubble in the coming Aftershock.

However, before we get to all that, we first need to tackle the reasons why gold had been seen as such a long-term loser by CW investors. These are smart and successful people with good track records in the past. How could they be so far off track now when it comes to the future of gold? Are they right or are we right? We invite you to review the basic macroeconomic evidence and decide for yourself.

Gold Was Golden for Centuries

Gold has been highly valued for a long, long time. We are talking millennia, not centuries. No one knows exactly when gold was first discovered and used by humans, but there is evidence that it may have occurred as early as 8,000 years ago. We do know that Egyptian pharaohs and priests used gold as an adornment beginning around 3000 BC, although at that point they still used barley, not gold, as a means of trade.

To the best of our current knowledge, gold was first used as money in about 700 BC. Since then, no other form of money has come close to gold's longevity or worldwide appeal. Regardless of the culture or the era, every form of gold—from gold nuggets to gold coins and gold bars, to gold jewelry and even gold teeth—have all commanded universal respect and buying power for more than 2,700 years.

In that time, people have found gold to be so beautiful, enduring, and scarce that it became more highly revered than merely money, and the elevated prestige of gold still continues today. Lovers seal their vows with gold rings. Kings and queens still wear gold crowns. Olympic winners still receive gold medals (although no longer solid gold). And a gold watch at retirement still symbolizes respect and accomplishment. Even our language continues to recognize the special status of gold with phrases like "our golden moment" and "his word is as good as gold."

Over the long haul of history, no other worldly substance has retained such a high and universal regard as gold. To say that this precious metal has staying power would be an understatement.

Paper Money Used to Be "Backed" by Gold

During the long evolution of money, beginning first with bartering and evolving to today's electronic money transfers, gold has played a prominent role. For centuries, gold, silver, and other metals were used for money, replacing the more perishable forms of currency, such as barley, seashells, and salt. After a while, as world trade expanded and economies grew, bags of metals-based money got too heavy to lug around (see the following sidebar) and paper money was created to make money more portable and easier to produce.

Heavy Metal

Did you know that gold is one of the heaviest metals around? With a specific gravity of 19.3, gold weighs 19.3 times more than an equal volume of water. That means just one cubic foot of gold (about the size of a basketball) weighs 1,206 pounds. That's more than half a ton! No wonder we eventually switched to paper money.

Of course, the ease of production of paper money naturally made people leery of its value. Gold and silver could be weighed and a trading value determined based on its physical size and purity, but not so with paper. This problem was addressed by certifying that the paper currency was "backed" by gold or silver, meaning there was a certain amount of precious metals set aside to back up the claim that the paper had any real value. Upon demand, this paper could be turned in for the amount of gold or silver it represented. Even when we went off of the gold standard in 1933, we still used gold to back our international transactions up until 1971.

Now the U.S. dollar is no longer backed by gold for either domestic or international transactions, and the Federal Reserve can print money whenever it wants. But even so, gold is still important today because people all around the world still think it is important. Gold continues to be considered a safe store of value by nearly every country. This includes the U.S. government, which reports owning about 8,100 tons of gold with an approximate market value of more than $330 billion, as of this writing.

Current Conventional Wisdom on Gold as an Investment: Stay Away!

Conventional Wisdom on gold has evolved as the uses of gold have evolved. For a very long time, CW thought gold was wonderful and wanted to own as much of it as possible. Even in modern times, CW still valued gold to varying degrees for most of the twentieth century. But more recently—especially since the early 1980s' stock market boom—CW's interest in gold as an investment has cooled off considerably.

A few mainstream investors may have a small percentage of their conventional portfolios in gold, particularly since the financial crisis of 2008, but they generally say that gold is a bad long-term investment for the following reasons:

- Unlike bonds, gold earns no interest.
- Unlike stocks, gold earns no dividends.
- Unlike real estate, gold earns no rent.
- Gold is not a safe haven, like bonds have been.
- Gold has no "real" value; it is mostly all speculative.
- The price of gold is volatile, and investing in gold is unpredictable and unsafe.

In short, CW thinks of gold as just a volatile commodity—perhaps a bit attractive under the right short-term conditions, but too dangerous in the long run.

Instead, CW investors are constantly telling us to stick with stocks. Why? Well, for starters, gold has not done as well as stocks over the past four decades, as Warren Buffett pointed out in his February 9, 2012, article in *Fortune* magazine. Mr. Buffett used the comparison in Figure 10.2 to show gold's relative performance. Gold still does well, especially compared to bonds, but not quite as well as stocks.

However, since 2000, after the stock market boom of the 1980s and 1990s, the Standard & Poor's (S&P) 500 has gained only modestly. Meanwhile, during those same years, gold climbed almost 300 percent (see Figure 10.3).

What does Mr. Buffett have to say about gold outperforming stocks in the past decade? He advises us to pay no attention to that. He says rising gold is nothing more than a bubble. Funny how he doesn't think stocks are a bubble, even though the Dow went up over 1,000 percent between 1980 and 2000 while gross domestic product (GDP) went up only 260 percent. Mr. Buffett implores us to stick with stocks instead of gold because the main reason people buy gold now is in the hope that more people will buy gold later. He sees no fundamental economic reasons for gold to ever rise, so if it does ever rise, it has to be mostly because of speculation.

In the *Fortune* magazine article, he wrote:

> Gold has two significant shortcomings, being neither of much use nor procreative. True, gold has some industrial and decorative

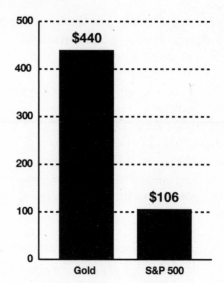

Figure 10.3   Gold versus Stocks since 2000

What $100 invested in gold or stocks in 2000 would be worth today. Since 2000, gold has far outperformed stocks.

Source: Bloomberg.

utility, but the demand for these purposes is both limited and incapable of soaking up new production. Meanwhile, if you own one ounce of gold for an eternity, you will still own one ounce at its end.

You see, according to current CW, since gold does not have utility value, it is not a worthwhile investment. Now Mr. Buffett would certainly agree that gold will have some short-term increases, as will many investments, but he says in the longer term, gold is not as good as stocks are now.

Fundamentally, his concerns have a certain amount of merit. But gold has risen in the past, even for long periods of time, despite its not having a utility value. More important, the recent past of 1965 to 2000 is not necessarily a good indicator of what's going to happen in the next couple of decades. The fundamental economic conditions could be, and will be, very different. These conditions will work very poorly for stocks and very well for gold.

Although Mr. Buffett has a better analysis than most CW investors who dislike gold, the bottom line for most CW investors is that, whatever the price of gold is today, that is the price at which gold is about to "top out," while stocks, at whatever price they are today, are almost always poised for long-term growth.

Why Current Conventional Wisdom on Gold Is Wrong

In the past, CW was deeply in love with gold. CW investors only stopped loving gold relatively recently, in favor of the stock market bubble, the real estate bubble, and the big run-up in bonds since 1980.

The irony here is that one of the reasons that CW does not like gold—because it is not driven by an income stream, such as interest, dividends, or rent (in particular interest)—will be the very reason that gold will do so well in the future, when high interest rates pop the other asset bubbles.

As discussed in detail in earlier chapters, rising interest rates (caused by massive money printing and the inflation it will create) will have a very negative impact on stocks, bonds, real estate, whole life insurance, annuities, and other interest-sensitive assets—some of which are already partially fallen bubbles. Rising inflation and rising interest rates will also pop our two remaining bubbles: the dollar and the government debt bubbles.

But there is one asset that rising inflation and rising interest rates will not be able to push down: GOLD. Therefore, by default, when most other assets are falling, gold is going to look increasingly attractive as people around the world begin to bail out of their sinking investments and pile into the gold lifeboat. Gold will be seen as a safe haven when the U.S. and world bubbles pop.

Greatly Limited Supply and Sharply Rising Demand Will Drive Huge Price Growth

A key reason that gold will do so well as the other bubbles fall is its very limited supply. Worldwide, only about 2,500 tons of gold are currently mined each year plus only about another 1,600 tons of gold per year are recycled, according to the World Gold Council.

Here is another way of looking at the relatively small size of total world gold. It would take less than three and a half Olympic-sized swimming pools to hold all of the gold ever mined—about

165,000 metric tons, most of which (about 85 percent) was mined in the twentieth century.

Despite the rise in gold prices in the past decade, the total output of gold mines, even with new mines coming on line, has actually declined or barely increased in recent years (see Figure 10.4).

There is *far* more value tied up in the world's stock and bond markets than in gold. For example, Apple's stock alone is worth more than all of the gold held by the U.S. government. And the U.S. government bond market alone is nearly 30 times larger than the value of all the gold the U.S. government holds. That means when these markets fall, investors will want to go someplace else, and that other place will be gold.

Right now, most Americans greatly prefer stocks over gold. But keep in mind that the United States is only 10 percent of the world's gold market. China and India now make up more than half the world's gold market, and they clearly love gold. There are now gold vending machines on the streets of Beijing, and Chinese banks hand out lots of brightly colored brochures pushing gold to their customers. People from India like gold so much they even have a gold-buying season when gold, mostly as jewelry, is traditionally purchased. Rising inflation in China and India has increased recent purchasing. Plus, in China, which has seen the highest growth in demand, interest paid by banks is very low, the stock market has done poorly, and real estate is very expensive for most people. So, the alternative investments to gold are not good.

So even if we don't generally like gold, the rest of the world is very pro-gold and they will not hesitate to rush into more gold in the future. That will make American investors highly interested, too, especially when our bubbles burst and they start looking for someplace to put what is left of their money.

Despite the CW assertion that there will not be enough demand to soak up future supply, just the opposite is true: Demand will far outpace supply, and that will rapidly push gold prices skyward. When the other bubbles pop, there will be a tremendous amount of money exiting stocks, bonds, and other investments. The tiny size of the gold market relative to stocks and bonds worldwide means that when people turn to gold, they will drive gold prices up fast and high.

Think of all the millions of investors around the world who will be trying to jump into those three and a half swimming pools.

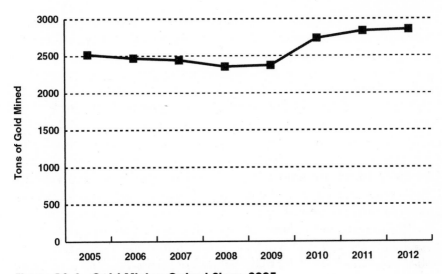

Figure 10.4   Gold Mining Output Since 2005

Gold mining output has not increased greatly despite a massive increase in the price of gold.

Source: World Gold Council.

Explosive demand and tiny supply will create the biggest asset bubble we have ever seen. And as we will explain later in the chapter, after this bubble goes up, it is not going to come down anytime soon.

Why This Investment Feels So Uncomfortable Now: Gold Is the Anti-Stock

What is really behind CW's refusal to see gold as a good investment, especially in the current fake recovery, is that a bet on gold is a bet against stocks, and for CW, betting against stocks is like betting against the home team—it's downright wrong!

In general, gold does poorly when stocks do well, and gold does better when stocks do poorly. The rise of the stock market in the first half of 2013 was created with massive stimulus, and the decline of gold in the same period was in part due to investors viewing the stock market more favorably. CW greatly prefers stocks over gold and will often see any positive news as a reason to shun gold and buy stocks. Heck, sometimes even *negative* news will get CW to shun gold and buy stocks.

This love affair with stocks is key to why CW doesn't like gold— they want their stock bubble back! Therefore, for CW, investing in

222 The Aftershock Investor

gold is equivalent to shorting America's bubble economy. People don't like that because they want America's bubble economy to last forever.

It won't.

What's a Savvy Aftershock Investor to Do?

The first step, once again, is to logically face facts. Continuing to bet heavily on a CW portfolio as we approach the Aftershock is simply not rational. All the CW arguments against owning gold (it doesn't earn interest, it doesn't pay dividends, etc.) are all irrelevant if stocks and bonds are going to fall with rising inflation and rising interest rates. Those are the same conditions that will make gold soar. Do you really need to worry about not earning interest when your investment is rising 300 percent or more?

Remember three things:

1. The other bubbles will pop.
2. Gold investments are very small relative to stock and bond investments.
3. Investors will pile into gold when other assets fall.

When you put aside all the emotional reasons for not liking gold, it just comes down to simple logic. Do the math: small supply plus huge demand will equal rapidly rising price.

The question is not whether you will buy gold. The question is *when* will you buy gold, and at that point how high will the price be and will you have the resources to buy it?

Gold Is Not Just a Commodity

Gold holds an unusual position in the minds of many people around the world as a store of monetary value. Hence, it is not really a commodity in the same sense as wheat or zinc or oil.

For this reason, long term, it will act very differently from other commodities in terms of its price. Other commodities are driven by commercial demand. Gold will be driven by demand for it as a store of monetary value in times of great fear of other financial assets.

In the short run, before the bubbles pop, the price of gold may at times follow the rise and fall of other commodities. But as the world's bubbles continue to pop, gold's attraction as a traditional store of monetary value will set gold increasingly apart from commercial commodities. Yes, the demand for gold as jewelry will fall since jewelry is a discretionary good, but that loss of demand will be more than offset by a big increase in investment demand. Furthermore, a great deal of gold jewelry that is purchased in Asia and the Middle East is often for investment purposes since it can be easily resold when the money is needed.

Gold Will Rise in Four Stages

Unlike any of the other investments we describe in this book, gold is a long-term investment that will actually do well before and during the Aftershock, despite its continued volatility. If you are in it for the longer term, there is really no bad time to buy gold. Buy now, buy later, or buy now *and* later. It is all good. Any price we pay for gold before the Aftershock is going to look like a bargain to us in the Aftershock.

Stage 1: The Recent Past and Now

Gold is up almost 300 percent since 2001, and since the financial crisis of 2008, gold has almost doubled. Although it pulled back in late 2011 and again in late 2012, gold rose 6 percent in 2012, up for the 12th consecutive year (far better than the stock or bond markets). Then in early 2013, gold dropped again for reasons we addressed at the start of this chapter. The price of gold continues to be quite volatile, which worries some investors, while others ignore the short-term action and see gold primarily as a good long-term investment as both a hedge against inflation and a place to make big returns when the other bubbles pop.

Stage 2: Short-Term Future

Going forward, we expect considerable volatility to continue. There also is some reason to think there may be a bit of manipulation of the gold price on occasion (see Appendix B). Don't count on gold's rising more than about 10 percent per year during this time, or gold could fall 10 percent or more. We don't recommend gold as a good short-term investment.

Stage 3: Medium-Term Future

As inflation and interest rates rise, expect to see stock, bond, and real estate values begin or continue to fall. Because gold is not interest rate-dependent, rising interest rates will not negatively affect gold. Quite the contrary—investors worldwide will be increasingly attracted to gold in a flight to safety as the interest rate–dependent assets fall. This trend will push gold up significantly.

Stage 4: The Market Cliff and Aftershock

As rational fear turns to rational panic, gold will shoot up just before and during the Aftershock. Here's a quick summary of why:

1. The gold market is very, very small compared to the stock and bond markets. Even a small shift of capital out of these larger markets and into gold will dramatically boost its price. And a large inflow of capital into gold will have a very huge, positive effect, indeed.
2. Gold is already viewed very positively as an investment in the Middle East and Asia, which are currently the biggest consumers of gold. When the U.S. dollar bubble pops, investors in those countries will move rapidly into gold when their economies tank even worse than the U.S. economy.
3. It is very difficult to quickly increase gold production. Gold mining will not be able to keep pace with demand.
4. Gold is often used as an illegal tax avoidance technique around the world. That is likely part of its attraction in China and India. We, of course, do not advocate illegal tax avoidance, but there's no denying that the world finds this appealing, further boosting the demand for gold.
5. Gold has traditionally been seen as an inflation hedge in the past, and in this case will be an extraordinarily good hedge against inflation in the future, so any significant rise in inflation in the United States or in other countries will drive the price of gold higher.

6. As the world's banking system comes under increasing stress, gold will have increasing appeal.

7. Dollar-based investors will get a double benefit by buying gold. If you buy gold with dollars, you are taking advantage not only of the price rise in gold, but also the fall of the dollar. As an example, if gold goes up four times, and the euro goes up two times against the dollar, your net increase is eight times.

Just before and during the Aftershock, there will be very few (if any) investment options as good and easy as gold. The rising gold bubble is your best bet for wealth protection and profits in the Aftershock.

How to Buy Gold

There are many ways to buy gold—some good, some not so good. We think the three best ways to buy gold are:

1. Buy Physical Gold from a Local Coin Dealer or a Reputable Online Dealer

Many people prefer to buy gold coins rather than larger gold bars. While coins are a bit more expensive per ounce than larger gold bars, coins are generally easier than bars to find buyers for later when you want to sell. Some of the easiest coins to trade are the Canadian Maple Leaf, the American Eagle, and the South African Krugerrand. Coins are usually one ounce in weight, but often also come in smaller half-ounce and tenth-ounce sizes.

You can buy gold coins from a local coin shop, but they will be a bit more expensive per ounce than buying online. However, there are no shipping and insurance charges at the coin shop. Some states may charge sales tax or, like Maryland, may require that you buy at least $1,000 worth of gold in order to be tax exempt. You can find local coin shops in the Yellow Pages or an online search. The U.S. Mint web site (www.usmint.gov/mint_programs/american_eagles/?action=lookup) also has a searchable database of coin dealers based on your location. Getting to know a local coin dealer now may help you later when you want to sell some coins.

Retail coin stores often charge a much higher sales commission or "spread," often ranging from 3 to 6 percent per ounce. One way to pay a lower spread is to buy online. Just like buying anything online, mail-order gold tends to be less costly because the vendors have much lower overhead than a physical store. You can simply type "gold bullion" into the search bar of your favorite Internet search engine and investigate your options, such as www.Kitco.com, www.bullionvault.com, and others. Bullionvault.com says it is the world's largest online investment gold service for buying, selling, and storing gold and silver, with more than $2 billion worth of gold owned by more than 45,000 users. Online outlets often require certified checks or cash to buy gold, or will ask you to wait until your check clears your bank before they ship or let you pick up your gold.

You can keep physical gold in a safe deposit box at a bank (even a small safe deposit box can hold quite a lot of gold), or in a lockable safe at home, which you can buy at any office supplies store.

2. Buy Gold Exchange-Traded Funds

Gold exchange-traded funds (ETFs) are traded like stocks on the New York Stock Exchange with the price roughly tracking one tenth of the price of an ounce of gold. First on the scene in the fall of 2005, gold ETFs now hold more than 1,000 tons of gold. The most popular ETF is GLD and is a product of State Street Global Advisors. Its competitor is IAU, which is very similar.

A different type of gold ETF is PHYS, which is actually a closed-end fund, rather than strictly an ETF. It holds physical gold in Canada. However, GLD and IAU also hold physical gold. GLD holds its gold in London. They actually list the serial numbers of the 400-ounce gold bars (London Good Delivery Bars) that they hold on their web site.

Many people prefer to buy gold ETFs because they offer:

- A way to buy and sell gold within a brokerage account, which more people are familiar and comfortable with than they are with coin shops and online gold sellers.
- Easy to buy and sell with a few mouse clicks or phone call.
- No storage needed.
- No insurance or other fees.

Gold ETFs have some tax disadvantages and expenses, but their trading convenience and small entry point make them quite popular with investors at every level, especially because they can be bought and sold through brokerage accounts, just like stocks. Also like stocks, ETFs can be bought on margin.

Gold ETFs are safe for now, but could become less safe in the future, particularly in the Aftershock, at which point owning only physical gold might be best.

3. Buy Gold Using a Gold Depository

An alternative to buying physical gold or gold ETFs is buying gold from a gold depository, such as Monex in Newport Beach, California. With a gold depository, you have ownership of the gold without necessarily taking physical possession, although at any time you can take physical delivery to your door. As soon as you buy it, they sign legal ownership over to you and deposit it with a separate legal entity. If the depository were to go bankrupt, the gold would still be yours.

Gold depositories solve the problems of gold storage and safety, and also give you the opportunity to buy gold on margin (see the section on leveraging gold later in this chapter). As we mentioned earlier, at some point, you may do best to take physical possession of your gold, which is very easy with a depository. That's not really feasible for most investors with current gold ETFs.

Later, taking physical possession of your gold may make the most sense if and when the government begins to take adverse actions against gold, such as restrictions on the purchase or sale of gold or very high taxes on gold transactions. Some investors may eventually choose to buy their gold offshore, depending on their circumstances. But we can't be certain about how safe that will be in the future, depending on how things may change in other countries. So for many people, having physical possession of their gold might be (or later become) the best option.

What About Gold-Mining Stocks?

Gold-mining stocks have the advantage of multiplying the profits that a gold-mining company can derive from mining gold. Hence, they

Figure 10.5 Gold-Mining Stocks versus Gold since 2000

Since 2000, gold-mining stocks (represented here by the Philadelphia Gold Miners Index) have performed poorly, both when gold is rising and when gold is falling, but these stocks are becoming a better value.

Source: Bloomberg.

can rise faster than the price of gold itself because you receive a multiple of earnings made from selling gold. Revenues rise as the price of gold rises, but operating costs do not. Therefore, as gold prices go up, gold-mining companies can do very well. That's the upside.

However, the downside of gold-mining stocks is that they can also go down faster than the price of gold. So, in general, the gold miners have been more volatile than gold (see Figure 10.5).

Gold-mining stocks can be affected by three key issues that are outside of the price of gold. The first is the overall stock market, which, when it falls, will tend to take everyone down, at least for a while. The second issue is that each gold-mining company faces the same company risks that any company can face. Remember, like Mark Twain once famously said, "A gold mine is a hole in the ground owned by a liar." Third, many mining companies, particularly the larger ones, are not pure gold plays. They often get the majority of their revenues from other metals, such as iron and copper.

Recently, as of this writing in mid-2013, gold-mining stocks have taken a beating. GDX, an ETF index of gold-mining stocks, fell 50 percent from its peak in October 2012 to now. Why did the gold miners fall more than physical gold? Because they have a high beta: they go down faster and up faster than gold itself. Also, even when the miners are generally on the rise, not all gold-mining stocks will perform equally.

Because the gold miners have come down so much recently, they are becoming a better and better value as prices drop.

Later, many gold-mining stocks will go down temporarily when the stock bubble fully pops in the Market Cliff, but then do extremely well—in some cases even better than the price of gold itself.

So there is a lot of money to be made in gold-mining stocks if you are aware of the risks we just mentioned. Long term, when the stock market falls and gold rises, there will be even better opportunities to buy gold-mining stocks. You need sophisticated investment research or competent guidance before going into any gold-mining stock. Another option is to purchase a diversified fund or ETF that holds a variety of gold-mining stocks, such as the ETF GDX.

By the time the gold bubble is rising rapidly, the stock bubble will have been pretty well deflated, so you will be buying gold-mining company stock at low prices.

Gold-mining stocks may be more attractive if your investment vehicle allows investments in gold-mining stocks but not directly in gold. But remember, great care is needed to avoid the downward pressure of a collapsing stock market on gold-mining stocks.

Leveraging Gold

One thing we've seen in recent years is that leveraging (borrowing money to fund part of the purchase of an investment) can light a fire under the growth of your assets. Hedge funds and private equity funds used leverage to create astounding returns for several years. But that fire can also burn you, as the hedge funds and private equity funds certainly found out.

The same goes for leveraging gold. There is no quicker way to make money on gold, and no quicker way to lose it. The greater the price volatility, the greater the risk, because even if you are right in the long term, you can be squeezed out by margin calls in the short term due to sharp short-term declines in the price. The price may jump back to its high very quickly, but you may have lost much of your money in the dip if you couldn't make the margin calls on your highly leveraged gold investment and had to sell your position at a low price.

Because we believe there will be greater volatility in the beginning of the gold bubble, we suggest you keep your leverage more limited in the early stages. However, as the gold bubble begins to take off with the dollar bubble pop, you could consider increasing your leverage.

If you decide to buy gold on margin, the amount of margin you can get is controlled by the government, like any brokerage account. But, depending on the volatility of gold, you can leverage three to five times. That means at a 3× leverage you can get $30,000 worth of gold for $10,000 cash. There are also significant interest costs associated with leveraging.

Gold now and in the future will likely be highly volatile, so be careful. We can't tell you how much leverage to use, since the amount of leverage you can take on is very much a factor of your wealth and willingness to take risks. All we can say for sure is that for most people leverage is like alcohol: use it in moderation.

What About Silver?

We have been focusing on gold in this chapter, but much of this discussion applies to silver as well, which is why we recommend buying one-ounce standard (meaning well-recognized) silver coins.

Silver is different from gold in that it is a hybrid investment. It is both a precious metal investment and an industrial commodity. About half of silver's production each year is consumed for industrial purposes, heavily electronics. That means that it is also much more vulnerable to downturns in commodities prices caused by economic downturns. That bodes poorly for silver. However, it is also cheaper and easier for many people to buy and is very much considered a monetary asset. Even our coins were made of silver up until 1965. So we expect that monetary value to keep silver following gold, but in a severe downturn silver will not track gold as well as it does now, given that industrial demand is still very high.

However, one offset to the downward pressure is that silver is heavily mined as a by-product from other metal mining, most notably copper. In fact, over 70 percent of silver production is as a by-product. So when demand for commodity metals such as copper

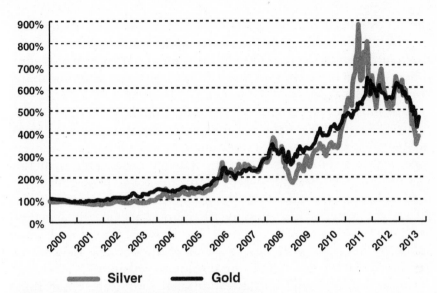

Figure 10.6   Silver More Volatile than Gold

When gold goes up, silver tends to go up a lot more, and when gold goes down, silver tends to go down a lot more. Silver is down more than 50 percent since its highs in 2011, unlike gold, which is down 30 percent.

Source: Bloomberg.

falls, so will production of silver. This will help offset some of the downward pressure on silver.

In general, silver tends to be more volatile than the already volatile gold price (see Figure 10.6), and we expect that to continue for the next few years, prior to the Aftershock.

However, we expect both gold and silver to do very, very well in the longer term. There may be times when one outperforms the other, but at the height of the Aftershock, gold will be king and silver will be the prince. Regardless of which precious metal you personally prefer, the world thinks of gold as number one and silver as number two (think of the Olympic first- and second-place medals).

Owning Gold as Part of a Well-Diversified Actively Managed Aftershock Portfolio

As much as we like gold, we would never recommend that you put all your eggs in one basket. Without reviewing an individual's specific financial situation, it is hard to say what percentage they should hold in gold. Many people are comfortable and can handle the volatility of 20 percent of their investment portfolio in gold, but others may be more comfortable with less and some would be more comfortable with more.

For most people, gold is the last remaining buy-and-hold investment, at least until we get a real economic recovery and the gold bubble finally declines (discussed later in this chapter). But even gold requires some ongoing active management, along with the rest of your portfolio. For many people, the active management of gold will mean increasing the amount of gold you own over time. As we get closer to the coming Aftershock, moving to a higher percentage of gold will be prudent. For those who want to do that sooner rather than later, there is no long-term harm, as long as you are prepared for the significant short-term volatility in gold and you don't mind sitting out any additional short-term upside that may be left in the stock and bond markets.

How High Will Gold Go?

The current conditions of low inflation, relatively strong U.S. dollar, strong bond market, good stock market, and fake recovery, all add up to a very negative environment for gold.

The Biggest, Baddest Bubble of Them All

Gold might seem like the silliest of all investments. People spend tons of capital, time, and effort trying to haul a bunch of rock out of the ground at enormous expense and smelt out tiny bits of gold, melt them together, and then do absolutely nothing with it—just store it in some vault. How much sillier can it get?

But gold is not just metal in the ground; it is considered a universal store of value, and that will make "silly" gold a truly smart and spectacular Aftershock investment. Huge amounts of money will be made—*and lost*—in gold. Gold will be a rising bubble on its way to becoming one of the biggest asset bubbles of all time. Second only to the fall of the dollar bubble, the bursting of the gold bubble many years from now will be quite impressive, as well.

What if this changes? What if instead of low inflation we have rising inflation, which we know is inevitable? What if instead of a strong dollar, stock market, and bond market, these are weaker? What do you think will happen to gold if the current strong negatives for gold turn into very strong positives for gold? In the longer term, when we hit the Market Cliff, gold will shoot up.

Many people like to ask us how high we think gold will go, and we generally hesitate to answer because we are not sure they will believe us. What we can say is that gold is up by more than 300 percent since 2000, during a gold-negative environment that included:

- Low inflation
- Decent stock market
- Bond market doing well
- Relatively strong dollar

If it can go up 300 percent in that kind of gold-negative environment, what if these four conditions listed above reversed so that we had rising inflation, falling stocks and bonds, and a weakening dollar? Certainly, we should be about to expect to see gold rise at least another 300 percent—and likely more.

But even if gold doesn't rise another 300 percent or more, and it increased only 200 percent or just 100 percent, how much better is that going to be than watching 50 percent (or more) of your CW portfolio fall off the Market Cliff and eventually go to Money Heaven?

When you take the emotions out of it and if you share even part of our macroeconomic view, investing in gold just makes sense.

Confiscation by Inflation

Will gold be confiscated or become illegal to hold individually, as it was during the Great Depression? Not likely.

Gold was much more important to the daily functioning of the economy during the Great Depression than it is now. It is almost an irrelevancy now; it wasn't then. Also, today, if the government needs money, they have a much more powerful tool for confiscating assets than confiscation of gold and that is: confiscation by inflation. When

(continued)

the government prints money, it is essentially confiscating certain assets, such as bonds, which will fall quickly as inflation and interest rates rise. Your stocks, real estate, pension, life insurance, and annuities will also decline as interest rates continue to climb.

Hence, you have little to fear from direct government confiscation of your assets, and much more to fear from indirect confiscation by inflation—unless you protect yourself. It's absolutely confiscation of people's assets, and it's a whole lot more powerful than confiscating gold. But the upside to confiscation by inflation is that, unlike government confiscation of the past, for those who are paying attention, this kind of confiscation will be easy to avoid.

When Will the Future Gold Bubble Pop?

Not for a long time. That's because it will be a long time before investors feel confident in other assets. For that to happen, we will need to start seeing some real economic recovery, which will give confidence in other assets. But that won't happen in the current money printing and government borrowing that is driving the fake recovery we have now, and certainly not the Aftershock economy we will have after the dollar bubble pops. We are going to need real economic growth driven by fundamental productivity improvements in order to get the U.S. economy fully back on its feet. When that happens, the gold bubble will come down.

However, the gold bubble will not exactly "pop" the way we will see many other bubbles crash. Instead, as the U.S. economy recovers, other economies will continue to struggle for a while longer. Investors in those countries will not be eager to sell off their gold quite yet, not while they still have no or limited growth. So the gold bubble is going to last a while. Unlike other bubbles, like the current stock bubble, the popping of the gold bubble will not be delayed by artificial government support.

That means, like many big bubbles of the past, you will see this one rising and falling, and you will have time to buy in on the way up before the Aftershock and time to sell out on the way down before the full worldwide recovery. Of course, that's only if you know it will pop and are not covering your eyes to the signs of a pop, unlike most people.

What if I Cannot Afford to Buy Gold? The Power of Grandma's Envelope

If you don't have a lot of spare cash to put into gold, do not despair. Here is a time-tested way to get a piece of the action, even if only on a smaller scale. *Some gold is better than no gold.*

Get yourself an old-fashioned envelope like our great grandparents used to save up enough money to pay the rent or buy a new pair of shoes. Write the word *GOLD* on the outside and hide your envelope someplace safe. Every time you have a little spare cash—even if it is just 20 bucks—stick it in your gold envelope. Try to do it regularly, like daily or weekly.

If you never seem to have any cash to spare, cut back on something you really don't need and start feeding that golden envelope whatever you can. Even just a few dollars here and there will eventually add up.

As soon as you have enough to buy a gold coin, take your envelope out to your local coin shop and buy yourself a gold coin. When you get home, hide your gold coin someplace safe and start feeding your gold envelope again. Even if you do this only once, you will have thousands of dollars more in the Aftershock than you do today.

PART

III

YOUR AFTERSHOCK GAME PLAN

CHAPTER

11

Aftershock Jobs and Businesses

The economic cheerleaders want us to believe that if we will just be patient and wait a little longer, strong future job growth will soon return. It is true that the big job losses we saw right after the financial crisis of 2008 have stabilized and some jobs have begun to return. Manufacturing jobs, for example, have made significant gains since the Fed began its first round of massive money printing (QE1) in March 2009. But more recently, the growth of manufacturing and other jobs has begun to slow again. And some jobs, such as construction, hardly came back at all.

As of this writing in mid-2013, overall new job creation for the first half of 2013 has been less than impressive: about 200,000 jobs per month. Just to keep up with population growth, we need to add 150,000 jobs per month. We certainly are not going to make up for the nearly 7.5 million jobs lost since 2008 at this slow pace.

Another important factor to consider is the quality of the new jobs currently being created. If you lost one good-paying, quality job and replaced it with two lower-paying, lousy jobs, the government statistics still counts that as two new jobs. But it isn't much improvement for you. Quality matters, too, not just numbers.

In any case, among working-age Americans, employment is not growing much. If this is any kind of recovery, it is one without much job growth, and that kind of "recovery" is no recovery at all. Strong and sustained job growth is essential to any significant future economic growth—not only for the country but for most people's personal economies, as well. Slower job growth means less income for many Americans and less tax revenue for federal and

239

state governments, which is a recipe for a deeper slowdown, not strong future growth.

That means finding and keeping a good job in this evolving economy of falling bubbles will become increasingly challenging as time goes on. Much of this you can do nothing about, but you do have some control over which jobs you try for and what you can do to keep your current job or prepare yourself to move to another potentially more secure job before the falling bubbles fully pop.

While the pressures on the slow-growing job market will continue and increase, all jobs and businesses are not created equal; clearly, some will fare better than others as the various bubbles continue to pop. The purpose of this chapter is to give you an overview of what is happening with jobs and businesses, and what to expect next.

The Rising Bubble Economy Created Huge Job Growth; Now the Falling Bubble Economy Means Fewer Jobs

As the conjoined real estate, stock, private debt, consumer spending, dollar, and government debt bubbles all rose in tandem from 1980 to 2000, the U.S. job market boomed, adding a whopping *40 million* new jobs during this time period. New employees were in such high demand in the late 1980s and 1990s that employment agencies and headhunters could hardly keep up.

But when the Internet bubble popped in 2000, much of that strong job growth began to unwind. Then the housing bubble pushed up job growth again, but nothing like it was in the 1980s and 1990s. So when the real estate bubble popped, jobs related to real estate—like jobs in construction and real estate sales—took an immediate and lasting hit.

But our job problems didn't end at the edges of the real estate landscape; we had other falling bubbles, as well. Because the rising real estate bubble was so key in driving up the private debt bubble and the consumer spending bubble, when real estate began to pop, much of the hot air escaped from those other bubbles, too. With less home equity to tap into and rapidly tightening credit, consumers naturally spent less, which only made matters worse for businesses and jobs.

So, along with the decline in housing-related jobs, big job layoffs were seen across the board, from the airline industry to

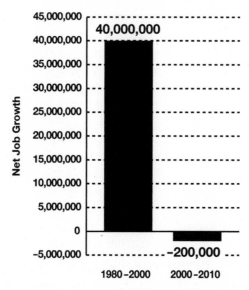

Figure 11.1   A Big Hole to Climb Out of: No Net Job Growth from 2000 to 2010

From 1980 to 2000, 40 million new jobs were created. However, from 2000 to 2010, we actually lost 200,000 jobs.

Source: Bureau of Labor Statistics.

shopping mall closures. And because the falling bubbles have not been entirely reinflated despite massive government stimulus to temporarily support them, many of those bubble-driven jobs have not come back. Most of the nonfarm jobs created during the rise of the real estate bubble are now gone.

The bottom line is, even with the new jobs that are being created by the massive government stimulus since 2008, we have had a very big hole to climb out of. While the number of jobs from 1980 to 2000 increased by 40 million, there was zero net job growth from 2000 to 2010. In fact, we lost almost 200,000 jobs (see Figure 11.1).

Conventional Wisdom about Future Jobs Is Based on Faith that the Future Will Be Like the Past

As with stocks, bonds, real estate, life insurance, and nearly everything else, Conventional Wisdom's faith in future job growth is derived from the assumption that what we had before (during the rising bubble economy) we will surely have again. CW loves to extrapolate trend lines—at least the trend lines they like. When things are going well, CW sees more great growth ahead; and when things are going not so well, CW says don't worry, the previous good trend line will naturally return very soon. For CW, good trend lines always continue, even if they happen to get temporarily sidetracked for a while.

For example, five years ago when the number of government jobs was growing significantly, CW said government job growth would always be strong. CW says all good job trends last forever. Not only that, CW also likes to believe that whatever is the current popular area of discussion—such as green jobs or nanotechnology jobs—will have strong job growth in the future. The CW winning formula for future jobs is the current trend line (or the recent past, if that looks better than today) plus whatever is in fashion at the moment.

One of the reasons that CW feels so confident about its views about the future is that extrapolating out the trend lines has worked pretty well for CW in the recent past. Naturally, in a rising multibubble economy, most positive trend lines have been remarkably reliable, and it has not been all that difficult for CW to be right on many near-term positive predictions in the recent past. This, along with the need to ignore unpleasant facts that threaten the status quo, has become the strong foundation on which CW now rests its firm faith that all good trends, including all good job growth trends, never end.

While this may sound like a bit of an exaggeration, if you look back at CW over the past three decades, you will see almost all the CW-oriented analysts and economic cheerleaders continuously telling us that everything is basically very good and will continue to be very good, even if we have a little down cycle occasionally. You never hear them say that a currently good trend is unsustainable because it is based on an unsustainable rising bubble economy. At this point, rising bubbles are considered both the norm and our American birthright. And, naturally, that will always include lots of good American jobs.

Even when CW acknowledges that many U.S. jobs have been moved overseas in recent years due to cheaper labor costs, there is no acknowledgment of how the rising U.S. bubbles created many jobs, nor how the falling bubbles have taken them away.

Why Conventional Wisdom on Jobs Is Wrong

Just as for stocks, bonds, real estate, life insurance, and nearly everything else, CW's views on future job growth are wrong for the same reasons that CW is wrong about all the rest: good past trend lines *cannot* be extrapolated into the future indefinitely. The future is not the past. Not even the present is the past. Good trends do not continue forever because *markets always evolve*, and this is certainly true for the jobs market as well.

The U.S. jobs market has always evolved over time, driven by real underlying fundamental economic drivers, not the latest fashionable interests. For example, more than a century ago, most Americans were actively involved in growing food, either for income or to feed themselves. However, farming jobs evolved and declined, as more manufacturing jobs were created in the rise of the Industrial Revolution.

There are countless other examples of how the job market has evolved over time, based on the evolution of the economy. In our current recession, unless the economy goes back fully to how it was before, the jobs are not going to come back fully to how they were before. Since economies never go backward, only forward, jobs evolve forward as well.

As discussed earlier in the book, the combination of the falling bubbles and the reality that there is no "natural growth rate," plus the coming future inflation (due to massive money printing by the Fed) is moving us forward to a new economic reality that we have not experienced before. It certainly will not move us back to the old rising multibubble economy, no matter how badly we may want our bubbles back. Once these jobs are lost, it is hard to bring them back without fundamental changes to the economy.

Does Government Stimulus Create Jobs?

The answer is most definitely yes! The stimulus of massive borrowing and massive money printing *does* lead to more jobs—as long as you keep pouring in more and more stimulus money to keep those new jobs going. But not long after the stimulus ends, so will the jobs. Why? Because big government stimulus does nothing to change the underlying reasons that jobs have declined in the first place; therefore, when the heat of the stimulus is withdrawn, the positive impacts of the stimulus will cool down quickly. That might not be the case in a normal, healthy economy going through a rough patch. In that case, a big temporary stimulus might help to get things back on track. But that won't work in a falling bubble economy. As soon as the stimulus is withdrawn, we are soon back to where we were before or worse than before.

Remember what we said earlier in the book: Try as we might, a falling bubble cannot be turned into a rising bubble for very long, if at all. We may be able to keep the bubble from falling further temporarily, but not forever. Bubbles eventually pop.

In the short term, the current government stimulus programs (massive borrowing and massive money printing) are helping to slow the rate of job loss, and they may even create new jobs in some areas, but the stimulus alone will not be enough to permanently save us from the deteriorating jobs market. Even additional "incentive" programs, such as tax credits to encourage employers to hire more employees, are likely to have limited impact. Until demand returns because the fundamentals of the economy change, the jobs market will generally continue to experience slow or no growth.

What's a Savvy Aftershock Investor to Do?

As we said at the start of this chapter, *not all jobs are created equal*; some jobs will do better than others, depending on what sector they are in. So understanding how each job sector will fare in the future (explained below) is key to understanding which jobs will likely hold up best as the bubbles continue to fall.

Although job opportunities in the Aftershock will not be the same as in the recent past, there are similarities to what has happened since the financial crisis and what will happen as we get nearer to the Aftershock. The best job prospects are in the medical industry, while the capital goods industries, such as construction and manufacturing, will be hit very hard. Figure 11.2 shows what has already occurred.

While the bubbles are still partially inflated and the government is still pumping in stimulus to keep them afloat, now is a good time to start planning your next move, whether it is a move

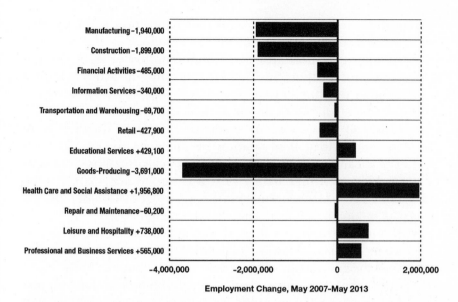

Manufacturing −1,940,000
Construction −1,899,000
Financial Activities −485,000
Information Services −340,000
Transportation and Warehousing −69,700
Retail −427,900
Educational Services +429,100
Goods-Producing −3,691,000
Health Care and Social Assistance +1,956,800
Repair and Maintenance −60,200
Leisure and Hospitality +738,000
Professional and Business Services +565,000

−4,000,000   −2,000,000   0   2,000,000

Employment Change, May 2007–May 2013

Figure 11.2   Gains and Losses by Types of Jobs, May 2007 to May 2013

Health care jobs have done the best, while manufacturing and construction have done poorly, as will be the case in the future.

Source: Bureau of Labor Statistics.

to a new job in a different sector or the same sector you are already in, or a new way to make yourself more valuable to your current employer or your customers.

But before we get to the details about each job sector, there are two important points to keep in mind, whether you are an employee or a business owner. First, keep your eyes open. Don't believe everything you see and hear from the economic cheerleaders about the so-called "recovery." We don't have one.

Second, please understand that this is not the recession of the late 1970s and early 1980s. What we have now is a falling multibubble economy, not just a typical economic slowdown. Don't expect big improvements to come quickly.

Some General Considerations for Employees and Job Seekers

- Understand that the overall economy and the job market are both evolving over time. A job that seems secure today may not be around in a few years. There is no need to panic, but now is the time to prepare for the changes ahead (see details about the job sectors below).

- Be willing to move from one job to another or from one job sector to another, but do not quit any job without having another one lined up.
- Consider your options for getting some extra job training, technical certificates, or academic degrees if they will help you move to a better-paying or more secure job, *but only if* this can be accomplished fairly quickly, such as in one to three years. Don't start a 10-year program and expect to be done with it before the Aftershock hits (for more details, see the section on college, later in this chapter).
- If you lose your job, consider taking a lower-paying job or doing temporary work, consulting, or even an internship (see the internship sidebar later in the chapter). Don't hold out for many months, waiting for the same job that you just lost to magically rematerialize. The further the bubbles fall, the less likely that will happen.

Some General Considerations for Business Owners

- Consider selling your business if it is in one of the more dangerous sectors of the economy (see details in the next section).
- If you were already planning to sell your business in the future, move up your time frame and sell it sooner, rather than later. It takes a fair amount of lead time to sell a business. Start now, before many of your potential buyers figure out what you already know about the future economy. The longer you wait to sell, the harder it will be to find a buyer and the lower the selling price, if you are able to sell it at all.
- Get as much cash as possible. If you must hold the note, make sure it is very short term. Try to keep it to less than five years—two to four years preferred. The more time that goes by, the less likely your buyer will be able to make your payments. Collect as much as you can up front.
- If you want to keep your business or start a new one, look for ways to cash in on or at least survive in the falling bubble environment (more details on this later in the chapter).

The Falling Bubbles Will Have Varying Impacts on Three Broad Economic Sectors

In assessing the impact of the falling bubbles, we find it helps to think of the U.S. economy in terms of three broad sectors:

1. *Capital goods sector*—cars, construction, major industrial equipment, and so forth.
2. *Discretionary spending sector*—fine dining, entertainment, leisure travel, high fashion, jewelry, art, collectables, cosmetic surgery, and the like.
3. *Necessities sector*—basic food, shelter, basic clothing, energy, basic health care, basic education, and so on.

In a normal economic downturn, we would expect to see the capital goods sector slow significantly, the discretionary spending sector decline somewhat, and the necessities sector to be mostly spared. But this is not a normal economic downturn. The impact of the Aftershock will be felt by all sectors, even the necessities sector. This time, all three sectors will suffer significant job and business losses, with the capital goods and discretionary spending sectors performing worst, and the necessities sector faring better, but not entirely spared. All three sectors will have some safe jobs and profitable businesses, but competition for these will grow as time goes on.

Right now, there are still jobs available but not as many as needed. Even with the creation of some new jobs since the 2008 crash, jobs have not been coming back equally in all sectors, as shown in Figure 11.2.

The Capital Goods Sector

In the Aftershock, high interest rates, coupled with a big economic slowdown, will be very bad news for the capital goods sector, including autos, construction, major industrial equipment, and so on. Rising inflation and rising interest rates will make borrowing money very expensive for consumers and businesses. This will have a very negative effect on the capital goods sector, which depends on its customers having access to low-cost capital. High interest rates will also add to the reasons why full economic recovery will take far longer and be far more difficult than in previous recessions.

Many Jobs in the Capital Goods Sector Will be Lost

Jobs in capital goods industries will be the worst hit in the coming Aftershock. If you have one of these jobs now, there probably isn't a lot you can do to protect yourself other than to gear up to move on to a job in another sector. Your best bet may be to rethink your career now with an eye toward joining an industry that will do better when the bubbles burst. We certainly don't recommend quitting one job until you have another in hand, but we also don't recommend waiting too long to make a move, if you want to do so.

If a major career makeover is not your style, you may want to consider making a move to a more stable area within your current industry. For example, if you work in the construction industry—which has already taken a terrible hit and is not coming back any time soon—you may find that moving into repair-oriented work, rather than new construction, will keep you busy while others sit at home. Of course, many construction workers will also get this idea after the bubbles fully pop, so the sooner you begin your transition toward repair work, the better. Most types of maintenance and repair work, such as automobile repair, will be in increasing demand, as people buy far fewer new cars and instead try to hang on to their older cars for as long as possible.

Most Businesses Will Fare Poorly in the Capital Goods Sector

We won't dress it up for you. The bottom line for business owners in the capital goods sector is not pretty. If you can sell now and get out, you probably should. No one can predict exactly when the Aftershock will hit, but even if it takes another two or three years, the marketplace for your business is unlikely to improve much during that time. The value of capital goods sector companies will not rise much under current conditions and will fall in value later, as unemployment continues to rise and the economy continues on its slow-growth or no-growth track. So if you have a business in the automotive, construction, industrial equipment, or any other capital goods industry, the longer you wait to get out, the more vulnerable you will be to significant losses.

As with selling homes and commercial real estate, your pool of potential buyers will get smaller and smaller as time goes by, so the sooner you go fishing in that pool for a possible buyer, the better. Selling any business takes time. Start now. Don't wait until the economy gets worse and most of your potential buyers have figured out that they should not own a business in the capital goods sector.

What will you do after you sell? Options include using your proceeds to invest in the kind of Aftershock portfolio discussed in this book. You can also be on the lookout for unexpected business opportunities in the Aftershock (discussed later in this chapter). If you decide to just hold it all in cash while you think about what to do next, be careful where you put it. Banks will be vulnerable leading up to and in the Aftershock, and the Federal Deposit Insurance Corporation (FDIC) will likely cover up to only $100,000 per bank account. Also, as inflation rises, the buying power of your cash is evaporating.

The Discretionary Spending Sector

As the economy continues to fall, Americans are not going to run out to the mall every night after work (if they have work) and squander their very limited cash and even more limited credit on high-priced designer handbags or the latest CDs. Discretionary spending on things like travel, restaurants, and entertainment is, well, discretionary. Many items and activities that we may currently still enjoy will simply be left off our shopping lists after the bubbles continue to fall and eventually fully pop. Over time, this will slow many businesses to a crawl and force others completely out of the game, further driving up unemployment.

But discretionary spending will still hold up better than the capital goods sector of the economy because some people will still have money, and they will keep spending their money, but they will spend at a lower level than before. So, instead of discretionary spending disappearing altogether, the people who can still spend will simply buy lower-priced discretionary items. For example, instead of shopping for designer handbags at Saks Fifth Avenue, they may downgrade to Walmart or Target.

The restaurant business will face this trend as well. As the bubbles fall, fewer people and businesses will spend money on eating out. That will certainly affect all restaurants. But some people and businesses will have money to eat out and will be quite happy to go to restaurants, as long as they don't have to spend as much as they used to. So the restaurant industry will continue to be a huge industry in the United States, but business will begin a long-term shift toward the lower end. For example, Mexican and Chinese restaurants will continue to survive and will gain increased market share, while high-end seafood and steak houses will be much harder hit.

To a large extent, this same trend will happen throughout the discretionary spending sector. Instead of brand names, we'll want bargains. We will still want to buy some stuff that we don't absolutely need, but we will buy less of it and we will want it at lower prices.

Because consumer spending drives more than two thirds of the U.S. economy, any decline in consumer spending has a big impact on the overall economy. This is a new situation for the United States. Back in the 1920s, when the nation was much less wealthy and was heading into the Great Depression, consumer spending represented a much smaller portion of our overall economy. So when the stock market bubble crashed in 1929, and the economy took a major downturn, the large dip in consumer spending back then had a much smaller impact on the overall economy because it just didn't make up that large a part of the economy. Other industries took a big hit, but people still had to eat basic food and buy basic clothing, so most of these industries just kept on going.

We are in a different situation today. Much of what we currently buy (and that keeps our economy going) we can easily do without. We may not like to skip the latest, high-priced fashions, but if we have to, we can easily shop at lower-end and discount stores. We can also survive quite nicely without $100,000 kitchen makeovers, complete with granite countertops and stainless steel appliances. As incomes and assets evaporate, Americans will learn to manage without these pricy pleasures.

While the discretionary spending sector will be hit less hard than the capital goods sector, the fact that discretionary spending has become such a big part of the current U.S. economy means a downturn in this sector will greatly accelerate the popping bubbles and make our postbubble recovery even harder.

Jobs in the Discretionary Spending Sector Will be Hit Hard

We've already mentioned how the slowdown in the discretionary spending sector will harm many businesses in the restaurant, retail, and home improvement industries. The travel industry has already taken a big hit, and that will continue as the bubbles fall. Leisure travel will be especially stalled, while more Americans will travel to locations that are closer and cheaper—such as into their living rooms to watch TV. Major entertainment destinations, such as Orlando and Las Vegas, will hang on due to liquidation of assets and to foreign visitors coming to spend their more valuable currencies in our cheaper playgrounds. Once the dollar bubble fully falls and the Aftershock begins, leisure travel by Americans going overseas will face the double whammy of minimal discretionary spending and a dollar that has fallen dramatically against foreign currencies.

Business travel will suffer, as well. Domestic business travel will decrease as the bubbles continue to fall and companies become more interested in cutting costs. Overseas business travel will be hit by high costs and the low value of the dollar, so only the most important overseas trips will continue. Once the Aftershock hits, our imports will be way down and there won't be much need for business travel overseas at that point.

If you are currently employed in the discretionary spending sector and are in a position to retrain for another career, this would be a good time to look for a job elsewhere, such as the necessities sector.

Businesses in the Discretionary Spending Sector Will Also Fare Poorly

Most businesses in this sector will experience some downturn as the bubbles continue to fall, and in the final pop and Aftershock, many will not survive. Businesses that have the best chances of survival during these increasingly leaner times will include low-end restaurants, low-end clothing stores, discount shops, used clothing and household furnishing stores, and businesses that cater to local or inexpensive travel.

If you own a business in the discretionary spending sector, you might want to give some thought to selling it. If you were already thinking of selling your business, you may want to move that time frame up and sell sooner rather than later. Waiting until many business owners start to realize that they need to sell will not be a good time to put your business on the market. Lots of sellers and not many buyers will mean prices will go way down.

In addition, you will be fighting against some demographics. Many businesses are owned by aging Baby Boomers, and as they get closer to retirement, they will become more risk averse and more likely to want to cash out of their businesses. Having more businesses for sale when you want to sell your business will make it harder for you to find a buyer. If you wait too long, you may risk facing the coming price drops.

Some Limited Good News: The Necessities Sector

Here is where we actually agree (somewhat) with Conventional Wisdom. Jobs and businesses in health care, education, and the government will do relatively better than in the other sectors. But even jobs in the necessities sector—such as health care, education, agriculture, government service, and utilities—not every job will not be perfectly protected before and during the coming Aftershock.

Historically, many of the jobs in this sector don't pay very well, and they will pay a bit less after the bubbles pop, when there are more workers available than jobs. But if you have a job in this sector, at least you have a job, and it will be much more reliable than most other jobs as the bubbles fall and later in the Aftershock. Even at lower pay, necessities sector jobs will be a godsend for families with a spouse who used to make more money than his or her mate but is now unemployed. The lower-paid, still-employed spouse, working as a nurse, teacher, medical administrator, or other necessities sector employee, will likely retain his or her job and be able to carry the family through the worst of the downturn.

But please understand that even in this sector, not all jobs will be equally protected. Many necessities sector jobs will not survive in the Aftershock. Why? Because they may not be "necessary" enough. So even in this sector, you will need to plan ahead.

The necessities sector is composed primarily of health care, education, utilities, basic food, basic clothing, and government services, usually run by government or other nonprofit entities. The private companies that supply these government and nonprofit entities have the potential to survive, as well. Of course, as the bubbles fall and eventually pop fully, the necessities sector will also take a hit because it currently contains a larger portion of discretionary spending (spending on high-end items within the necessities category) that will eventually be cut. So even within this relatively good sector, some jobs will not stay.

Health Care Jobs and Businesses

Health care is currently a very strong element of the U.S. economy, and it will continue to be the best bet in the necessities sector as the bubbles fall and fully pop, but there will still be some negatives, especially as unemployment rises and health care revenues decline.

Health care capital goods, such as radiology machines and hospital construction, will not do very well. However, businesses providing services and supplies to the health care industry will continue to do okay, even though they, too, will experience some downturn. Health care services jobs that will do the best include:

- Nurses
- Primary care doctors
- Psychiatrists
- Nurse practitioners
- Physicians' assistants
- Medical technicians, support personnel, administrative staff, and others involved in primary care medicine (not specialties)

Specialists and their supporting staff and services will not do well, with surgeons taking the biggest hit due to falling demand. Elective procedures, such as cosmetic surgery, already had a downturn during the financial crisis. If you can, transitioning out of these kinds of nonessential medical jobs into more basic areas of health care would be ideal.

Health Care Could Become 20 Percent of the GDP When the Bubbles Pop

Health care will be one of the safest havens for business owners and workers in the Bubblequake and Aftershock. Currently, the huge health care industry accounts for about 16 percent of the nation's GDP. As other industries decline, especially in the discretionary spending and capital goods sectors, the more stable health care industry will naturally take up a larger percentage of our economy. We've seen this before on a smaller scale. For example, during the oil bust in the 1980s, the percentage of the Houston economy represented by non-oil industries grew dramatically.

Add to this an aging population with increasing demands for health care, and it is quite possible that health care could take over a staggering 20 percent of our economy after all six of the bubbles pop, even if we have what could be a 50 percent cut per person in medical care costs, primarily by limiting procedures and reimbursable rates.

That means that not only will the safest jobs and businesses be in health care in the Aftershock, but also that the nation's hopes for regaining significant productivity growth in the postbubble economy will lie with dramatic productivity advancements in the health care field.

Government Jobs and Businesses

After health care, the next best positions in the necessities sector will be government services jobs, such as police and firefighters. As in past recessions, government services will still be needed. However, unlike in past recessions, in the Aftershock, government services will have to take deep cuts when the government can no longer borrow money after the government debt bubble pops. Before the Aftershock, government service jobs will hold on and may seem protected, but they could be pulled out from under you later, when things get worse.

This will be particularly true for private companies that have contracts with the federal government or states. Businesses and individuals who supply capital goods or construction services to the government will be hit. Road construction and maintenance, and transportation in general, will do poorly as the money for these expenditures dries up. Businesses that can make the switch to repair work and repair-related services will fare far better.

Education Jobs and Businesses

Along with health care, the demand for public education will continue, so businesses that supply education or health care products or services to the government will benefit from strengthening their marketing and business ties to these areas and increasing their percentage of sales in these sectors.

Jobs in education will be more secure than in, say, the restaurant business (discretionary spending sector), but do not make the mistake of thinking that *all* education jobs will be fully protected as the bubbles fall. As tax revenues drastically drop at both the state and local levels, funding for education will fall. Long term, jobs at primary and secondary schools will hold up better than those in higher education. Some number of elementary, middle, and high school math and science teachers will still be in demand, but as class size expands, many math and science teachers will not find a job.

Music and art teachers will face more layoffs, along with extracurricular personnel. Once the bubbles are fully popped and the Aftershock begins, we may find that seniority and union membership won't matter much. Instead, if you want to get or keep a job in education, you will need to be very good at your job, be willing to teach more classes to more students, and be loyal to your school's administration.

The picture for higher education will be tougher. Strong departments in practical fields, like engineering and computer science, especially at top colleges and universities, will fare better than those in "soft" departments (sociology, English, etc.) at liberal arts schools. Don't count on tenure to save you if your department has to take big budget cuts. If you are lucky enough to be retained in a strong department, be prepared to teach more classes for less pay.

Broader Job Trends

One of the obvious job trends as we near the Aftershock will be growth in cash businesses and jobs. Expect that jobs in restaurants will increasingly be paid with cash and many people will be able to find temporary jobs or consulting jobs that pay cash and will be willing to work at lower rates. The underground cash economy will likely grow substantially, as it has in other countries experiencing a major economic downturn. Jobs in repair, as we mentioned earlier, will be more resistant to the downturn and are the type of jobs that can be easily paid for in cash.

Also, another current trend that will continue into the Aftershock, and especially afterward, will be higher pay and growth in demand for highly skilled blue-collar jobs. Although highly skilled blue-collar workers will be hurt like most job seekers, this area will still offer reasonable pay and decent opportunities even during the Aftershock. This is especially true if these skilled jobs also involve difficult working conditions, such as being an electrical lineman who has to repair electrical lines in storms. Such jobs will continue to pay relatively well and there will be decent demand,

Free Internships—Not Just for College Students Anymore

Free internships have been a good route for college students to potentially get a paid job by working for free. For the student, an internship provides an opportunity to get a foot in the door of an employer, as well as getting some on-the-job training. For the employer, the internship offers a chance to get to know the intern in the work environment before deciding to hire or fire, while also getting some work out of them for free, making the internship an effective win-win for both parties.

What is beginning to happen now, and will be more common in the future, is unpaid internships for adults who are not college students. In an increasingly tight job market, workers who are willing to work for free for a period of time will have a competitive advantage. Like college students, they will have the chance to get their foot in the door, while also gaining training and on-the-job experience. The value to the potential employer is obvious: free labor.

As the bubbles continue to fall, and even more so after they fully pop in the Aftershock, unpaid internships for non–college students will become increasingly common.

If there is a job you are going after now and they don't currently offer an unpaid internship, there is no harm in suggesting one. The company may not be set up to accept your offer, but you never know. Everyone likes a freebie.

mostly because many people with skills don't like those kinds of jobs. Even now, there are lots of vacancies for these types of jobs and significant turnover in many of them. Although conditions will tighten considerably in the future, this will still be an area for employment simply because of the skills required and many people's unwillingness to work under bad conditions.

Should I Go to College?

For high school students or recent graduates, planning to go to college still makes sense. Even though the economy may be falling during that time and you will likely emerge from college in a difficult work environment with fewer jobs and business opportunities than before, it is still a good idea to get a college education if you can. The longer you wait, the less likely you are to go back to school, and a college degree will still mean something, even in the Aftershock.

However, spending too much on college is not a good idea. In figuring the costs and benefits of continuing your education, it is important to be realistic. (Please see the next chapter on spending, savings, and debt for an in-depth discussion on paying for college, including student loans.)

In general, the financial value of an expensive four-year college degree in the liberal arts has been going down recently, while the value of a two-year college degree in a practical field, or a diploma or certificate of completion from a trade or technical school, has gone up.

While additional education is no guarantee of landing employment, it will definitely increase the odds of getting a job after you graduate and will also improve your chances of getting a higher-paying job. Obviously, you will do better picking a field in the more favorable job sectors mentioned earlier. If you already have a secure, full-time job, going back to college may not be worth it, unless you can get your degree in a year or two.

Opportunities after the Bubbles Pop: Cashing In on Distressed Assets

In nearly every industry in all three sectors of the economy, there will be some opportunities to benefit from falling asset values. Just as high-priced office furniture from bankrupt dot-com companies ended up at auction sales for pennies on the dollar after the relatively small Internet bubble popped, there will be countless auctions of every description after our multibubble economy pops. Opportunities to make large profits by buying, selling, and servicing distressed businesses and other assets will actually become one of the good sectors in the postbubble economy.

As always, timing will be key. One of the biggest mistakes many people will make is buying distressed businesses or other assets too soon. In this very unusual economic downturn, involving the fall of multiple bubbles, we will face very high interest and inflation rates that will take a lot longer to come down than anyone might imagine. It will be easy to mistakenly think the worst has passed and the time is right to start buying up distressed businesses and assets, when actually the price of these bargain properties will likely fall *even lower*. For maximum profits, think years, not months. Many people in the real estate market are making this mistake right now. They think that because an asset has lost 25 to 50 percent of its peak value, it is a bargain. That is true only if it is not going to fall further.

That said, there can be some shorter-term opportunities to "flip" a distressed asset even before the Aftershock hits and assets fall even further, if you can find a willing buyer.

Once the Aftershock hits, the servicing of distressed assets and businesses will be an instant and long-term winner. People and companies who buy, restructure, manage, and resell distressed businesses and other assets will have the opportunity to make huge incomes and profits, including:

- Accountants and financial analysts involved with forensic accounting and distressed properties accounting.
- Consultants, bankers, managers, and others involved in the acquisition, restructuring, and management of distressed businesses and other assets.
- Bankruptcy attorneys.
- Liquidation companies and auction houses.

Dig Your Well Before You Are Thirsty

The title of Harvey MacKay's excellent book *Dig Your Well before You Are Thirsty* makes a lot of sense in these pre-Aftershock days before the full bubble pop. Now is the time to network among colleagues or make new connections that you can draw on later, as needed.

Now is also the time to show your boss (or your customers) just how great an employee (or business owner) you really are. Make yourself indispensable before any downsizing occurs. And, of course, never leave a job or income source before having another one in hand.

If you find yourself without a job or other income, don't be too proud to take whatever you can get as soon as possible, while you continue to look for better work. This will not be a good time for holding out for something better.

If you do find yourself temporarily out of work, please remember that your net worth is not your self-worth. And perhaps more important, please show that same respect to others. Everyone, regardless of income or wealth, is equally worthy.

CHAPTER 12

Aftershock Money Smarts

SPENDING, SAVINGS, AND DEBT

How well you prepare for the coming Aftershock goes beyond what you do with your investment portfolio. It is also about countless other big and small decisions, made consciously or unconsciously, about how you spend, save, and borrow money.

As we approach the Aftershock, continuing to live your life as if nothing is about to change is foolish. The new economic future requires new ways of thinking. Just as with your new investment thinking, in some cases the old rules for spending, savings, and debt may no longer apply.

Don't Let Spending Become the Achilles Heel of Your Aftershock Preparations

Over the past several decades, shopping for many Americans has become more than just a necessary task; it's become a national pastime. With more malls, shopping centers, warehouse stores, buying clubs, online merchants, mom-and-pop joints, and more places to buy-buy-buy than ever before, much of the country has turned into a coast-to-coast spending arcade. Even our airports now offer more on-site shopping opportunities than the entire economies of some of the countries they fly to.

Beyond whatever it is that we are buying, the shopping experience itself has become the main attraction for many people, so much so that recent studies show that on average Americans tend to become mildly depressed when they are kept from shopping for more than a few days.

Shopping is not just important for the American psyche, it's been vital to the American economy as well. In fact, more than two thirds of the U.S. economy depends directly or indirectly on consumer spending. That's why after the terrorist attacks of 9/11, one of the first things that then-president Bush said to the country was "please go shopping" to keep our economy going.

And, of course, U.S. consumers have been keeping many other economies going and growing as well, such as China, India, and others. Rising home equity and low interest rates helped boom the consumer spending bubble, and for many decades America's rising consumer spending and other bubbles have been the growth engine of the world's rising bubble economy. So U.S. spending has been a powerful propeller of many economies, both bubble and nonbubble.

But for us as *individuals*, how much spending is too much spending, especially in light of what we know is ahead? Putting aside any other potential impacts, how is your current level of spending affecting your personal finances, besides perhaps filling up your house? And, more importantly, how will what you are buying now impact you later when the Aftershock hits?

Stop Spending as if There's No Tomorrow

Cutting spending is one of the simplest ways to prepare now for the worldwide economic troubles ahead, and yet most people find it the hardest to do. Even if you have a decent income, a nice car, the latest cell phone, and a wallet full of credit cards, if you are spending at close to the rate that you are earning, you are headed for future trouble if that income declines. Even in a healthy economy, overspending is a mistake. In a falling bubble economy—where you may eventually see both your income and your assets fall—overspending now will turn out to be a really big mistake later.

Even if you aren't spending at maximum speed today, there are likely places you can cut back. And if you have already done some cutting back, there are probably a few places where you can prune further. Study after study has shown that once a certain minimum standard of living has been reached, continuing to buy more and more stuff does not lead to more happiness. It can, however, lead to more future problems when they money you are spending now could have been put to better use to maximize your safety later.

Before the Aftershock: Cut, Cut, Cut!

As we head for the Market Cliff (described in Chapter 4) that will cripple not only the markets but employment across the country, it is highly advisable to cut spending while you still have your current income. Even if you hold on to your job before and during the Aftershock (see Chapter 11), your income is unlikely to keep up with rising inflation. So, ideally, you'll want to save money now and put it into Aftershock-safe investments.

The obvious place to cut spending is at the margins. Opting for lower-cost items and items that come with lower maintenance costs is a great way to reduce spending without impacting your daily life too drastically. If you need or want to buy a new car, buy the car, but does it need to be a Mercedes? If you have a big event coming up, such as a wedding, consider spending less on items that can easily be had at lower prices without a major downgrade in the overall experience. If you need a new refrigerator, forego the extra cost of a built-in TV or other nonessential add-ons that add significantly to the cost. With every major purchase, ask yourself, do I really need this?

The big items are not the only place to look for spending cuts. The cost of the small stuff, like buying a cup of gourmet coffee on the way to work, adds up to more than you might think. It may help to make note of each and every thing you buy for a full month. It will be a nuisance, but be as accurate as possible. Then review with the goal of trimming where you can without making your life miserable. Bring coffee from home, cut out the cable TV channels you don't watch, trim the phone bill, stop magazines you don't read or can get at the library or online, buy the lower-priced store brands, and get into the habit of skipping or choosing less expensive options for little things that don't matter much. One big money eater is dining out at restaurants. You may be surprised at how much you can cut spending by eating out less often or replacing lots of trips for fast food with one nicer dining experience.

Something else to consider is holding off on some purchases altogether. Once the Aftershock hits, many goods and services will be dramatically cheaper—but *only for those who have protected themselves!* If invested for the Aftershock, money that could be spent on big-ticket items like high-end housing, high-priced cars, and collector's items today, would ultimately be able to purchase much, much more when the world's bubble economy bursts.

Whether you are running a household or a business, make cutting spending a priority; it can really add up. We know this isn't fun and might seem trivial now, but it can make the critical difference in your prosperity before and after the Aftershock. If you start feeling too deprived, remember that people generally get more pleasure from experiences than from owning objects. Find fun things to do that don't cost too much, and when you do occasionally spend money, make it something that will make you happy.

During and After the Aftershock: Many Great Bargains

For those who have saved and invested well for the Aftershock, spending in a post-Aftershock environment will be easy and even fun. Nearly everything will have gone down in real prices (adjusted for inflation). But gold and other Aftershock-safe investments will have grown in value. And unlike any wealth you may have now, which is mostly bubble money, your post-Aftershock wealth will be real wealth—meaning it will last.

This brings up a key point about the Aftershock. Despite depressing the economy and bankrupting individuals, businesses, and governments around the world, the Aftershock will see more real wealth made by more people in a smaller time frame than any other time in history. Think of the smart investors who in the Great Depression saved their money and later bought great stocks and picked up other bargains. Only this time it will be on a much larger scale.

In the post-Aftershock world, those with money will be able to buy just about anything they want, from gorgeous waterfront property and fast cars to fine art and rare collector's items, for pennies on the dollar. The whole country will be like a giant yard sale. Cut your spending and invest well now so you can be in a good position to be a buyer later.

Savings: How Much Is Enough?

There are two big reasons to save now for the Aftershock (saving for a rainy day and saving for retirement) and one big reason not to save too much (future inflation).

Saving for retirement is covered in detail in the next chapter, so here we are going to focus on saving for potential loss of income. It is absolutely essential that you have some money put aside to cover your essential living expenses in case your income declines or disappears before or during the Aftershock. Experts typically recommend setting aside at least six months of expense money—and that's in a healthy economy, not in a falling bubble economy that will eventually pop.

Americans are notoriously bad savers, and few people could maintain their current lifestyles if their incomes suddenly dropped or stopped. As a culture of spenders, the idea of savings is not too appealing, especially when the stock market is up and the economy seems to be doing well. In bad times, we get a little bit more interested in putting some money aside, which explains why after the 2008 financial crisis, the U.S. savings rate rose modestly.

More recently, however, as massive money printing has created this temporary fake recovery, people have gone back to saving less and borrowing more—in part because the economy seems to be doing better and in part because of persistent unemployment. Whether people are saving less due to more optimism or lack of income (or both), the lack of significant savings in the United States is stunning (see Figure 12.1).

If you are among those who haven't put aside much for a rainy day, *please start now.* If you don't know where you will find the money, cutting spending will help with that. Don't think of it as deprivation; think of it as smart preparation. Even if you already have some rainy day savings, now is the time to bump it up to storm level.

Given the approaching Aftershock and the rising unemployment it will bring, the typical advice for putting aside six months' worth of money may not be enough. How many months you plan for is really a personal decision and may have more to do with making you feel more comfortable now than it will have to do with actually covering all your needs later. In a non-Aftershock economy,

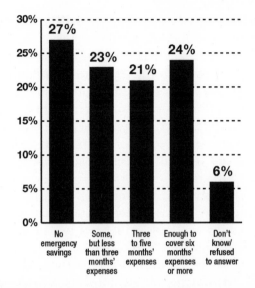

Figure 12.1   The Majority of Americans Live Paycheck to Paycheck

A June 2013 survey revealed that three out of four Americans don't have enough savings to cover six months' worth of living expenses. About half don't have enough to last even three months, and 27 percent have no savings at all.

Source: Bankrate.com.

putting money aside to cover a short-term income loss can be calculated based on how many months you think it will take you to get back on your feet, either with a new job or another business. But in an Aftershock economy, it may not really matter how many months' worth of savings you have put aside if your lack of income lasts longer than your savings account.

So the better question than "how much savings is enough?" is to ask yourself to focus on developing an overall game plan for the Aftershock, one that includes cutting spending, putting some savings aside, being smart about your job or business, and creating an actively managed Aftershock investment portfolio (see Chapter 14). If you are thinking you will rely on your savings alone, without developing a bigger Aftershock protection plan, no magic number of months of savings alone may be long enough to cover you—which is why it is so important to also have some wise Aftershock investments for the future, such as gold.

Even if you have plenty of cash, there is another big reason why you shouldn't rely on your savings alone. . .

The Buying Power of Your Savings Will Evaporate with Inflation

As we enter and go through the Aftershock, inflation and interest rates will rise and asset values will fall, putting many types of investments at risk, including stock, bonds, real estate, pension funds, and life insurance. Making matters worse, jobs will be at risk, and many people's incomes will suddenly stop. Even those who manage to remain employed or find new employment will face downward wage pressures.

Under these conditions, one might think that the best defense is having the biggest possible savings account. Certainly, having some money set aside will be a big help and you absolutely need to do that, but don't assume that if some savings is good then more savings is even better, without limit. Once inflation kicks in, the buying power of your money will begin to evaporate.

For example, if you have $200,000 in savings and we see inflation rise to just 10 percent (remember, inflation went to 14 percent in the 1980s, so 10 percent isn't unrealistic), then each year that inflation continues, your savings will lose 10 percent of its buying power. That's like having $20,000 *per year* stolen from you. A few years of that would reduce your savings pretty quickly.

Now imagine that, instead of 10 percent inflation, we get 20 or 30 percent inflation. This is not out of the question, especially given that the Fed's money printing has already increased the U.S. monetary base by more than 300 percent and the money printing continues. In fact, by the time the money printing finally stops, the peak inflation rate could go higher, at least for a while. That means keeping too much money in cash just before and during the Aftershock will be like leaving your wallet unattended at a rock concert. It's going to disappear fast.

So what's the answer? Give up saving altogether? Absolutely not! Savings will never be more critical to your safety than in the years before and during the Aftershock, so if you don't already have some put aside, the time to build up your savings is now. Although cash is fine for now, in the longer term you may not want to leave too much of your savings in cash, and opt instead for more Aftershock-safe investments, as outlined in Chapter 14.

Where to Stash Your Cash?

For centuries, the classic answer to this question was to put money under the mattress or bury it in your backyard. Also historically popular was to hold gold, jewelry, and other precious objects, hide those wherever you could, and then sell them later when you need the money. With the rise of the modern banking system, however, methods of saving money have grown much more sophisticated— but not necessarily a whole lot safer.

Many investors have opted to keep their savings in bonds, whole life insurance, and annuities (primarily bonds) because they pay interest. More recently, keeping savings in home equity and stocks became more popular due to their appreciation of wealth, especially during the rising bubble economy. By now we know the risks associated with keeping savings in tied up in bubble assets. It's lots of fun on the way up, but it's not a good long-term plan.

Before and during the coming Aftershock, the best places to stash cash are:

- FDIC-insured *checking* accounts.
- Safe deposit boxes.
- In-home safes.

Even if you don't have an in-home safe, keeping some amount of spare cash where you can access it quickly is smart, just in case the banks and ATMs are temporary closed for a short period of time.

Will My Bank Be Safe in the Aftershock?

Probably not, but it doesn't matter as much as you might think. Many people familiar with our predictions are worried about their banks collapsing when the Aftershock comes, asking us where they should keep cash to protect it. While many banks will fail in the Aftershock, we see no need to put money under your mattress or dig holes in the backyard. If your bank goes under, the contents of your safe deposit boxes will still be yours. And even during the worst of the Aftershock, the government will still ensure that deposits in *checking accounts* in U.S. banks will be liquid. Any check written against a U.S. checking account will continue to be redeemable in a matter of hours.

The reason for this is that the cost to the economy of letting the checking accounts payment mechanism fail is simply too high, and by comparison it's relatively cheap for the government to keep it going. Yes, it will involve more money printing, but even in the depths of a mega-depression, this will be a worthwhile trade-off. The Fed will always make sure money in checking accounts is safe and easily transferable regardless of the amount.

Note that we said "the Fed" and "regardless of the amount." In other words, we're not talking about FDIC insurance, which will certainly be overwhelmed by the Aftershock and quickly out of money. So don't count on FDIC saving accounts, only checking accounts. Also please note that we are not talking about certificates of deposits (CDs) in banks. These accounts are less liquid, and if a bank goes under, so will most of the funds in savings accounts and CDs. In some cases, for people who have lost money in savings accounts and CDs that they rely on for basic living expenses, there will be some hardship payments. But these will still likely be much less than the original value of the FDIC-insured accounts.

There is no need for immediate panic, and we are not saying you must run out today and shut down all your savings accounts and CDs. There's still time to put your Aftershock protection plan in place as you see more evidence that our predictions are right. When you are ready to make some changes, keep in mind that checking accounts in the United States will be fine for the long haul, but money in savings accounts and CDs will be at risk.

Later in the Aftershock, in order to keep their depositors, the banks will have no choice but to offer some amount of incentive in the form of low or no fees and/or better interest payments on deposited funds. This will slightly compensate you for the significant amount you will lose to inflation. Money in checking accounts will be needed to maintain some liquidity. The money will still lose wealth over the long term, but it will be a slow drain on what should be only a small portion of your overall protection plan, including some precious metals and an actively managed Aftershock portfolio.

How Much Cash to Keep in an Actively Managed Aftershock Portfolio?

The general rule is that when inflation and interest rates are low, you should keep more in cash. Conversely, when inflation and interest rates are high, you should keep less in cash. Given that rule, it's generally best to keep cash a small part of your portfolio as we head for the Aftershock. But there are a number of factors to consider, given the changes in economic climate we can expect over the next few years.

Right now, we generally recommend allocating about 6 percent of a portfolio to cash. Everyone needs some liquidity, and there's very little risk right now. There's no perceived inflation, and interest rates are still very low.

Eventually, inflation will rise—both in reality and in public perception. In a perfect market, interest rates for storing cash would exactly match and correct for risk, inflation, and taxes. In reality, they don't, and they certainly won't in the Aftershock economy. When inflation does rise in earnest, interest rates will also go up, but interest paid on saving accounts will fall short of the inflation rate and taxes. So if you keep too much cash in your portfolio during high inflation, you're going to lose wealth.

However, because you still need liquidity, you'll still need to keep *some* cash in your portfolio. That's why we'd recommend trimming at that point from 6 percent down to maybe 3 or 4 percent, but not much lower than that. This will vary according to your liquidity needs. (Please see Chapter 14 for more details about building an actively managed Aftershock portfolio.)

Borrowing Money before, during, and after the Aftershock

On the way up, America's Bubble Economy used borrowed money like jet fuel. Without low interest rates and lots of money borrowing, the bubbles could not have grown as big or as fast as they did. Now, as the government resorts to massive stimulus to prop up the sagging bubbles, money printing is keeping interest rates low and making even more borrowing possible. While many people did cut back on their personal and business debt a bit right after the financial crisis, consumer and commercial debt is starting to pick up again.

Some people believe that *all debt* is bad and should be eliminated as soon as possible for all individuals, businesses, and governments. We don't share that point of view. *Debt is a tool, not necessarily a problem.* Problems arise when any tool is used stupidly. There is

smart debt and there is dumb debt. What we want to talk to you about now is how to limit or eliminate dumb debt, the kind that could hurt you later in the Aftershock.

In assessing whether you have smart debt or dumb debt, it's important to take into consideration a variety of factors:

- *What is the debt for?* Does the debt help you make money in the future, such as borrowing for an education that will lead to a good-paying job or borrowing to start a profitable business? Or will the debt help you lose money in the future, because of high or rising interest payments or because whatever you bought with the debt was a bad investment?
- *What is the interest rate?* Typically, the lower the rate, the smarter the loan. But not always. You also have to ask . . .
- *Is it a fixed-rate or an adjustable-rate loan?* A low-interest, fixed-rate loan is much smarter than an even lower interest adjustable-rate loan because as inflation rises you can pay off the fixed-rate loan with "cheaper" dollars, while the adjustable-rate loan will rise with inflation and climbing interest rates, making your payments larger and larger.
- *How easy would it be for lenders to collect on this debt?* Not that you are planning on defaulting on your obligations, but if push comes to shove and you can't pay, it's better to have a debt that is harder to collect than one that is easier.

Mortgage Debt

In today's environment, the conventional wisdom is that mortgage payments should take top priority. This is because we are in an environment in which mortgage lenders will make strenuous collecting efforts if a homeowner misses a payment, and will quickly move to foreclosure and eviction if payments can't be collected, costing the debtor both their home and any equity it may have had. Those are pretty strong incentives to keep up payments.

However, in a post-Aftershock environment, the situation will be very different. With an overwhelming number of homeowners defaulting on their mortgages, eviction will become a very difficult process for mortgage lenders. On top of that, when the value of homes has collapsed across the board, lenders will have little or nothing to gain by going ahead with expensive foreclosure proceedings.

Today, missed mortgage payments can ruin your credit score, which is a disaster when credit is so easily available at low rates. But in and after the Aftershock, when there will be little borrowing going on anyway, and most people's credit scores will be lower than they are today, it won't matter so much, if at all. At that point, for those with underwater mortgages, for those with adjustable-rate loans, and those who earlier had prioritized a rapid mortgage debt repayment, continuing to make mortgage payments will naturally be a low priority.

For those who manage to secure a long-term, *fixed-rate* mortgage before the Aftershock, though, life will generally be a little easier. Over time, inflation will dramatically diminish the value of monthly payments—meaning your income will go up but your monthly mortgage payment will not, so you are paying it off with "cheaper" dollars. In this case, homeowners may end up owning their homes outright, having paid a fraction of its value.

Prior to the Aftershock, there might be some lean years, so having a cash cushion is important for covering your home loan if your income drops or stops. As real estate values fall, having an actively managed Aftershock portfolio (see Chapter 14) will help make up for your loss of home equity.

If you have a home equity line of credit (HELOC) loan, it is likely at an adjustable rate. If so, do your best to pay the loan off fairly quickly or to refinance it to a low, fixed-rate loan, if the lender is willing. Another option is to roll your HELOC loan into a mortgage refinancing, if you can't pay off the HELOC and it's the only way for you to turn it into a fixed-rate debt.

Remember, when inflation hits, paying off any *fixed*-rate loan with "cheaper" dollars is smart. Trying to keep up with rising payments on adjustable-rate loans is not.

Credit Card Debt

Just before and during the Aftershock, there will be only two good reasons to pay off credit card debt: (1) you have a lot of income and assets that can be repossessed, or (2) you have some business need for a good credit record. Otherwise, there's little reason to worry much about credit card debt in the longer term. That's because in an Aftershock environment, there won't be much the credit card companies can do to collect. Interest rates can be raised, but regulations make it difficult, and there are limits. Also, credit scores will no longer be an issue. Most people will have terrible scores and there will be far less money available to lend, so it won't matter. Many people will be forced to ignore their credit card bills. And when there's little income and few assets to go around, there isn't much credit card companies can do to collect. Eventually, the industry will go bankrupt.

However, before the Aftershock, you will want to keep up with your credit card payments and when possible pay them off if you can, assuming the balance is reasonable. If you can't pay it off quickly, don't fall prey to making only the minimum payment. That can turn even a small credit card debt into a much larger one, as interest keeps accruing.

However, if your credit card debt is large relative to your income and especially if it is approaching your annual pay, you may want to seek bankruptcy relief, depending on your situation.

In general, it is smart to use credit cards for everyday spending and larger purchases in order to gain various bonuses (like airline miles or cash back), but only to the extent that you can pay the balance off quickly. It's not so smart to use credit cards to buy things you really cannot afford.

Car Loans

Car payments will generally be among the most important to make just before and during the Aftershock. Why? Because chances are, you will need your car to get to work or to look for work. Cars are very easy to repossess when payments aren't made—there's no expensive foreclosure and eviction process as with homes. This will leave you without a car, and if you have no cash, buying another one will be nearly impossible. There will be no more loans available. The exception to this might be if your car is unnecessary to your life, or if you have a particularly expensive car. In those cases, you might simply prefer to let the car be repossessed and not worry about the payments.

Like credit cards, prior to the Aftershock, you will likely do better to keep your car payments up or sell or trade in the car while you can get more value for it. If you are considering a new car loan before the Aftershock, make sure you buy something reliable for the long haul. Or consider buying a late-model used car. They're a whole lot cheaper.

If you are deciding between paying for your car with cash or financing it, a low fixed-rate car loan is a good idea if you can put your money to work in other ways for a higher return. In any case, never opt for an adjustable-rate car loan. Stick with fixed-rate only.

Business Debt

If you own a business, the outlook for business debt is the opposite of that for personal debt. It is important to reduce business debt as much as possible, and preferably go into the Market Cliff (see Chapter 4) with little or no debt.

The reason for this is that collection on business debt is much easier than collection on personal debt. Businesses have assets and earnings, and creditors can take over a delinquent business and sell it for whatever they can get. It's true that inflation will reduce your fixed-rate business debt over time, but if a business has significant debt heading into the Aftershock, default is very likely and creditors will move in long before inflation has taken effect.

If your business does have existing debt, the best approach is to reduce it in any way you can. However, there is another, potentially even better option: sell your business sooner rather than later, and jettison the debt along with it. This could lead to a big equity gain, and you can put that money into Aftershock-safe assets. If the business is not of great sentimental value to you, this is a great way to turn it into a gain ahead of the Aftershock while most businesses will be struggling later. Waiting too long to sell will likely result in no sale at all.

Saving and Borrowing for College

Conventional wisdom's approach to saving and borrowing for college, like most of CW's advice, makes sense in a normal, healthy economy and also in a rising bubble economy. However, it makes less sense in a falling bubble economy.

Saving for College

Traditional savings plans and college investment instruments are not going to fare well as inflation rises, interest rates climb, and many investments fall. Simple savings accounts that don't grow faster than the inflation rate will mean a loss over time. And investments, such as 529 plans, that are vulnerable to the Market Cliff certainly are not ideal.

We are not big fans of many 529 plans for the following reasons:

- Most 529 accounts are heavily invested in stocks and bonds, which will not hold up well in the Aftershock.
- Most 529 plans do not allow alternative investments.
- Most 529 plans allow you to change your portfolio allocations only once per year, at a prescheduled date, regardless of changes in the markets.
- Even if you go to all cash in your 529 account, rising inflation in the Aftershock will diminish the value of that cash.

If you will be tapping your 529 account in the next two to four years, you may be able to escape a big drop in your college savings before we hit the Market Cliff. However, if college is not around the corner, we recommend you put college savings into a well-diversified Aftershock portfolio, as described throughout this book and summarized in Chapter 14.

Financial Aid

In addition to saving and investing for college, students should also actively pursue any and all public, private, and institutional financial aid available, including:

- Federal student aid, such as Pell Grants.
- State student aid, grants, and scholarships.
- Grants and scholarships offered by educational institutions.
- Private grants and scholarships offered by many organizations, such as local community associations, nonprofits, and private donors.
- Lower-interest federal student loans.
- And as a last resort, higher-interest private student loans.

Student Loans

Student loans, both federally backed and more expensive private loans, are still an option. But with U.S. students now owing an average of $26,600 at graduation, education loans have become a big burden at the start of adult life, and will only become even more burdensome when good-paying jobs become increasingly harder to come by as we approach the Aftershock.

This isn't just a problem for the individual borrowers. Total student loan debt in the United States is now more than $1 trillion—accounting for almost 9 percent of all consumer debt, up from just 3 percent in 2004, according to the New York Federal Reserve. Student loans have become a massive debt bubble (see Figure 12.1) that will eventually pop.

How Much Should I Borrow?

In general, keeping debt as low as possible is a good idea, but for a variety of reasons, student loans may be a different story.

Typically, student loan experts recommend borrowing no more than what you think your first year's salary will be after graduation. Right now, student loans cannot be discharged in bankruptcy, and student loan lenders, both private and government, go after student loan payments fairly aggressively. So under normal

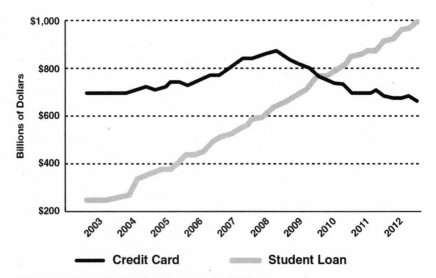

Figure 12.2   – Student Loans Top $1 Trillion

Student loan debt is now greater than all U.S. credit card debt.

Source: Federal Reserve Bank of New York.

circumstances, it makes sense not to borrow more than you can reasonably handle in monthly payments after you graduate, and not to borrow more to go to an expensive school when a less expensive option is available and likely just as good for whatever your particular goals.

However, the coming Aftershock changes the outlook for student loans dramatically. That $1 trillion student loan bubble we mentioned earlier is poised to burst—meaning more and more of these loans won't be paid back. Even now, about one third of student loans are already delinquent, and clearly that number will rise as unemployment rises before and during the Aftershock.

Student Loan Repayment in the Aftershock

If we were predicting a typical recession, we would tell you to be careful about your student loans: don't take on too much debt and pay it back in full. However, the Aftershock will not be a typical recession. Many colinked bubbles will pop, including student loans.

Most student loans are government guaranteed, meaning that if the student doesn't repay the loan to the lender, the government will. So in the shorter term, the government will exercise its power to push hard to collect on these loans because if they don't, they will have to cover the loss.

But in the longer term, when unemployment is high in the Aftershock, it will become increasingly unpopular with the public for the government to try to force student loan repayment. Just as the recent recession made the government more relaxed about the repayment of mortgages in default, we will probably eventually see the government become more relaxed about the repayment of student loans. It will be difficult to force collection and very politically unpopular, as well as increasingly unfruitful due to lack of employment.

Instead, the government will simply print more money to cover the student loan losses, adding even more inflation in the future. In the Aftershock, many student loans will be written off when default rates may go as high as 70 to 90 percent, with little chance of collection because people will have few assets and little income to seize.

Certainly, those who have significant assets and/or income will have to continue making payments on student loans for some time. Failure to make payments may result in assets being seized

It's Getting Harder to Pay for College

A 2013 Sallie Mae survey revealed that parents cannot help with college costs as much as they used to. In 2010, parents coughed up 37 percent of their students' college costs, but now that's dropped to 27 percent because of dwindled savings and less income. Nearly 70 percent of students said they had to eliminate some schools from consideration due to costs, up from 58 percent in 2008.

Meanwhile, student have to borrow more than ever, with loans now contributing 18 percent of total college costs, compared to 14 percent in 2009. And the need for grants and scholarships is also increasing, with two thirds of students requiring grants and scholarships in 2012, up from only about half needing the free money about five years ago.

All this is due to both the rising costs of college and the decreasing ability for students and their parents to pay for it—a trend we can expect to see for many years.

or income being garnished. But remember that eventually inflation will eat away much of these low, fixed-rate loans, so even if you must continue making payments, you will be paying it back with "cheaper" dollars.

In the meantime, prior to the Aftershock, we recommend fixed-rate, low-interest student loans on which you can defer repayment as long as possible. If you are out of school and have a job, *it's best to make your minimum student loan payments, as required.* If you are out of school and unemployed, seek hardship deferments for as long as you can.

Get these low-interest student loans while you still can. After our falling bubbles finally fully pop, there will be far less money available for student loans even at high interest rates, so if you want to borrow money to go to college, now is the time to do it.

Summing It Up

Here is the bottom line for what to do with spending, saving, and debt before and during the coming bubble pop and Aftershock:

Before the Aftershock

- Cut spending. Start today and keep looking for more ways to cut.
- Put aside at least six months' worth of living expenses.
- As we get closer to the Aftershock, move savings accounts and CDs into checking accounts.
- Keep some quick access cash at home (and don't spend it!).
- Savings should be just one part of your Aftershock plan, not counted on as your only protection.
- Choose only low fixed-rate loans (or refinance to them) and keep up with the payments.
- Pay off high-interest loans faster, if you can.
- Don't accelerate payback of low-interest loans (pay off with "cheaper" dollars later).
- Borrow for your education and make minimum required payments (for now).
- Don't borrow for things you don't really need or cannot afford.

During the Aftershock

- If you did not prepare well, cut spending to the bone, apply for all available support programs, and share housing and other expenses with others.
- Request hardship support if you've lost savings that you need to live on.
- If you don't have much income or assets, don't pay back loans that most others are not paying back, like student loans.
- If you have income and assets, pay off fixed, low-interest-rate loans with cheaper dollars as inflation rises.
- Those who prepared well for the Aftershock will be able to buy many depressed assets for pennies on the dollar.

CHAPTER 13

Aftershock Retirement and Estate Planning

For those who are nearing or already in retirement, the Aftershock couldn't come at a worse time. The vast majority of retirement portfolios are still focused primarily on stocks, bonds, and real estate. And in time as those bubbles begin to pop, so will most people's retirement plans. What worked well for a good retirement in the past will turn out to be not so good for retirement in the future.

Making matters worse, many people simply have not saved enough over the years to retire comfortably, even without the threat of future popping bubbles. In general, Americans have not been especially good savers for the past few decades, and more recently the low savings problem has been compounded by rising unemployment and low wage growth, leaving many people with less income available to save. The numbers on retirement savings are pretty dismal (see Figure 13.1).

But even if you have plenty of retirement savings and limited exposure to the vulnerable asset bubbles (stocks, bonds, and real estate), there is another ugly retirement problem looming on your horizon: *rising future inflation.* Any amount of inflation is a negative during retirement, when everything costs more as inflation rises and your dollar buys less.

Inflation matters because rising costs will compound the rising expenses of retirement. One of the myths about retirement is that you will spend less than during your working years. In fact, for

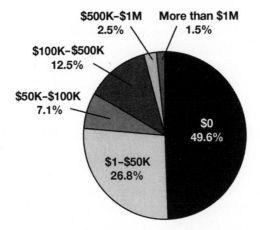

Figure 13.1 Most Americans Don't Have Enough for Retirement
More than 75 percent of U.S. households have less than $50,000 in retirement assets.
Source: CRS analysis of the 2010 Survey of Consumer Finances.

many people, spending goes up. Retirees have much more leisure time, and many want to fill that time with travel and activities they consider necessary for a good retirement. So spending more and prices rising is not a good combination.

Even if you tighten your belt and cut back on spending, for retirees living on a fixed income, inflation is the enemy. The more inflation goes up, the less buying power your money has. Each year that inflation continues, it's as if you are becoming poorer and poorer.

The threat of future inflation—which will be quite significant, given the Fed's massive money printing—means that keeping too much of one's retirement savings in cash in the future will be a bad idea. But if you limit cash and try to grow your retirement savings in a typical conventional investment portfolio, as most people do, your investments will eventually hit the Market Cliff and be wiped out in the Aftershock.

Back in the retirement-friendly days of the rising bubble economy, successful retirement investing—like all investing—was a whole lot easier. In this new environment of increasingly vulnerable asset bubbles and looming future inflation, planning for retirement has become far more challenging, even scary.

But that doesn't mean you can't protect your retirement investments now, while you still have some time. In fact, if you reorient your retirement portfolio before the bubbles begin to pop, you can limit your downside risks as we approach the Market Cliff and even come out ahead in the Aftershock. Well-placed investments now can save you from a lot of difficulty down the road. Active management is key (see Chapter 14).

Why Conventional Wisdom on Retirement Is Wrong

Conventional Wisdom says that stocks, bonds, and real estate are all recovering or will recover soon. As long as people simply hold on to their diversified stocks and bonds, and stick with real estate, everything will be fine. Pensioners, 401(k) holders, and other investors will be able to retire comfortably for years to come.

In previous chapters, we explained why we can't count on stocks, bonds, real estate, annuities, or whole life insurance to hold up well during the Aftershock; therefore, conventionally invested retirement portfolios that contain these vulnerable assets—including conventionally invested 401(k)s, individual retirement accounts, and all the rest—will not do well.

For pension funds, the situation is a bit more complicated, but the outcome will eventually be very much the same. Conventional Wisdom says not to worry about pension funds. Even with some recent concerns about underfunded corporate pensions, most people generally tend to rest easy about them. After all, corporate pensions are overseen by managers with many years of experience with investing in stocks and bonds, and many pension funds are restricted to bonds with the highest ratings and better-quality stocks.

Even if those stock and bond holdings go bad, the company is still on the hook to cover the payments of their retirees. And if all else fails and the company goes bankrupt, there's the ultimate safety net: the federal government. Many pensions in the United States are insured by the Pension Benefit Guaranty Corporation, or PBGC, which collects premiums in return for covering pensions in the event that they fail. If the PBGC fails somehow, it's pretty much understood that the government will do what it has to do to guarantee pensioners get what they were promised, even if it has to resort to more borrowing and printing money to do so.

This is a pretty extensive list of protections for pension plans, and every single line of defense must fail before pensions collapse. That's never happened before, so it's understandable that many people think it never will.

But, in truth, many pension plans throughout the United States have been notoriously underfunded and poorly managed. There are protection levels in place, but those were designed to handle individual failures, not widespread multiple pension plans going bad en masse, as we will see when all the bubbles pop. In fact, each level of protection has serious vulnerabilities.

Let's start with managers. While many pension managers are chosen for their qualifications and judgment, in practice these people rarely outperform market indexes. And if they haven't outperformed the market in the past—under stable conditions—why would they be able to keep their pension funds afloat in the case of a serious market crash?

Next are asset categories. Being invested primarily in bonds won't help these pension funds much because we know that rising inflation and rising interest rates will be poison to the bond market. Ratings? The ratings agencies showed catastrophically poor judgment in the recent past, when they contributed to the 2008 financial crisis. They haven't changed much about how they operate, yet people still expect them to deliver good results. (What's that line about the definition of insanity?)

If and when bond issuers go bankrupt, bondholders will still have a high priority in liquidation proceedings, but if many companies go belly up at the same time, there will be a lot of sellers and very few buyers. Their assets will bring in only pennies on the dollar. Bad news for bondholders. Corporate backing for pensions is the same story—corporations will face failed pensions and collapsed earnings at the same time. Bankruptcy will be the only option.

Last is the federal government, which will certainly do its part, at least for a while, in making sure pensioners get what they need. But the PBGC is not well funded to begin with and will quickly be overwhelmed. The government can still step in and help for a few years, but eventually there are simply too many guarantees to cover—not just with pension plans, but everywhere—and the Fed can't keep printing money forever. And down goes the last line of defense for pension plans.

Of course, long before a company goes bankrupt or the federal government has to step in, bonds can lose an enormous amount of their value as interest rates rise, as detailed in Chapter 7. Stocks and real estate are also very vulnerable, as described in Chapters 6 and 8. So, even if there were no corporate bankruptcies or no need for government bailouts, pensions can lose much of their asset value and, hence, their ability to pay those pensions.

Unfortunately, defined contribution plans, like 401(k)s, aren't in much better shape. Because most offer relatively few options based on traditional investing strategies, they make it very difficult for an individual to beat a total market failure while also protecting against inflation. When stocks, bonds, and real estate all fall, 401(k) plans will fall with them. In 2008, for example, some 401(k) plans fell in value by 40 percent. This is just a taste of what's ahead.

Will Social Security Still Be Around?

If you've been in the workforce for a while, you probably qualify for Social Security benefits. Yet even if you work up until age 65, the benefits probably aren't much. In fact, Social Security was never meant to provide for *all* retirement needs (let alone comforts), but it has provided something of a safety net to millions of retirees for generations.

In recent years, the program's future has come into question, and for good reason. Social Security is an unfunded program, meaning that the Social Security taxes you pay today are being used directly to pay current beneficiaries. In other words, it's a transfer payment, not a pension plan. For decades, Social Security was running surpluses, and the government was borrowing those surplus funds to finance other parts of the budget. Now the surpluses are gone and things aren't going to get any better in the Aftershock.

There's a good chance that many people reading this will never collect a nickel in Social Security benefits. The government will still offer basic assistance, particularly for the elderly, but Social Security will be means-tested (meaning if you don't really need it, you won't get it.) Even that level of support will depend on severe income tax rates on all working Americans. Since the government will no longer be able to borrow money easily, and since printing money will become self-defeating, the government will have to strike a delicate balance: taxing enough to provide for those in need but not so much to discourage people from working, particularly if the alternative is to collect welfare payments.

So there will still be *some* Social Security benefits for *some* people, but the payments won't be very much. Social Security recipients will also need to rely on other forms of support, including potentially living with family members or friends.

What's a Savvy Aftershock Investor to Do?

With such an ugly outlook for pensions and other retirement plans, it's hard to know how to proceed. Unfortunately, the simple answer in most cases is to get out of your employer's plan, so you have more control and can put it into assets that will hold up in the Aftershock. However, *when* and *how* to get out are crucial questions. Because of the tax advantages in most retirement accounts, you often face steep penalties if you pull your retirement money out early. In addition, as we write this, stocks are doing well and bonds are doing not so well. Now and over the years ahead, you will need to strike a balance between maximizing your portfolio for the next few years and making sure your retirement savings will hold up in the Aftershock.

To determine your best option, we'll break down each category of retirement plan and the best way to protect yourself as much as possible.

Defined Benefit Pension Plans

Defined benefit plans guarantee retirees a certain amount of money, like an annuity, in monthly payments depending on considerations such as how long they worked at the company and what their salary was. Many defined benefit plans, however, offer the option of taking a lump sum at retirement as opposed to an annuity. This is great news for those approaching retirement in the next few years. Taking a lump sum and putting it into Aftershock investments—which you actively manage, of course—is an easy way to minimize the risk of ever-shrinking payments down the road. Better yet, you can put the lump sum into an individual retirement account (IRA) and enjoy the benefits of tax-deferred growth. (See the section on IRAs for more information on this approach.)

For those who don't have the option of a lump-sum payment and are instead forced to take regular payments, the situation is more difficult—especially for people near retirement or already retired. Remember, those are fixed payments, so when inflation kicks in, it will eat away much of their value.

When things get bad, you can expect the federal government to step in and provide hardship payments, with pensioners among the first in line. But those payments will be limited—probably not much more than $1,500 per month (in 2013 dollars)—since the government will have to rely on tax revenues to cover their cost. But it will be better than nothing. People facing this scenario may need to plan on drastically reduced living expenses as they approach their retirement years.

One option offered in certain defined benefit plans is to borrow against your pension. There are limits to how much you can borrow, and the terms may be somewhat strict, but for those with no other option it is worth looking into. Timing is important here. If you borrowed against your plan today and had to repay it with interest a year from now, it probably wouldn't work out so well. But as we progress to the Market Cliff (see Chapter 4), it may become better to borrow and invest the money wisely than to end up losing everything.

Younger readers with defined benefit plans may not be as concerned about retirement, but it's worth looking into your options now regardless of your age, so you know what your options are. Does your plan allow for early withdrawals? Paying a relatively small penalty now or in the next few years is almost certainly better than being wiped out later. What about early retirement? What are the costs and the benefits? If you're thinking about changing jobs, or if you lose your job, can you roll over your retirement benefits into a self-directed IRA?

No matter how close you are to retirement, if you're covered under a defined benefit plan, you need to know the choices your employer is making on behalf of your future. If you work at a small company, you can always request changes to the plan. Even if your employers aren't sold on the Aftershock—and many employers are resistant to these ideas—they might be willing to offer options for employees who want to protect themselves with alternative Aftershock investments, such as gold.

Defined Contribution Plans (401(k))

For a classic defined contribution plan, such as 401(k) and 403(b), in which your employer pays into an annuity-like fund with no input from employees, the options are basically identical to those of a defined benefit plan.

For 401(k)s and other defined contribution plans that do have some element of self-direction, the problem is that they limit your options. If you can invest only in traditional stock and bond funds, your retirement account is going to suffer when the stock and bond markets collapse. In most cases, employees with 401(k) plans have no good Aftershock options.

At some point, obviously, you'll need to get out. But not so fast. There are some mitigating factors that can make holding on to a 401(k) worthwhile, at least in the near term. First of all, you can always ask your employer for more diversity in investment options, including a gold or foreign currency fund that is more likely to hold its value in the Aftershock. If you work at a smaller company and several employees feel the same way, you might have enough sway to convince your employer to make a change.

Even if you are stuck with limited options, there are still legitimate reasons to continue making contributions to a 401(k) *in the meantime,* before the Aftershock. For one thing, if your employer offers matching contributions, that alone may be reason enough to keep making the minimum contribution to get that match for the next few years, while things are still relatively stable. After all, employer contributions are free money. Another factor to consider is whether you are close to being fully vested in your plan, or at least will be more vested than you are now. Employees in that situation should stay with their current plan, as the increased vesting could mean a substantial difference in potential income down the road.

If you're going to remain, what should you invest in? In the immediate future, cash-type investments, such as money market funds and short-term Treasury funds, are the safest options. These funds still may lose value as inflation and interest rates rise, but the declines will be mild at first, and your employer's matching contributions should easily cover the difference. Better yet, investing in Treasury inflation-protected securities (TIPS), will give you some protection against inflation in the short term. However, as we've said elsewhere in this book, *you must be out of the U.S. stock and bond market before the Market Cliff.* This even includes Treasuries and TIPS.

Of course, sooner or later, if your 401(k) plan doesn't offer options that will hold up in the Aftershock, you may want to see if you can get out of it altogether before things get too ugly, even if you have to take some penalty. Borrowing from your 401(k) fund is an option. This can be risky—and you should make sure you understand the terms of the loan up front—but if you wait for the right time (based on the timeline we provided in Chapter 4) it can certainly be a better option than losing a significant portion of your retirement account.

Hardship withdrawals are also available, but they may not be an option for those looking for other investment opportunities (except, in some cases, for buying a home).

For older workers, the choices are a little easier. If you're already older than 59½, or will be soon, some 401(k) plans will allow you to take an in-service withdrawal based on your age, even if you're not ready to retire. That way, you can simply take a lump-sum payment, preferably rolling it over into an IRA account, where you can invest as you wish.

Even if an age-based withdrawal is not allowed, early retirement may be the right option for you, depending on your financial situation and life plans. Some 401(k) plans even allow you to retire as early as 55 and begin withdrawals without penalty. (One caveat: If you roll these funds into an IRA, you'll still have to wait until you turn 59½ to begin taking withdrawals without a penalty.)

For younger employees, the answers aren't as simple, but you still have some solid options. First, some employers offer a partial rollover, allowing you to take out a portion of your 401(k) funds—usually not more than 50 percent—and put it into a qualifying IRA of your choosing. This may not solve all your problems, but it's a pretty good start.

Second, if you change jobs, you can roll over your 401(k) funds into an IRA. For some people who are on the fence about their current employer, this may be enough to help them make their decision.

Note: You can also take this option if you're fired or laid off. While that's certainly not an ideal situation, the silver lining is that you can invest your retirement wisely and perhaps come out richer for it in the long run.

If none of these options are available, you *may* be able to withdraw your 401(k) funds early. You'll likely face a 10 percent penalty for the amount you take out, and the funds will be treated as ordinary income. If it's a significant amount, it could easily push you into a higher tax bracket for the year. But if the alternative is to lose too much of your retirement savings, this may be a price you're willing to pay. Like we said, you likely have a couple more relatively stable years between now and the Aftershock, giving you some time to preserve and even grow your portfolio. This is a big step. It's worth looking into all the ramifications ahead of time so you will be prepared to get out when the time comes. You can make up for the losses if you invest wisely.

We should also emphasize that for younger employees who haven't yet opened a 401(k)—assuming there is a significant employer matching contribution—it can still be worth doing so *even if later you'll have to take the penalty to get out* in a few years. Remember, the employer's matching contribution is essentially free money, and if you're sticking with cash-based investments like money markets and short-term Treasuries, even a 25 percent gain because of your employer's contribution (let alone a 50 or 100 percent return) is a very impressive return on investment, especially in these slow economic times.

One note for readers in other employment categories: This advice also applies if you have a 403(b) plan, which carries the same rules and penalties for early withdrawals. If you have a 457 plan, you have an added advantage—you can still withdraw funds early without the added 10 percent penalty, though you'll still owe ordinary income tax on all withdrawals. Similarly, people with Keogh plans, simple IRAs, and SEP IRAs should follow the same advice—invest in Aftershock-safe assets. But the great advantage of self-employment is that you get to make the choices yourself.

Stock Options Better than Company Stock

Some companies encourage employees to invest their retirement money in company stock by offering it at a discount to the market price. But allocating a large amount of your retirement portfolio in your employer is a risky proposition under any circumstances. If your company hits a rough patch, you could lose both your job and your retirement savings at the same time. You might think this is unlikely, but it's happened all too frequently in recent years, and will only become more common in the future. You are already invested in your employer's success by working there. No need to double down.

Employee stock options are a different story. Options allow you to lock in the price at which you can buy company stock. The best part is that if you don't want to buy when the time comes, you don't have to. You usually have a long window of time before you need to make this decision. In the long term, there may be some upside to employee stock options, but there isn't any downside—they're risk free.

IRA Rollovers

One of the great features of IRAs—both traditional and Roth—is the *rollover* function. If you have a 401(k)—or 403(b) or 457, for that matter—and are leaving your employer, whether it's due to a job change or involuntary termination, you can transfer your 401(k) funds into a self-directed IRA account without paying taxes or penalties. This gives you far more investment options than a typical retirement plan, letting you put the funds in Aftershock holdings.

This is also a great option for those who are entering retirement. You can take your withdrawal in a single lump sum and roll it into an IRA, invest the funds as you wish, and continue to enjoy the tax advantages for the life of the account.

Here's another nice option: The total contribution you can make into your IRA is capped each year, but there's no limit to the number of IRA accounts you can have. You can put some funds into a gold IRA and another portion into a discount brokerage account, and still another portion into a full-service brokerage account (you just can't go over the maximum total for the year). The only potential drawback to this is that your broker may charge fees for transfers and for setting up new accounts. But if you have substantial retirement funds and you want to diversify, IRA accounts provide a great vehicle for that.

Federal Employee Retirement Plans

Because the federal government guarantees the retirement plans for its workers, those plans will hold their dollar value—though not necessarily an inflation-adjusted value—until the government defaults, which won't happen until we are well into the Aftershock. The downside is that retired federal workers could face serious problems before that. After all, once inflation kicks in, it will eat away much of the value of their monthly payments.

The biggest problem with the defined benefit plan for federal workers is that they don't allow you to take lump-sum payments. Instead, the government makes distributions on an annuitized basis, which means that you can't depend on these plans over the long term. Fortunately, as we discussed in the defined benefit section, if these plans run into problems, federal-service pensioners will be at the front of the line when the government makes hardship payments.

For federal employees who take part in the Thrift Savings Plan—which effectively functions like a 401(k)—you can take a lump-sum withdrawal when you retire, or a one-time, age-based withdrawal if you are older than 59½. That gives you some measure of control and lets you pick Aftershock assets. But if you're younger than that and still working for the government, you're out of luck. The TSP doesn't allow early withdrawals for current employees. Even if you were willing to pay the 10 percent penalty, you can't do it. This puts younger federal employees in a bind—they may have to consider changing jobs over the next few years or risk a significant loss down the road in the retirement savings they've already accrued. Again, if you're involuntarily separated from your job, this could be a silver lining.

Should I Use a Retirement Calculator to See if I am on the Right Track?

Retirement calculators can be valuable tools, but they won't be accurate unless they include Aftershock assumptions, and we don't know of any that currently do. In fact, while calculators are a way to gauge your progress, it's more important to get the fundamentals right and invest properly in an Aftershock-based portfolio.

Should I Take Social Security Early?

In the past, traditional advice would say to not take Social Security early because it made more financial sense to get more money later than less money earlier. However, because future inflation will make your Social Security payments less valuable to you and because getting the money sooner rather than later means you may be able to invest it in Aftershock investments that grow rather than fall in the Aftershock, we generally recommend taking your Social Security benefits as soon as you can get it, even though the amount of the payment will be somewhat lower than if you had waited until a later time.

Plus, in the future, Social Security payments could become smaller or even disappear (see sidebar), so taking it while you can might be best.

Estate Planning: Making the Most of Your Assets for Yourself and Your Heirs

For hundreds of years, estate planning was simple. You created a will that stipulated how your assets were to be distributed after you died. But things became much more complicated in the early twentieth century, when income taxes and estate taxes were first introduced. These extra costs motivated people to plan their estates in ways that helped them avoid taxes and the increasing cost of probate.

Probate

If you don't leave a will, your local probate court distributes your assets according to "intestacy" laws, which vary from country to country and state to state. Typically, this means equal distribution among heirs with no personal control over who gets what. For example, you might want one of your children in particular to inherit your wedding ring, or you might want to leave a certain amount to charity. Without a will, intestate distribution doesn't allow that.

Today, even if you have a will, your heirs have to go through probate to implement its provisions. Probate can be a trying process—it often results in long delays before a will can be executed, along with legal fees that can eat away much of an estate. If a judge ends up appointing an executor and attorney for the will, some of those professionals will try to wring as much money out of the estate as possible. It's well worth your efforts to avoid a complicated probate situation.

If you have limited assets, you can accomplish much of this through a process known as "titling." In practice, titling simply means establishing control and ownership over something. For example, you can hold a bank account jointly with a spouse or another heir, stipulating a right of survivorship. That way, if you die, your spouse simply takes over the account outright, and it doesn't become part of the estate. Life insurance is another example—if you specify a beneficiary, it becomes a simple transaction when you die: the insurance company pays the beneficiary directly. If you're planning to distribute assets this way, it's critical to keep your records up to date. If you've remarried or had a new child, out-of-date documents could lead to problems.

Titling assets appropriately works well and removes the potential for disputes, but it has limited application. If you have complex inheritance situations, you can't handle them through titling alone. Another, more powerful method is to use a revocable living, or inter vivos, trust. You put the assets you want to distribute into a trust, and you control it during your life. Once you die, the trust is controlled by the trustee or by the successor of the trustee to continue to protect or to distribute the assets according to your instructions. It's an effective way to distribute assets and avoid probate. You can keep the entire inheritance process private. The process of creating a living trust usually requires an attorney, though some people do it themselves.

Estate Taxes

Estate taxes can be complex, but they're a lot less relevant today than they were in the past. As of 2013, the first $5.25 million of any estate is exempt from any taxes, and the remainder is subject to a flat 35 percent tax. That means that most people don't need to worry about this issue. Even some people who have estates above the $5 million limit will simply make a large donation to their favorite charity to get the overall estate below the cap. However, the rules are changing all the time, and it's difficult to predict how they might change even a few years from now.

A word of caution here: It's illegal to engage in *any* activity the IRS deems a deliberate attempt to avoid paying taxes. We don't condone tax evasion and are not recommending it. That said, there are some completely legal ways to pass assets to your heirs while minimizing taxes.

For example, people often minimize their potential tax liability by giving gifts to their heirs while the giver is still alive. The IRS sets a cap each year on the amount one person can give to another without a tax consequence (as of 2013, the cap was $14,000). That sounds small, but if you have multiple children and grandchildren, it can add up.

Another common practice is to put appreciating assets into a generation-skipping trust. This means that heirs are considered "life tenants" of the trust—they can benefit from the interest generated by the trust, but not the principal, which gets passed on to the next generation. In years past, the principal passed through tax free. However, Congress has since created a special "generation-skipping" tax to close this loophole, but again, only for amounts over $5 million.

A more recent development in estate planning is the family limited partnership. This structure consists of a general partner who retains control over the assets (typically a parent), and limited partners who have an ownership stake but no control (typically the children). A limited partnership offers several tax advantages. For example, it allows you to transfer ownership of assets to children over time through the standard annual gifts up to the IRS cap within the partnership, meaning you retain control of the assets. Above that amount, your family will have to pay gift tax only on the "fair market value" of any ownership transfers. And because the limited partners receiving the assets don't have control over them, this fair market value is often considerably less than the actual asset values.

To use this approach, you need a qualified appraiser to assess the value of any gift in a family limited partnership to determine the appropriate taxable amount. It is also good to consult a good estate planning attorney.

Estate Planning in the Aftershock

The biggest issue for estate planning in the Aftershock is that most traditional assets—stocks, bonds, real estate, whole life insurance, and annuities—will be worth only a small fraction of their former value. For people who lose most of their wealth, estate planning will be moot because they won't have much left to give to their heirs. Of course, if you're reading this book, we're going to assume that you have protected yourself with safe investments and still have plenty of wealth to distribute.

When the government can no longer borrow or safely print money, its only recourse will be to dramatically raise taxes on those who are employed and have assets. That means the estate tax will become a much bigger issue and impact more people. We expect progressive estate tax rates in line with income tax rates, which will be higher than current levels. There will probably still be an exemption—maybe even as high as the current $5 million—but it won't necessarily be adequately indexed for inflation. And remember, $5 million in the Aftershock won't be what it is today.

Estate planning is rarely simple, but in an Aftershock environment it gets even more complex, especially for estates with various types of assets. If you have multiple assets you're trying to protect, you will likely need multiple strategies. For domestic assets, such as a house, car, or furniture, an inter vivos trust is usually the best approach. For assets like a family-owned business or real estate holdings, a family limited partnership is generally the best way to go. As discussed earlier, you can use joint titling with right of survivorship for assets like bank accounts that you want to be transferred quickly after death. Also, you may still need a will for any residual assets.

Finally, you'll need to take capital losses into account. Capital losses are an almost negligible aspect of estate planning today, but they'll be critical in the Aftershock, as all kinds of assets will lose a great deal of their value. Realizing capital losses in your stock portfolio and other assets could help offset any income from wages or capital gains and could substantially reduce tax liability. There are some fairly restrictive rules today about using capital losses to offset income, so this strategy does have its limits.

A Good Retirement

The good news is that you still have time to save aggressively and invest intelligently. This means diversifying funds, moving assets into Aftershock-safe investments, and actively managing your

Aftershock portfolio over the next several years. It won't be easy, but it is doable.

Changing from CW investing to Aftershock investing may feel uncomfortable at first, but it is the only way to have a shot at a decent retirement in the Aftershock. If handled correctly, it could work out even better for you than you originally planned. But you must make the switch, either gradually or all at once, to an Aftershock portfolio. In the next chapter, we'll show you how.

Please remember, regardless of your retirement plans, that a good retirement is not entirely about money; it's also about enjoyment. Some of the most financially successful people prior to retirement do not succeed at being happy in retirement. We should all plan to create as much nonmonetary fulfillment as we possibly can. As we always say, self-worth is not net worth. Find what brings you peace and contentment regardless of your finances, and start planning for that today regardless of your age.

CHAPTER 14

Your Actively Managed Aftershock Portfolio

Throughout this book we have been referring you to this last chapter, the place where we finally put all the pieces together. We didn't do that just to string you along. We did it because if we told you earlier what we are about to tell you now, you wouldn't know the reasons behind our advice. We hope that at this point in the book our unconventional macroeconomic view is looking a bit more plausible.

Even if you don't yet believe that we have a multibubble economy on the way down, logic, history, and solid research shows us that massive money printing and massive money borrowing will eventually have some negative impacts. To think otherwise is just wishful thinking and at some level even our biggest critics know it.

The fact is that massive money printing will eventually bring us rising inflation, which in turn will bring rising interest rates. And massive borrowing will bring us even greater total debt. Even without the popping bubbles, the negative impacts of inflation, high interest rates, and big debt would not be good for *any* economy.

So you needn't buy our entire macro view to have some concerns about the future of your investments. Even if the bond market doesn't melt down, there are still big long-term problems to contend with, such as rising interest rates. Even if the stock market doesn't melt down, there are still big long-term problems to contend with there as well, such as slowing revenue growth. The same is true for real estate: certainly, rising mortgage rates are not going to help. It won't require a big multbubble pop and Aftershock for all these assets to fall to some extent in the future.

Even if all we eventually get are interest rates that were typical back in the booming 1960s—which were absolutely benign compared to the high interest rates of the 1970s and early 1980s—even that level of interest rates (about 6 to 8 percent) would cause real problems for stocks, bonds, and real estate values, given their very high prices today.

You must be prepared for interest rates to rise and asset values to fall.

This Economy Is Evolving—Your Investments Should Evolve, Too

Massive money printing will cause inflation and interest rates to eventually go up. But it's not as if a bomb will drop and the next day inflation and interest rates will be sky high. This economy is evolving over time—rather gradually at first, then faster over time, and then very fast as we approach the Market Cliff and Aftershock. As we keep saying, even without an Aftershock, this economy is evolving forward, not cycling backward to the former easy bubble-money days.

Therefore, your investment portfolio must evolve, too. We are not talking about changing your portfolio once and then leaving it alone, like we used to be able to do with buy-and-hold investing years ago. Now your investment portfolio must continue to change along with the changing economy and changing investment environment.

That is the basic requirement of active portfolio management: to keep changing as the markets and economy keep changing. It doesn't matter which way the wind blows as long as you change with the wind. And to do that you must have the *correct macroeconomic view* of where we're headed so your investments don't end up gone with the wind!

At the very least, you need to be prepared for lots of volatility. We think there will be an Aftershock at the end of this volatility, but even if there isn't, you need to at least be prepared for the volatility in the future and the likelihood of diminished returns from traditional investments.

To do that, let's get into more details now about the elements of a well-diversified Aftershock portfolio and how to actively manage it. In particular, what are the overall portfolio goals, strategies to meet those goals, and best ways to limit losses and maximize gains at each stage ahead?

The Three Goals of an Actively Managed Aftershock Investment Portfolio

The basic goals of a well-diversified, actively managed Aftershock portfolio are sensible and straightforward:

1. Preservation of capital
2. Less volatility than the stock market
3. Reasonable returns

Goal 1: Preservation of Capital

The term *preservation of capital* should be defined since it is used by many money managers. Most often, what conventional wisdom (CW) money managers mean by preservation of capital is lots of safe long-term bonds, some safe blue-chip or high-dividend stocks, and maybe an annuity. We have discussed each of those in detail in the book, so you know by now that keeping those investments for a long period of time will not preserve your capital. It will do just the opposite.

So CW says safe bonds and safe stock are the way to go. We say those aren't safe for the long term anymore. What we mean by preservation of capital is protection against a long-term decline in the stock and bond markets and high inflation down the road. Those are the real threats to your hard-earned wealth.

The fact that stocks and bonds are not good long term doesn't mean that they have peaked today. In fact, they probably haven't. Timing is always an issue in investing, and it's hard to time the market. We'll talk more about how to handle the timing issue later in this chapter.

Goal 2: Less Volatility than the Stock Market

Minimal volatility isn't too hard to define, although exactly how little volatility you want depends on your financial tolerance for volatility. Also, there's no free lunch. To get higher returns you will have to accept somewhat higher volatility. But you can shoot for a happy medium that is less volatile than the stock market but still gives you returns that are comparable to a modestly rising stock market today.

Ideally, if you properly implement a good Aftershock investor strategy, your returns should look similar to the straight line in Figure 14.1. It should not look like the line that looks like a "W," which shows the stock market moving violently up and down. Of course, no one can hit a straight line, but that should be the goal.

Some people don't like that goal. They want to profit on every upswing and be protected from every drop. That is a lovely fantasy, but it is not very achievable. Timing every dip and rise in any market is very hard to do. Instead, you want to be the straight line, not the "W" line because you need to be prepared in case the downstroke on the W doesn't rebound, which is what we think will eventually happen.

So, right now, the goal is not so much to beat stock market returns, although you may still do that; the more important short-term goal is to maintain your returns in a way that doesn't leave you exposed to the downstroke on the W. In other words, *it's better to be defensive for the longer term than greedy in the shorter term* because we can't know exactly when the market will hit the wall. That doesn't mean you can't make some profits along the way. It means that aiming to maximize profits is not as good as aiming to maximize safety, and this will only become more and more true as we approach the Market Cliff.

Very high returns are probably not a smart goal right now because they carry too much risk and volatility. What you want is reasonable returns and limited exposure to what is potentially a big downside in the stock market and bond market. That's your biggest threat over the next five years. Maybe not this year and maybe not next year, but within the next five years, which is far more important for most investors, and that's what you need to focus on.

Remember from Chapter 4 ("The Market Cliff") that once we get to the point where the normal remedy for boosting the stock

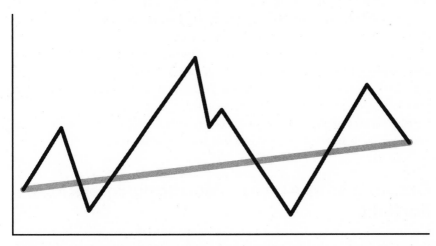

Figure 14.1   Ideal Aftershock Portfolio Performance in a Moderately Increasing, Volatile Stock Market
Shaded gray line is the performance of an Aftershock portfolio; the black line is stock market performance.

market (massive money printing and massive borrowing) has increasingly less positive effect and then eventually has a negative effect, the final big stock market drop will occur and it will not rebound. This market isn't being kept up by economic fundamentals; it is being kept up by artificial means that the government has used effectively, in combination with stock cheerleaders, to maintain a bubble stock market valuation.

Goal 3: Reasonable Returns

Reasonable returns are harder to define in part because the definition of "reasonable" varies based on the context of the times. For example, six or seven years ago it was very reasonable to expect a 5 percent return on a safe bond. Today, that kind of a return is typical of a low quality junk bond, and therefore going after a 5 percent return today is very risky. The key is what level of risk you are taking to get what level of return. If you are getting a high return, you are likely taking a high level of risk. In conventional investing, this is called the *risk-adjusted rate of return,* which is often expressed as the Sharpe ratio (the higher the Sharpe ratio of an investment, the better the rate of return you are getting relative to the risk you are taking).

Of course, we are seeing certain investments as risky long term that the market is currently not seeing as risky. So our risk-adjusted rate of return would be different from standard investing analysis. Nonetheless, the concept is correct, and we are advising a lower rate of risk taking now for most people, and that will result in a lower rate of return. But it's better than losing your money. Also, you can make very high returns as we near the Aftershock, but you will be taking more risk and will get higher volatility.

Creating Your Actively Managed Aftershock Portfolio

Conventional investing attempts to reduce risk with broad diversification, but only within one or two asset classes, such as stock and bonds. An actively managed Aftershock portfolio also seeks to reduce risk through broad diversification, but rather than diversifying only within one or two asset classes—which does nothing to protect you from the risk of these markets falling—an actively managed Aftershock portfolio limits overall market risk by diversifying *across multiple asset classes*. In other words, merely owning a diversified range of seats on the *Titanic* is not as good as also having some seats on a different boat.

Often, the best way to diversify across multiple asset classes is to use exchange-traded funds (ETFs). These are very similar to an index mutual fund in both cost and structure. ETFs tend to be relatively cheap since they are not managed like normal mutual funds. And, depending on the asset class, ETFs may be the only way to buy and sell some investments, such as gold, within a brokerage account, making them more convenient than directly trading the asset itself.

The following are key components of an Aftershock portfolio. Because you are building an *actively managed* portfolio, it is important to remember that your mix of investment types and proportions will certainly change over time. *Timing* is everything, as we will explain shortly.

Here are the types of assets to consider:

- Physical gold and gold ETFs
- Stocks
- TIPS (Treasury inflation-protected securities)

- ETFs for foreign currencies
- ETFs for commodities
- ETFs that short stocks
- ETFs that short bonds

Gold

This is an important element of any Aftershock portfolio, and it will become increasingly important in the future. When we say gold, we mean physical gold and not gold-mining stocks. Please see Chapter 10 for more details about investing in gold.

The big problem with a very large allocation of your portfolio in gold right now is the volatility. However, prior to recent months, gold has been a very stable performer on a year-to-year basis for more than 10 years, and the fundamentals for the future of gold have never been better. (See Figure 14.2.)

As the Aftershock comes closer, and you are more convinced that it is coming, you should increase your gold holdings accordingly. But buy some now even if you aren't very sure of the Aftershock. It could easily go down for a while after you buy it, but best to get your toes

Figure 14.2   GLD, a Gold ETF, from mid-2008 to mid-2013

Gold has shown strong long-term growth over the last five years, despite being down over the last two years. It remains up 40 percent from the beginning of 2008, as opposed to the S&P 500 which is only up 5 percent.

Source: Bloomberg

wet now so that you will feel more comfortable buying gold in the future. Right now, many people don't buy gold because they missed it at a lower price earlier. Don't fall into that trap. Just start now by buying a smaller amount and increase over time.

Don't sweat the short-term volatility in the price of gold or try to pick just the right entry point. Any price we pay for gold in the short term is going to look like a bargain to us in the longer term. In the shorter term, we can expect to see continued ups and downs in gold, in part due to possible manipulation (please see Appendix B) and other short term factors.

An easy way to add gold to your Aftershock portfolio is with ETFs, such as GLD, IAU, or PHYS. Other options include physical gold stored in a home safe, bank safe deposit box, or private gold depository. You can also own gold in a specialized individual retirement account (IRA) that allows ownership of physical gold.

Stocks

Isn't this one of the assets we said the cheerleaders would suggest? Yes, it is. The difference is that we are not recommending stocks as a long-term hold. You will need to move out of stocks well before the overall market goes way down.

In general, going long in the stock market will continue to be a better money maker than bonds or real estate, for as long as direct and indirect government intervention to support the market continues, and for as long as Animal Spirits (investor psychology) remain strong. We have been saying for many years that continued money printing by the Fed could push the stock market back up to and even higher than previous highs. That is exactly what happened and it could easily continue with continued massive money printing and continued positive investor psychology. But keep in mind that we have to have both money printing and upbeat investor psychology. Money printing alone will not do it.

Recently, Animal Spirits have started to lag just a bit. Time will tell if this is a deepening trend or just momentary. However, we do know that over time, especially as inflation and interest rates rise, we can expect to see a significant dampening of Animal Spirits, with continued money printing having a decreasing positive impact on the stock market.

Eventually, the positive impacts of more money printing will end entirely, but until then we have to assume the general trend will be up or at least flat, not generally sharply down.

The trick, as we have said repeatedly, is getting out before investor psychology turns firmly negative and we go over the Market Cliff. For some, that might mean exiting now or soon. For others who want to take their chances, there are still opportunities to profit on stocks in the short term.

High-dividend stocks provide a short term buffer against the volatility of the current market and a decent dividend income as well. We particularly like pharmaceutical, consumer staples, and electric utility stocks. The ETF tickers for these categories are PPH, XLP, and XLU, respectively. Electric utilities stocks did well in 2012 but, like bonds, they are down in 2013 and they may not do as well in the future as they did in the past in part because they tend to behave somewhat like bonds, falling as interest rates rise. Therefore, we favor consumer staples and pharmaceuticals. (See Figure 14.3.)

Figure 14.3   PPH, a Pharmaceuticals ETF, from late 2012 to mid-2013
High-dividend paying stocks, such as pharmaceutical companies, have performed well along with the stock market. They also tend to be more resistant to market downturns.
Source: Bloomberg

TIPS

Treasury Inflation-Protected Securities, or TIPS, are bonds that are adjusted for inflation. The principal of a TIPS increases with inflation, as measured by the Consumer Price Index. The coupon rate does not adjust for inflation but the principal does. So, they are somewhat inflation protected. We say *somewhat* because a TIPS is adjusted by the CPI, which is not a particularly accurate measure of real inflation.

Daily prices are influenced by investors' expectations of future inflation, which are fairly low right now. TIPS become most effective when investors are expecting inflation to rise in the future. Hence, they perform more like a regular bond currently and have not been particularly good investments in the past year, although they did quite well in 2011. Nonetheless, they will do better than a typical long term bond, which is not adjusted for inflation, as we near the Aftershock.

The ETF TIP holds longer term TIPS with an average maturity (as of this writing in mid-2013) of about 8.5 years. The ETF STPZ (see Figure 14.4) holds shorter term TIPS with an average maturity

Figure 14.4   STPZ, a Short-Term TIPS ETF, from mid-2011 to mid-2013

TIPS is a type of bond that is inflation-adjusted. However, with little inflation, they have been flat over the last two years, especially shorter-term TIPS.

Source: Bloomberg

of about 2 years. Like all shorter term bonds, the shorter term TIPS funds will have less volatility but also have less potential for price appreciation than longer term TIPS.

Foreign Currencies

These are a trickier category because they are fairly volatile, especially with the European debt crisis, so the dollar could be stonger for a while longer. Therefore, we see foreign currencies as a longer-term play. There is probably too much volatility now for most people to work with this asset category and not enough upside to make it worthwhile. However, longer term, when inflation rises and foreign investors become wary of the United States as a safe haven, the dollar will fall, and foreign currency will become a good buy.

It's hard to invest in any given currency because it can be affected by country-specific issues. However, a good and relatively stable one for the future will likely be the Canadian dollar. The ETF for investing in the Canadian dollar is FXC (see Figure 14.5).

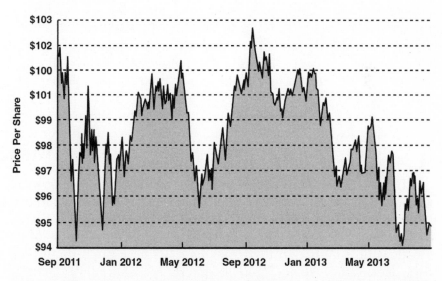

Figure 14.5   FXC, a Canadian Currency ETF, from mid-2011 to mid-2013

Foreign currencies, such as the Canadian dollar, have not performed well in the last two years because the U.S. dollar has remained a safe haven. That will change as we near the Aftershock.

Source: Bloomberg

Another currency option in the future (not now) is to short the dollar index. The dollar index is a basket of foreign currencies measured against the dollar. As the dollar index falls in the future, the short will go up. The ETF for shorting the U.S. dollar index is UDN.

Commodities

Commodities are a broad category. Within that category we're going to focus on four groups of commodities: 1) Agricultural 2) Non-precious metals 3) Oil and 4) Natural gas. Long term, there will be downward pressure on commodities due to the declining global economy. Short term there will also be downward pressure due to a slowing Chinese economy. Since the financial crisis of 2008, China's growth has been the primary supporter of commodity prices. Offsetting some of the long term pressure on commodities prices is that they generally adjust fairly rapidly for inflation.

So, the story of commodities is to some degree a story of how each category will be affected by a slowdown, and eventually an Aftershock, in the world economy. The first category, agricultural commodities, will be one of the best long term commodities and is also likely to do relatively well short term. Short term, it won't face the same downward pressure from slowing Chinese demand as metals or oil, and long term the falling dollar will help support agricultural prices since agricultural goods are easily exported. Plus, people will still need to eat in the future even if they have far less money for discretionary consumer goods.

DBA is an ETF that holds a basket of agricultural commodities. It's an easy way to invest directly in agricultural commodities that is also diversified among various types of agricultural commodities. (See Figure 14.6.)

The second category of commodities, non-precious metals, such as copper, steel and zinc, will feel the full brunt of a slowdown in the world economy. These metals are heavily used in construction and the manufacturing of durable goods. Both sectors will be hit hard in any downturn. Although there may be short term opportunities in these metals, they are not a good long term Aftershock investment.

The third category, oil, is in an unusual position because we will likely be a net oil importer for some years to come. That means that when the dollar falls, the price of oil will go up. Even with past increases in U.S. oil production, we will likely only

Figure 14.6   DBA, an Agriculture ETF, from mid-2011 to mid-2013

Commodities have been under some downward pressure recently from a slowing Chinese economy. But agricultural commodities will do well when the dollar falls.

Source: Bloomberg

produce around 7 million barrels of oil per day in 2013, according to the U.S. Energy Information Agency. Since we consume about 18 million barrels of oil per day, we will be an importer for some time to come. Even if the U.S. can increase production by 500,000 barrels per day for the next 10 years, and that is a big assumption given the rapid production declines for the new oil shale wells being drilled, we will still be a net importer. Of course, consumption will decrease in a recession but it is likely that the price of oil will still be governed by the imported price of oil for some time. That will hold up the price of oil produced in the U.S. or imported into the U.S., but the global price will fall due to falling demand.

USO is an ETF designed to track the movements of West Texas Intermediate crude oil. It is one way to invest directly in oil. There will be a lot of volatility in investing in oil over the next few years and hence, is not one we highly recommend although we do think the long term outlook for oil in the US is good. Investing in oil company stocks is another way to invest in oil but it is primarily an investment in stocks, which will do very poorly when the Aftershock hits.

The fourth category, natural gas, is also in an unusual position because we import very little natural gas. In fact, we now import less than 5 percent of our annual natural gas consumption (almost entirely from Canada).

So, the price of gas won't be determined as much by the fall in the dollar. However, the cost of producing gas in the US is rising. The new gas shale wells are much more expensive than traditional sandstone wells. Most of our old sandstone wells are rapidly declining in production as they age, especially in the Gulf of Mexico, our largest single production zone for natural gas. Hence, rising production costs will force rising natural gas prices.

UNG is an ETF that tracks the price of natural gas futures. Because it is based on futures, it is not always a good reflection of daily natural gas price movements. In 2013, UNG actually worked fairly well to reflect price movements. Long term, we are very bullish on natural gas prices. We are also bullish in the short term since drilling for natural gas has fallen over 70 percent since 2009. The lack of drilling should produce upward pressure on natural gas prices in the shorter term.

However, this is really only for more sophisticated investors, and the window of greatest opportunity is still a ways off since commodity prices will first fall before they recover due to the falling dollar.

ETFs that Short the Stock Market

There are probably few instruments more difficult to work with than short ETFs or inverse ETFs. They are simple to buy and sell, but they are difficult to profit from in the current market, especially while so much money printing is still occurring.

Inverse ETFs are also rebalanced daily, so that's a technical issue that means they don't always follow the long-term trend precisely. Hence, they are best used when the trend is in your favor, and that can be hard to predict. In the shorter term, inverse ETFs can be most effective as a hedge, or "insurance," against some long positions.

Clearly, at some point, there will be a time when these can be used to make money, but it won't be until we start to see real weakness in the stock market. If you do use inverse ETFs in the next couple of years, don't be afraid to take profits. Markets can move against you quickly, and you can quickly lose whatever you have gained. But if you are using inverse ETFs mainly as insurance, this is less of a concern.

One of the most popular inverse stock ETFs is SH, which shorts the Standard & Poor's (S&P) 500 (see Figure 14.7).

Also, you have to be especially careful about 2× or double-short ETFs. These are leveraged, so you can make twice as much money, but you can also lose twice as much money. Plus, the technical problems with daily rebalancing can have a greater negative effect on tracking long-term trends with leveraged ETFs than nonleveraged.

Please see Appendix A for more details about shorting stocks.

ETFs that Short Bonds

The same issues that apply to inverse stock ETFs apply to inverse bond ETFs. Bonds will likely turn bad earlier simply because interest rates have fallen so low that even a modest upward movement could damage bonds quite a bit and create nice gains for inverse bond ETFs. However, many investors have been hurt by thinking the bull in Treasury bonds has run its course, including the King of Bonds himself, Bill Gross.

In our opinion, the bull run for bonds is now over, but there is a limit to how low they will fall in the short and medium term because the Fed will limit that fall for as long as they can. So, we don't expect a bond Market Cliff in the near future.

One of the most popular inverse bond ETFs is TBF, which shorts the 20-year Treasury bond and is not leveraged (see Figure 14.8).

Active Portfolio Management: Timing Is Everything

By "timing" we don't mean *perfect timing* for when to enter or exit markets because that is impossible. For example, as we explained in Chapter 4, if you want to exit the stock market at the *perfect* time, you would have had to get out in 1999, prior to its fall in 2000 and then put your money in gold before its massive rise. That way you would have avoided the long period after 2000 until now when the market has fallen relative to inflation, but have cashed in on the massive gains in gold since 2001. Too late for that now. You are not

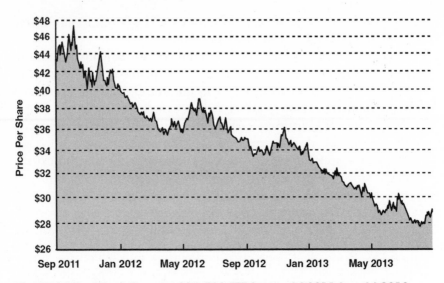

Figure 14.7   SH, an Inverse S&P 500 ETF, from mid-2011 to mid-2013

Inverse ETFs can be risky, and clearly don't do well in a rising market supported by printed money. But when the magic of money printing wears off, the opposite will be true.

Source: Bloomberg

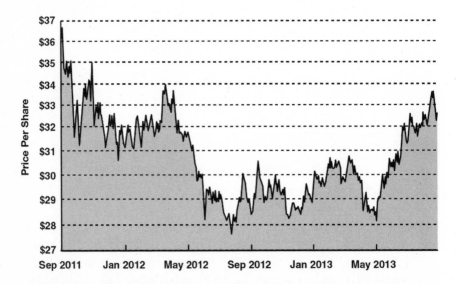

Figure 14.8   TBF, an Inverse Long-Term Treasury ETF, from mid-2011 to mid-2013

Although bonds have been a good bet for a long time, that trend is changing. Shorting the bond market will become an increasingly profitable trade.

Source: Bloomberg

going to get in at the perfect moment nor get out at the perfect moment, so please forget about that.

When we say "timing" in this context, we are talking about getting in and out of assets in a way that maximizes your odds of *approaching* the three idealized goals mentioned earlier: preservation of capital, minimal volatility, and reasonable returns.

Notice we said "approaching." We are rarely going to fully reach these goals. Instead, the strategy is to approach these goals by paying close attention to timing—that is the essence of active portfolio management.

Attempting to describe this kind of timing in any book is challenging. Optimal active management could easily require you to change your portfolio allocation mix as often as quarterly, monthly, or even more frequently, depending on what is going on in the world and the markets at the time.

There are some longer-term Aftershock investments, such as gold, that can be held through the shorter-term ups and downs, if that is part of your longer-term strategy. But most of the other investments we mentioned earlier will need to come and go in your portfolio, depending on the changing economy—and perhaps more importantly, depending on *changing investor psychology*, which ultimately determines all market movements.

So trying to advise you about these sorts of moves in a book is close to impossible—which is why we have monthly newsletters and other services. However, we've been promising you some details about how to actively managing your investments prior to the Market Cliff and Aftershock. What follows is our best estimation of what to do and when to do it, based on what we know as of this writing in mid-2013.

Remember: Active Aftershock Portfolio Management Is Different from Investing during a Normal Recession

Typically, the strategy in a normal recession is to shift your portfolio away from risky stocks into safer stocks and also into safe, highly rated bonds. However, the Aftershock will be no ordinary recession. Some stocks, like those in the necessities sector, will still fare better than others in the Aftershock and beyond, but that's not saying much. In the Aftershock, while the capital goods sector

may be hit hard, and the discretionary spending sector may be devastated, the necessities sector will do relatively better, but will still
suffer losses. Most stockholders wouldn't consider themselves winners if their portfolio loses more than 50 percent of its value.

So beyond short-term investing, there's no way to pick a good
stock for the Aftershock. Everything will be hit across the board.
For those who don't get out in time, we suppose you could say it's
better to retain 10 percent of your stocks' value after the Market
Cliff than to have only 1 percent or zero percent.

In the case of bonds, issuers with a great track record (like the
U.S. government or blue-chip companies) may hold up longer than
others. But soaring inflation and rising interest rates will greatly
reduce the value of any fixed-rate bonds. On top of that, once it is
clear to investors that risk-free bonds are not as risk-free as adver-
tised, the bond market will essentially collapse.

As for real estate, the story isn't much better. The real estate market has grown utterly dependent on low interest rates. Once mortgage
interest rates soar, demand for real estate will fall, and those holding
investment properties will have little to show for their investment.

As we said in Chapter 4, the most important consideration in
choosing investments is that you get out of conventional investments, including all stocks and bonds, before we hit the Market
Cliff. Naturally, we don't expect everyone to call their broker immediately and sell everything right now. But as we get closer to the
Market Cliff, and as the proof becomes more apparent, you'll want
to position yourself more and more in Aftershock-safe investments.

In the meantime, if you aren't entirely convinced and you want
to keep a certain amount of your portfolio in conventional investments (i.e., stocks and bonds), that's fine. We're not going to give
you a template for picking conventional stocks and bonds. There are
plenty of books and online resources available that can help you with
that. But we can give you a rough template of the safest places to be,
if you want to stay in stocks and bonds a while longer. The key is to
focus on investments that are not too sensitive to rising interest rates.
Let's take a stage-by-stage look, following the timeline in Chapter 4.

Stage 1

As we said in Chapter 4, Stage 1 has already occurred. It didn't turn
out well for most people, and many are still struggling to get back

to where they were—with plenty of assistance from the Fed's money printing, which is temporarily supporting the stock market and helping to create the current fake recovery.

Stage 2

In Stage 2, which we are now beginning to exit, our focus was on capital preservation. In the stock market, this meant stocks that pay high dividends. This may also have included electric utility or pharmaceutical stocks, for example, and other stocks with a high necessities sector component.

For bonds, the focus was on those that have been the least sensitive to interest rate changes. This means short-term bonds issued by the government or very highly rated corporations. This was also a good time to invest in TIPS and STPZ, which will remain advantageous—at least for a while until inflation begins to take off. Progression out of late Stage 2 and through early Stage 3 will depend on the effectiveness of continued government interventions in the markets, both indirect and in some cases direct (see Appendix B for more details).

Stage 3

We are now beginning to enter Stage 3, in which we have an oscillating stock market that the Fed will have difficulty stabilizing with more money printing. Over time, this will become increasingly less effective. The stock market may go up and down, but the overall longer term trend later in Stage 3 will be down—with the valleys getting deeper and deeper and the peaks getting lower and weaker.

When that happens it will become much more difficult to succeed in the stock market. High dividend stocks may still do better than most, but they are still unpredictable and it will be harder for the market to overlook languishing revenues.

Later in Stage 3, rising inflation and interest rates will significantly hurt the value of most bonds. Some very short term bonds may be able to retain much of their value, but the imminent collapse makes this a good time to transition away from most bond investments, if you haven't already.

Stage 3 is a good time to capitalize on TIPS. TIPS rise in value with inflation, but their value on the secondary market also rises on inflation expectations. With inflation already kicking in and more on the way, investors holding TIPS can do very well by selling TIPS at this stage. You don't want to hold on to them past the Market Cliff, when the bond market will be devastated.

For those who still want to play the stock and bond markets, you will have to carefully time the oscillations up and down. This is not easy to do, and requires a sophisticated hedging strategy to avoid losing too much if you guess wrong. Limit orders are easier than puts and calls. Don't make them too tight or you will be stopped out with small changes in the markets.

Stocks in Stages 2 and 3

In general, we divide businesses and their stocks into three sectors:

1. *Stocks in the capital goods sector.* Capital goods include houses and cars. This is the sector that generally gets hit the hardest in a recession. Demand drops, and the scarcity of capital makes it very difficult for people to invest in capital goods.

2. *Stocks in the discretionary spending sector.* Discretionary spending is exactly what it sounds like: goods and services that are purchased with discretionary income, after basic expenses have been paid. This might include entertainment, eating out, or lots of unnecessary or designer label clothing.

   The definition of the discretionary sector is somewhat fluid. Many items that are necessities have a discretionary component. You have to buy food, but you don't have to pay extra for organic raspberries. You have to buy clothes, but they don't have to be made by a famous designer.

   In a recession, there is less discretionary income floating around, so the discretionary spending sector is hurt, but not as badly as the capital goods sector. It is easier in a recession to pay an extra $50 or $100 for a few clothing items or for a night on the town than it is to pay for a new house or car.

3. *Stocks in the necessities sector.* Necessities include health care, education, utilities, food. These are the goods and services people really can't do without. In a recession, the necessities sector will generally be the safest place to be. However, as we said, necessities generally have a discretionary component

built in. McDonald's is much closer to the necessities end of the spectrum than a highly rated sushi restaurant in Manhattan. But even McDonald's can suffer as more people buy food from supermarkets to prepare at home. So the question in evaluating what sector a business belongs in is just how necessary is it?

Bonds in Stages 2 and 3

As we mentioned before, we see little upside left for bonds and increasing risk as interest rates rise. Timing each stage of the demise of bonds is tricky and depends on many moving parts that are hard to predict in a book that will be published before many of these events will take place. We know what will happen but we don't know the exact moment that each new development will occur.

If you are not ready to get out of all bonds yet, Table 14.1 summarizes our current thinking about bond risk, with a ranking of A, B, and C at each stage prior to the rapid crash of bonds to XXX when we hit the Market Cliff.

In the Aftershock that will follow, most previously issued bonds will be essentially worthless. Clearly, you will want to be out of *all bonds* before their A, B, or C score crashes to XXX. Please don't let all your bond investment capital go to Money Heaven before then. Remember to keep your eyes open and stay alert as these vulnerable markets evolve.

Stage 4: The Market Cliff

At Stage 4, you must already be *out* of the stock, bond, and real estate markets in the United States. Those who aren't out by now not only will lose most of the value in those investments, but it will be impossible to get out of these markets when everyone is running for the exits all at once. Similarly to what happened with the bankruptcies of 2008, many people will just end up stuck with worthless or nearly worthless assets.

Real estate in Stage 4 will be in a mess because the mortgage market will have effectively disappeared temporarily. People who own rental properties will have to deal with unemployed and

Table 14.1   Our View of the Relative Risk of Various Bonds before the Market Cliff (Stage 4)

Type of Bond	Stage 1 Recent Past and Now	Stage 2 Best Guess: 2014–2016	Stage 3 Best Guess: 2015–2018
Short-term U.S. Treasuries	A	A	B
Medium-term U.S. Treasuries	A	B	C
Long-term U.S. Treasuries	B	C	C
TIPS	A	A	B
High-grade corporate bonds	A	B	C
High yield	C	C	C
Municipal bonds	B	B to C	C
CDs/Money markets	A	A	B
Savings bonds	A	A	C
Mortgage-backed bonds	A	B	C

At each stage, a bond score of A = good, B = okay, C = more vulnerable.
Source: Aftershock Publishing.

bankrupt tenants who simply cannot pay their rent, and eviction through the backed-up courts will be a long and difficult process at this point.

In Stage 4, gold will be skyrocketing in price and will be one of the very few places investors can turn for safety. Those who invested in gold early, whether it was in 2000, 2008, or 2014, will be rewarded handsomely. Even those who bought gold at its earlier high of about $1900 in 2011 will be richly rewarded in Stage 4.

Warning: Active Management of *Short Term* Investments is Riddled with Potential Danger

Active management is not day trading but it does mean actively buying and selling various investments at certain times, not simply setting-and-forgetting what's in your portfolio. Unfortunately, perfect timing is impossible, good timing is rare, and even OK timing is very hard to do. That did not matter so much in a generally rising economy and or a rising asset bubble. As long as the overall market is going up, simply getting in and staying in for as long as possible is best. That was the basis for "value" investing: Find good buys (usually good companies with relatively low P/E ratios) and stay in while they rise.

Now that we are in a different investment environment, instead of value investing we are turning to active management, which requires making trades not necessarily at the "right" time but at least at a profitable time. And getting in and out at a profitable time is a whole lot easier to do with longer term investments, such as gold, than it is for shorter term investments, such as stocks and bonds. It can be done, but opportunities for losing money on shorter term investments are lurking at every turn.

So although we have just given you a list of possible investments to consider for your actively managed portfolio, you must keep in mind that the active management of any investment involves considerable risk because getting the timing right on each buy or sell trade is very difficult, and the active management of *short term* investments is the most difficult of all. Therefore, trying to actively manage a portfolio full of short term investments, particularly stocks and bonds, is risky and for many people not advisable. For many people, simply exiting these markets in stages as we approach the Aftershock—even though it may mean missing out on some gains—is far better than risking losses.

There will be lots of gyrations ups and downs, and there are those who can profit from it. As these moves get bigger, more conservative investors should not try to run the trends because the trends will be very short-lived.

Better to Move Too Early than Too Late

As we said before, perfect timing is impossible. You already missed your opportunity for perfect timing in the past, and perfect timing in the future is pretty unlikely other than by random luck. So, you have to assume that your timing will not be perfect and therefore you will either be a bit too early or a bit too late on each of your portfolio moves.

Which one do you prefer? Clearly, being a bit too early is far better in this case than being a bit too late.

You may kick yourself because of the money you could have made if the stock market rises after you sell. Certainly, other people will kick you for sure! They don't like to see people selling out of the market. It's bad for business if you're a stock salesman, and it's bad for others who hold stocks, which is a lot of people. Don't expect their support, whether it turns out in the short term you were right or wrong. If you were right and stocks go down, it's like salt in the wound to others. If you're wrong and stocks go up, then that's more reason for others to feel good about owning stocks and proving to the poor fools who aren't as smart about stocks that they were wrong.

Because timing cannot be perfect, moving too soon is better than moving too late. When in doubt, get out. Better to miss out of some gains than to participate in too many losses.

Ultimately, if you share our macroeconomic view, you know where the stock market is heading: over the Market Cliff! If you pull over to the shoreline sooner than the last minute as other boats continue going over the waterfall, that isn't so bad. Remember, everyone cannot exit at the same time, so the earlier seller makes out a lot better than the later seller.

Government Intervention Makes Active Portfolio Management More Difficult

The biggest change since the great stock collapse during the Great Depression is that government intervention in the stock, bond, and real estate markets now is enormous. Never before have we seen such massive intervention, both indirectly and directly, in those markets. And that intervention is being done worldwide, sometimes, in a very coordinated fashion. The United States certainly doesn't have a monopoly on government intervention.

This government intervention makes timing even trickier, since it can be more difficult to predict the exact timing of their interventions. More importantly, it is very hard to predict exactly when investor psychology will turn more negative and therefore make the interventions much less effective.

Although government intervention sometimes responds quickly to market forces, it isn't driven by market forces in the same way a normal market would be. Hence, just following the financial news doesn't tell you *when* or *how much* the government will intervene at any given time. And it doesn't tell you how investors will view it—as a positive or as a negative. So far, investor psychology has stayed mostly positive.

It's much like a very unusual fire. You can predict that the fire department will try to put it out, but since it has never dealt with such an unusual fire before, it is difficult to predict exactly how it will react at any given time in its attempt to put it out.

Government Intervention, Not Market Forces, Will Have the Biggest Impact on Your Aftershock Portfolio for the Next Few Years

Because government intervention has been so massive, as discussed earlier in this book, it will be the most important factor impacting your Aftershock portfolio. It will be what fundamentally drives investor confidence, consumer confidence, economic recovery, housing, and even retail sales. Although there are other factors driving those aspects of the economy, the size of the government intervention in the economy and the markets is so large that most of those other factors are driven at least in part by the government intervention as well. Remember the chart in Chapter 1 that compared the amount of growth in our economy to the amount of increased government borrowing from 2008 to 2012? Increased government borrowing was far larger than the *entire* growth in the economy during that period. Government intervention is huge. It's of absolutely historic proportions.

And that has just an indirect impact on the stock and bond markets. Through its money-printing operations, it is also having a very direct impact on the stock, bond, and mortgage markets. So, let's take a final look at how this all important intervention will impact these markets over the next few years.

So what went wrong that made the government and the banks turn to market interference? And, more important, why can't they just stop doing it and let things return to normal?

We've already discussed how productivity growth slowed down in the 1970s. At this point, possibly facing an endlessly stagnating economy, a little artificial stimulus for the markets didn't seem like such a harmful idea, and it might not have been. But borrowing large amounts of money and not paying it back (both government and private borrowing) is like a drug: The more you use it, the more it takes to achieve the same results. And after a while, it becomes impossible to stop without serious, painful consequences. And the United States has been on this drug for several decades now.

So when we talk about the consequences of ending market interference, we're not talking about minor withdrawal symptoms but consequences that affect our very way of life. First, for many in the financial sector (and elsewhere), it's not just a matter of losing their jobs but their entire careers. Add to that the loss of most of their life savings, as well as potentially compromising their children's futures.

More broadly, letting go of the way things have been done for many years means, in a way, letting go of the American Dream—that is, the stability and upward mobility of the upper and upper-middle classes. Families that have been wealthy for generations will see much of that disappear. For such people, it's critically important to protect the status quo. They will take risks well beyond what would normally be acceptable, and they will welcome anything that keeps their lives undisturbed and relatively prosperous, altering their thinking to downplay any long-term consequences.

Do It Yourself or Bring In Help?

It's not an easy decision. Either way, there are problems. It's hard to actively manage an Aftershock portfolio entirely on your own. Emotion gets in the way. Plus, it takes a certain amount of time and a *lot* of mental energy. It's not that it takes a lot of time, but it's hard not to focus on it a lot of the time. And all that focus energy can wear on you. So we tried to outline a plan in this book that will reduce your focus time by protecting you from a big decline in the various markets, but like we said, there is no good set-it-and-forget-it option right now.

Bringing in some help makes sense, but in today's market, that's almost always going to be a cheerleader of some sort. It's hard to find a sensible alternative. And you don't want a cheerleader who says they will invest the way you want because if they don't really understand it, they can't really do it, even if you are telling them how. And if you are telling them how to do it, why are you hiring that person? So if you can find the right person, then great. Otherwise, you sort of have to do it yourself.

The Bottom Line

In case we haven't made this clear enough yet, we'll say it one more time: The key is to *get out early*. You may often hear about opportunity costs and kick yourself when a stock rises after you've sold it. But it should be clear by now that any potential short-term gains are nothing compared to the huge costs of staying in the markets too long. The fall is likely to be sudden and unpredictable, and it will be very easy to get trapped. Those who wait until things have started to collapse will find themselves surrounded by a massive sell-off with hardly any buyers. Everyone simply cannot fit through the exit door at the same time, so prices will plummet.

For those who do get out early, though, life can be prosperous for years to come—much more so even than before the Aftershock. Think of all the people who put their assets into gold during the 2008 crisis when it was below $800 per ounce. They're pretty ecstatic right now. And they aren't alone. In fact, those who bought gold in early 2008 are up more than 75 percent today, compared to the S&P which is only up about 16 percent in that same time period. And gold will only go up even more and even faster when times get truly tough for other investments.

You're Not Alone—People Are Already Moving Out of Stocks in Big Numbers

If you think you are alone in being nervous about the stock market, you are not. Enormous numbers of individual investors have already left the stock market, even with the more recent rebound. Some people say this is stupid money leaving the market. But we say it is not stupid money leaving the market, as stock cheerleaders would have you believe. It is people who are not investing OPM (other people's money), so they really need to protect their capital and be careful—not just keep their high-paying money management jobs by investing in a stock market that has increasing risks of a long-term downturn.

The Fact that the Alternatives Aren't Very Good Doesn't Mean You Should Do Nothing

A lot of investors are concerned about the economy and agree with much of what we say. However, since the alternatives, such as gold, are uncomfortable, and other alternatives like TIPS or cash don't earn much money, they decide it is best to do nothing and just stay in the stocks.

Unfortunately, this is a big mistake in the long term. As we just explained, you can get caught in a market downdraft and not be able to get out quickly. Also, the fact that there are no good alternatives doesn't mean you should stay in and lose a lot of your money. There's a popular myth that there is a bull market somewhere "out there," all the time. This simply is not true, was never true, and certainly won't be true in the future. Sometimes there just aren't any stocks moving up for a period of time, whether we like it or not.

When Charlie Merrill (cofounder of Merrill Lynch) told his colleagues in 1928 that it was time to get out of the stock market, it wasn't because he had spotted a bull market somewhere else. He didn't tell his colleagues to move out of stocks and put the money in another investment. He just told them to get out—period.

True, there weren't many good alternatives other than cash. Even gold was a bad alternative then. And, yes, he was early in making that very good call. Many who took his advice probably kicked themselves for missing out on the big gains in stocks that their friends were getting after they sold too early. But, he was still right. Long term, Merrill's colleagues who heeded his advice and got out of the market early were much better off than those who stayed in, even with missing some upside. Having a good alternative to stocks was entirely irrelevant. What really mattered was to get out before you lost your money.

The Cartoon that Sums It All Up

We end this book with our best and most important cartoon. Everybody loves a bubble, and *no one* wants to lose it. That's perfectly reasonable. But when the bubbles burst, it's time to move on and recognize that a new era of investing has begun. Unfortunately, what many people want is to think that the bubble will somehow come back. This is fantasy (a great fantasy, but a fantasy nonetheless). Even worse, it makes you blind to other bubbles. So we use the cartoon below as a fun way to tell an important message.

Leave this book with a laugh. Humor has been and always will be a valuable commodity. You'll need even more of that in the future and, unlike other commodities, it won't fall in value, even with a greater supply. There will always be strong demand for good humor.

"I want my bubble back."

Staying Afloat in a Sinking Economy

We did not write our series of books in order to get you to buy something from us. All our current products and services grew out of reader demand over many years. For those who want to prepare for, not just read about, the coming Aftershock, we offer the following:

You are welcome to visit our web site (www.aftershockpublishing. com) for more information as we approach the Aftershock. While you are there, you may sign up for a two-month free trial of our popular

Aftershock Investor's Resource Package (IRP), which includes our monthly newsletter, live conference calls, and more. Or you may reach us at **703-787-0139** or info@aftershockpublishing.com.

We also offer **Private Consulting** for individuals, businesses, and groups. Please contact coauthor Cindy Spitzer at **443-980-7367** or visit www.aftershockconsultants.com for more information.

Through our investment management firm, **Absolute Investment Management**, we provide hands-on, Aftershock-focused asset management services on an individually managed account basis. For details, please call **703-774-3520** or e-mail absolute@aftershockpublishing.com.

APPENDIX A

Additional Background on Stocks and Bonds

In Chapter 6 (on stocks) and Chapter 7 (on bonds), we purposely left out some of the more technical details in order to not interrupt the flow of the chapters. Not everyone wants so much information, and we wanted to focus primarily on the evolving macroeconomic story that will lead us to the coming Aftershock. After all, it is pretty easy these days to look up definitions online or in conventional investment books, but harder to find information about what is really going on, from our nonconventional point of view. We saw no point in giving you yet one more mainstream investment guide.

So here are some of those more technical details we left out of these chapters. This is hardly an exhaustive guide, but it will give you a bit more background on stocks and bonds if you have an interest. For more information than the brief explanations here, we recommend you visit some educational web sites, such as www.investopedia.com and others.

Stocks

Basically, when you buy a stock, you are making a bet that the future earnings of a company will grow. The company initially sells stock certificates in order to raise capital, and the stockholders then own a part of the company. After the initial offering, company stocks can then be sold and bought on the stock market in a giant trading game, where those who want to bet on more future growth are buyers and those who are done with their bet (at least for the moment) are sellers. Like any investment, traders naturally want to sell for more than whatever they paid to buy—that is the only way to make a profit on your stock investment. Once you sell and realize a profit on your investment, you generally have to pay taxes on that capital gain.

Of course, there is much more to the story. Here are the stock topics we will discuss in this appendix:

- Understanding the public offering.
- Knowing the difference between common stock and preferred stock.
- Options for buying stocks.
- Making sense of stock and company data.
- Using a registered investment adviser.
- Securities Investor Protection Corporation (SIPC) protection.
- Knowing your options for "short" selling, including put options and long-term equity anticipation securities (LEAPS).

Understanding the Public Offering

The goal of any well-run company is to keep growing. In order to do this, a business requires capital. In the early stages, a business might rely on earnings, private equity, bank loans, or bonds. But, eventually, many businesses turn to the public offering, allowing common investors to buy shares in the business in exchange for the opportunity to profit from the company's growth. These investors may also get a voice in determining the company's direction, but with only a percentage of the company's value up for grabs, and shares going in various portions to numerous investors, the voice is a small one.

To begin an initial public offering, or IPO, a company generally goes through an investment bank, which assesses the value of the company and underwrites the sale. That is, the investment bank purchases the portion of the company that's being sold—assuming all risk for the company's value—then divides up the shares and sells them to the general public, the "primary market." The bank then collects a small fee while passing on the proceeds to the company. By "small fee" we mean percentage-wise. If you were an investment bank selling $16 billion worth of Facebook shares, for example, a 7 percent fee would amount to more than $1 billion. Not a bad payday.

Once the initial shares have been purchased, they are tradable on the open market, or "secondary market." All the major stock markets you've heard of—the New York Stock Exchange, the Nasdaq, the London Stock Exchange, for example—are secondary markets.

Knowing the Difference between Common and Preferred Stock

Common stock is generally what we mean when we discuss the stock market. Common stock represents an ownership share in a company, which, in addition to investing the shareholder in the future of that company, often grants the shareholder certain voting rights, such as in electing the company's board of directors.

Note that we said that common stock invests the shareholder in the future of that company. That's important because, generally speaking, the company doesn't owe common stockholders anything other than due diligence in managing the company's affairs. If the company grows and the value goes up, the shareholders are happy. If it falters and the price goes down, they may be unhappy and they may complain, but there isn't much they can do about it, other than sell their shares at a cheaper price and take their money elsewhere. This is why common stock is among the most volatile investments: plenty of room for growth, but plenty of room for losses, too.

Common stocks are traded on stock exchanges all over the world. The oldest exchange in the United States is the Philadelphia Stock Exchange, established in 1790. The largest exchange in the country, and in the world, is the New York Stock Exchange (NYSE), located on Wall Street, along with the American Stock Exchange, or "Amex." Other major exchanges in the United States are located in Boston, Chicago, Cincinnati, and San Francisco. You've probably also heard of the Nasdaq, the world's first electronic stock exchange. A primary exchange for high-tech business, the Nasdaq has one of the highest trading volumes in the world.

Many common stocks pay dividends on a quarterly basis, dividing up their profits among shareholders. Some pay more than others. High-dividend-paying stocks can be a strong incentive for investors, but keep in mind that dividends are optional, and if a company starts to struggle, common stock dividends are often the first thing to go.

Preferred stock, in addition to representing a share in the company, also represents a debt obligation from the company to the shareholder. Before any dividends are paid to holders of common stock, the company must pay a fixed dividend to preferred shareholders. And in the event of liquidation and any monetary distributions that might come from it, preferred shareholders are in line ahead of common shareholders, who usually won't receive any compensation at all (although preferred shareholders are still behind bondholders).

Of course, preferred shareholders don't always get their dividends either. This is what makes preferred stock a useful tool for companies that need to raise capital. Because preferred stock is a hybrid investment—not quite a stock, not quite a bond—companies have some flexibility in choosing to defer dividend payments when capital is running low. Preferred stocks are rated just like bonds, but they naturally come with lower ratings to begin with, and a company's credit won't be affected too significantly by holding off on dividend payments to preferred stockholders. (Doing the same thing to bondholders would be a default and carries major consequences.)

So, preferred stockholders don't have all the rights that bondholders have, and they also don't have all the rights that common stockholders have. Most notably, preferred shareholders have no voting rights in the company, except in certain special circumstances. Also, preferred shares usually come with a call feature, which allows the company to repurchase shares of preferred stock at its discretion.

Options for Buying Stocks

If you want to buy a stock, you don't walk down to Wall Street, hop on the trading floor and make your bid. You have to have a broker execute the trade for you. Traditionally, a broker offers an array of services for clients, gets to know their clients' portfolios and provides research and investment advice, while charging heavy commission fees in return.

These full-service brokers are still in abundance, but a popular alternative that has developed in recent years is the *discount broker.* Discount brokers are for investors who don't need or want the hand holding of a full-service broker, and instead just need a way to execute trades based on their own research and analysis. Discount brokers often charge a very low, flat fee for trades, and often have very low minimum account balances. They are a popular way to get involved in stock trading for people who aren't ready for (or don't want) a traditional broker. But they also pin all responsibility on the investor.

Another advantage of discount brokers is that, unlike many full-service brokerage firms, discount brokers don't risk their own money in the market. This is important because accounts at a discount brokerage may be in less jeopardy in the event of a major market downturn. Plus, discount brokers sidestep the temptation to unload their own bad positions on their clients, a temptation that has gotten many full-service brokerage firms in trouble.

Whether to go with a full-service or discount broker is a personal decision, but if you're going to go with a full-service broker, first, be sure they really know what they're doing and have your best interests at heart. Furthermore, even though someone else is doing much of the work for you, you still have a responsibility to be an informed investor and to not let yourself be pressured into positions you know aren't good for you. Before deciding on a full-service broker, it is important to check with the Central Registration Depository (CRD), which provides information about an individual broker's history, including employment history and any complaints filed by former clients, In addition, relevant information about many brokerage firms can also be obtained here.

Making Sense of Stock and Company Data

If you decide to go with a discount broker and make your own trades (or even if you have a traditional broker and want to be better informed), you have a wealth of real-time information available to you thanks to the Internet. Looking at the data for a particular stock may be daunting, but the numbers aren't really so complicated. You'll see things such as the bid price (the last price a buyer was willing to pay for it) and the ask price (the last price a seller was willing to sell it for). You'll probably also see the range of prices the stock has sold for over the past year, the average daily trading volume, and the price-to-earnings, or P/E, ratio. Most financial web sites have a key for you to look up the more difficult-to-understand numbers and how they've been calculated.

Using a Registered Investment Adviser

For those looking for a little more help with their investments, a registered investment adviser, or RIA, may be the answer. RIAs are basically money managers and will make decisions about your investments based on your goals and their own investment philosophy. RIAs often require large minimum investments, typically at least $100,000, and possibly going as high as several million dollars.

An RIA will manage your investments through your brokerage account, with authorization to buy and sell assets on your behalf. This sounds like a set-it-and-forget-it strategy, and indeed RIAs can make trades without notifying the client every time, but this doesn't mean investors should forego all responsibility for their investments. It's important to find an RIA who not only understands your financial goals but also shares your macroeconomic view of the near and longer-term future. And it is also important to stay up on what's happening with your money and continue confirming that it's in good hands.

RIAs collect their fees based on the total amount of funds under management, generally never more than 3 percent (usually around 1.5 percent). This gives an RIA a strong incentive to make money for clients because, unlike with a broker who collects fees based on commissions, the success of an RIA's investments directly impacts the RIA's fees. If your assets shrink, so does the RIA's takeaway.

Be careful that your RIA does not overcrowd your portfolio with mutual funds. Aside from the problems with mutual funds (which we'll get to later), remember that a mutual fund is a managed fund, and you are already paying your RIA for that. If your RIA heavily uses mutual funds, you are essentially being charged twice for management, paying double the fees.

SIPC Protection

In order to protect investors when their brokerage firms go bankrupt, Congress set up the Securities Investor Protection Corporation, or SIPC, in 1970. The SIPC is a nonprofit organization that collects insurance fees from member brokerage firms in return for insuring customer accounts up to $500,000 each. Any brokerage firm that is part of the National Association of Securities Dealers (NASD) is a member of the SIPC.

This provides some peace of mind for investors. In addition, many brokers carry their own insurance on accounts in addition to the SIPC insurance. But the problem is that these insurance policies, like everything else, are designed with the rare occurrence in mind. They aren't designed for a system-wide failure in the markets. This is a big reason why we prefer brokers that don't risk their own money in the markets—they are more likely to survive the future Aftershock.

Understanding Short Selling, Put Options, and LEAPS

Short selling is what some investors do when they think the price will go down. Short selling is effectively three transactions rolled into one. The first transaction is the sale of a stock at the current market price, or close to it. The second transaction is borrowing that stock—generally from the broker executing the trade—in order to give it to the buyer. Finally, the third transaction is buying the stock later when the loan period is over to repay the broker and hopefully make a profit (assuming the buying price is lower than the earlier selling price).

During the period between selling the borrowed stock and buying the stock to repay the loan, the investor has a "short" position in the stock or commodity. (In contrast, if the investor owned shares of the asset, that would be considered a "long" position.) If the asset price goes down during that period, the investor makes money by buying it for less than he or she sold it for. On the flip side, if the asset price unexpectedly goes up, the losses are potentially unlimited, since the short seller is obligated to buy the stock to pay back the original loan (plus any fees that might be associated with the loan).

Put options are an alternative to short selling. An investor can purchase a put option on a security, which gives him or her the option to sell that security at a specified price (the *strike price*) to the seller of the option during a specified time period. If the price of the stock goes down during that time, the buyer of the put option can simply buy the stock and sell it to the other party at the agreed-upon price, pocketing the difference. If the price doesn't go down and the buyer doesn't exercise the option, the loss is limited to the price of the put option. A put option is the opposite of a call option, which gives the buyer the right to buy a security at a specified price.

Put options (and call options, for buying instead of selling) are generally limited to terms of a year at most.

LEAPS (long-term equity anticipation securities) are like put options for a longer period of time. LEAPS can have terms extending more than two years. One quirk is that equity LEAPS always expire in January, so the term is determined by the expiration year of the option. The further out the expiration date, the more expensive the option will be.

Bonds

A bond is essentially a loan made to the bond issuer in exchange for future repayment of the principal of the loan plus interest. Various factors affect the interest rate offered on the loan (which were discussed in Chapter 5). Once a bond is issued, it may be sold and bought on the bond market, which adds layers of complexity for a number of reasons. Primary among these is the fact that current interest rates change, making previously issued bonds either more or less valuable, depending on the details of the bond. In addition, other things change as well. For example, the creditworthiness of the bond issuers may change over time, which impacts the value of the bond on the bond market. Also, changes in the inflation rate matter, too, because if inflation goes up, it subtracts from the value of the bond.

Chapter 5 provides a basic explanation of bonds and the bond market. For this discussion, we will now focus on:

- The call.
- U.S. Treasuries
- Zero-coupon bonds and Separate Trading of Registered Interest and Principal Securities (STRIPS).
- Treasury inflation-protected securities (TIPS).
- Savings bonds.
- Mortgage-backed securities.
- Municipal bonds.
- Corporate bonds.
- Certificates of deposit.
- Money market funds.
- Bond sensitivity to changes in interest rates and inflation.

The Call

Even if an investor does not sell a bond for a gain when prevailing interest rates go down, having a relatively high interest rate locked in is a pretty nice perk. This perk is eliminated if the bond has a *call* feature. Some indentures give the bond issuer the option of paying off the principal before the maturity date, thus ending the debt obligation and any future interest payments to the bondholder. In many cases, this option may be triggered at a certain length of time into the bond's life span.

Why would a bond issuer want to do this? Just like if you wanted to pay off a mortgage early and refinance at a lower rate, the bond issuer would be at a great advantage by refinancing if interest rates go down. It's easy to see that this feature benefits the bond issuer, and only the bond issuer. If interest rates go down, the issuer has every incentive to execute the call feature, refinance, and leave you to find another suitable investment. If interest rates go up, however, when you would *want* the call feature to be executed, the issuer has no motivation to refinance. The bond issuer can keep paying you at a lower interest rate until the maturity date. Many indentures may specify a premium to be paid in the event of a call, but it is sure to be paltry compared to the interest that would be earned over the remaining life span of the bond.

U.S. Treasuries

As the name suggests, U.S. Treasuries are bonds issued by the Treasury Department of the United States. When people talk about public debt in the United States, they are talking about outstanding U.S. Treasuries. Treasury securities are owned in huge amounts by big government agencies and corporations, such as the governments of China and Japan, as well as our own Federal Reserve, but these securities can be purchased by individual or institutional investors.

Backed by the full faith and credit of the U.S. government, U.S. Treasuries have traditionally enjoyed the highest investment grade awardable. As a result, they tend to offer among the lowest yields of any bonds, but this is acceptable to many investors, who view our Treasuries as risk free. This view took a small hit in the summer of 2011 when Standard & Poor's downgraded the Treasuries' credit rating to AA+, after 70 years at AAA. U.S. Treasuries are still considered a rock-solid investment, especially given the current turmoil and potential risks in Europe.

Another reason Treasury securities can afford to offer low yields is that the interest paid on them is not subject to state and local taxes. This makes Treasuries especially attractive to investors in states with high income tax rates, but less so to those in states like Texas or Washington with no individual income tax. Treasury interest is, however, subject to federal income tax.

Standard-issue Treasuries are divided into three categories based on their lengths of maturity. *Treasury bills*, or *T-bills*, usually range from 90 days to 12 months, *Treasury notes* range from 2 to 10 years, and *Treasury bonds* can take up to 30 years to mature. Keeping this terminology straight can be difficult, and you might hear some people use the terms interchangeably if they don't know the difference. If you have trouble remembering which is which, the blanket term *Treasuries* works just fine (as long as you know when the maturity date is, of course).

Most Treasury securities make payments just like any other bond. T-bills, however, don't make interest payments due to their short maturity. Instead, you buy the bill at a discount, and receive the full face value at the maturity date. The difference between the price you pay and the amount you receive is the interest.

Zero-Coupon Bonds and STRIPS

A zero-coupon bond is just what it sounds like: a bond with no coupons. Interest is accrued and reinvested in the bond, to be paid back in one sum at maturity. In many cases, this means taxes must be paid on the interest before the investor receives it. This drawback can be eliminated by purchasing zero-coupon bonds through an individual retirement account (IRA).

STRIPS are another kind of zero-coupon bond. Back when bonds were issued on paper, they would literally have their coupons "stripped" by brokers before sale. An example of this type of bond is U.S. Treasury STRIPS, which are not sold by the Treasury itself but through private brokers. The bond is separated from its coupon payments and sold by itself at a discount. As a result, taxes on reinvested interest are not an issue with these bonds. The difference between the amount paid on the market and received at maturity represents a capital gain.

The market value of zero-coupon bonds tends to be subject to more volatility than that of regular bonds. Be careful about purchasing zero-coupon bonds if you're not planning on holding them until maturity.

TIPS

TIPS are designed to keep the bondholder's investment current based on inflation. TIPS come with fixed-interest payments just like other Treasuries, but the principal amount is adjusted twice a year, according to the current Consumer Price Index (CPI). For example, if you invested $10,000 in TIPS at a rate of 0.5 percent, you would continue to receive that 0.5 percent annual interest until maturity, but you might be earning 0.5 percent interest on $10,500 or $11,000 at some point, depending on current inflation.

The fixed rate of TIPS tends to be relatively low, and in fact we have even seen it effectively drop below zero recently. When fear of inflation is up, many investors are willing to take a small hit now in order to protect themselves from inflation later. (This doesn't mean that bondholders will get a bill when the coupon payments are due. What happened is that bidders agreed to pay a small premium for these bonds at auction, and the premium effectively canceled out the even smaller coupon payments at the current rate and then some.) If inflation rises significantly, the par value of these bonds goes up and a bondholder can come out ahead. We will discuss inflation and its effect on bonds a little later.

Savings Bonds

Unlike other Treasury securities, U.S. savings bonds are not exchanged on the open market. They are tied to the bondholder's Social Security number (or tax identification number), which means no one but the bondholder can redeem them. Savings bonds can be purchased in many different denominations ($25 and up), which, along with the fact that they can be owned by minors, has made them a favorite investment tool for parents and grandparents to give to children, often to save for education.

Savings bonds are zero-coupon bonds, so both principal and interest are paid in one sum when the bond is redeemed. Interest is accrued regularly, and the current value of any given savings bond can be calculated at www.treasurydirect.gov, though there is a small penalty if you redeem before five years have passed since issue. Current savings bonds offered are the Series EE (formerly Series E) and Series I bonds.

Series EE bonds have a maturity of 20 years, but continue to earn interest for another 10 years after maturity. Formerly, the interest rate on Series EE bonds was adjusted based on current rates, but bonds issued after April 2005 earn a fixed rate. Patriot bonds are a paper version of the Series EE bond. As of January 2012, these bonds (along with all paper Treasuries) are no longer available.

Series I bonds are savings bonds that are linked to inflation, much like TIPS. Series I bonds come with two different interest rates: a fixed rate that doesn't change over the course of the bond's term, and a variable rate that is adjusted twice a year based on the CPI. The adjustable rate might be negative during times of deflation, but the combined rate of the bond cannot fall below zero percent.

Mortgage-Backed Securities

Mortgage-backed securities include those issued by government-sponsored agencies Ginnie Mae (Government National Mortgage Association), Fannie Mae (Federal National Mortgage Association), and Freddie Mac (Federal Home Loan Mortgage Corporation), as well as some securities issued by private corporations. Ginnie Maes are unique among the group in being backed by the full faith and credit of the federal government, just like Treasury securities.

Mortgage-backed securities are issued using a pool of home mortgages as collateral. Because most mortgages are paid monthly, most of these securities pay interest monthly as well. Because mortgage loan principal is prepaid in various ways and at various times (such as extra payments or paying it off all at once), the time to maturity varies widely.

Municipal Bonds

Municipal bonds, or *munis*, are issued by state and local governments to finance new projects or to improve infrastructure. Munis have the advantage that interest paid is exempt from federal taxes, and in some cases from income taxes in the state in which the bonds are issued.

There are two principal types of municipal bonds. *General obligation* bonds are backed by the full faith and credit of the issuing government, based on its ability to raise revenue through taxes. *Revenue* bonds are backed by revenue to be raised from the specific project the bonds are funding—for example, bonds used to finance the building of a toll road or an airport.

The tax advantage is generally the key attraction for these bonds. The higher the tax bracket you are in, the more attractive munis become. The way to assess the value of a tax-exempt interest rate is to calculate its *taxable-equivalent yield*. The formula is to take the yield of the tax-exempt bond and divide by 1 minus your tax bracket percentage. For a bond exempt from state taxes, you would combine federal and state tax percentages in the calculation.

Corporate Bonds

Private corporations also issue bonds in order to finance and/or expand their business operations. Many companies that issue corporate bonds also have shares traded in public stock markets. But owning a corporate bond is very different than owning a share of a company.

When you buy stock in a company, you are buying ownership in that company, and the value of that share will rise or fall in accordance with the company's market value. You might receive dividends from company earnings, but this is not at all guaranteed (especially if the company has no earnings), and dividend payments can be very low compared to the stock price. But when you purchase a corporate bond, you are making a loan to the company, which has an obligation to return your principal and make interest payments. If the company's fortunes rise, you will still get only the amount that was agreed to in advance. You might lose your investment if the company goes bankrupt, but as a creditor you will be ahead of shareholders (even preferred shareholders) in line to receive money in a bankruptcy settlement. So while purchasing bonds has a speculative element to it, it is not nearly as speculative as purchasing stock.

Most corporate bonds are *unsecured*, meaning the debt is not tied to any collateral, and the bondholder is relying on the general credit and continued solvency of the business. Secured bonds may be backed by claims on specific assets of the company, possibly including new equipment that the bonds were used to purchase. Other bonds may be backed with stocks and other securities, or can even be guaranteed by a company other than the bond issuer. Owners of secured bonds will take priority over owners of unsecured bonds in the event of bankruptcy.

Corporate bonds are available on the New York Stock Exchange or over the counter (directly from the issuing companies). The advantage of corporate bonds is that the coupons tend to be higher than government-issued bonds. But, of course, these higher yields come with higher credit risk. Some investors will take the higher risk along with the higher payment, even going after junk bonds issued by companies with poor credit ratings. But if capital preservation is your goal, corporate bonds are generally not your best bet unless you stick with rock-solid companies with great track records, and only if you get out well before the Aftershock hits.

Certificates of Deposit

Certificates of deposit (CDs) behave similarly to zero-coupon bonds, in that you deposit money for a certain amount of time and receive principal and interest back at maturity. The differences are that CDs are offered specifically by financial institutions to their customers and that they are usually insured by the federal government. CDs fall under the category of *time deposits*, meaning you lock up your money for the specified period, and they cannot be sold on the open market or called by the issuing bank before maturity.

CDs tend to offer lower rates than comparable bonds, but interest rates can vary depending on a number of factors, including the size of the principal, the length to maturity, and the size and reputation of the financial institution, among other factors. On the plus side, interest is usually compounded monthly, which can be an advantage for deposits of longer time periods—as long as interest rates don't rise. Unfortunately, both inflation and interest rates will rise, and CDs will not fare so well. Because they are guaranteed by the government, CDs have a reputation for being virtually risk free. That is not a reputation that will survive the coming Aftershock.

Money Market Funds

If you've ever had an account at a brokerage firm, you have probably had cash in a money market fund. Money market funds invest in a highly diversified pool of securities, with maturities usually no more than two or three months. These include government bonds, CDs, and commercial paper (short-term, unsecured debt obligations issued by corporations with rock-solid credit). The aim for a money market fund is to keep a constant share price of $1, with yields paid as dividends that can be reinvested.

The short terms of the investments and the solid credit ratings of the issuers make money markets very low risk, relatively speaking. If investments do fail and the share price of the fund falls below $1, it is referred to as *breaking the buck*, something that is never supposed to happen. It was an especially rare event before September 2008, when Lehman Brothers' bankruptcy and the ensuing panic led to the Treasury Department's setting up an insurance program for many money market funds.

Bonds Vary in Their Sensitivity to Rising Interest Rates

Changes in interest rates impact some bonds more than others. Long-term bonds are much more reactive to interest changes than short-term bonds. Long-term bonds can punish or reward the bondholder long after interest rates have changed. It does not take much of an increase in interest rates to push the value of long-term bonds down significantly.

Changes in interest rates also have a greater impact on the value of bonds issued by less reputable companies than on high-grade bonds issued by solid corporations and agencies. This is because of the combined concerns about both rising interest rate risk and credit risk. Bonds rated from AAA to BBB are considered investment grade. Anything below BBB– or Baa is considered to be speculative. Traditionally, most experts would advise sticking only with bonds among the A to AAA categories because they are considered the safest bets to get your money back, even if they don't come with the highest interest rates. However, in this economic environment, it's sometimes necessary to look past a good rating. Even very good ratings can drop very quickly and unexpectedly, as we'll see later on.

To limit the risk of rising interest rates, many investors turn to inflation-protected or floating-rate bonds, such as TIPS. These are less sensitive to interest rate changes than fixed-interest-rate bonds because they adjust with prevailing rates. Therefore, rising interest rates are not expected to lower the value of inflation-protected or floating-rate bonds as much as they will lower the value of fixed-rate bonds. But do not be fooled into thinking that these floating-rate bonds are risk free. As interest rates go up, credit risk will also go up significantly. Remember, it doesn't matter how good your interest rate is if your bond issuer is unable to pay.

Under normal economic circumstances, bankruptcies are relatively rare, especially among larger corporations and banks, not to mention governments. And even when bankruptcies happen, even debtors holding unsecured bonds still usually end up getting back at least a portion of their principal from the settlement. So it is understandable that bonds, especially those issued by governments and blue-chip companies, have traditionally been viewed as safe from credit risk. But there is one circumstance that is always bad for bonds: *inflation.*

Inflation, Interest Rates, and the Aftershock

The conventional wisdom is somewhat divided when it comes to the impact of inflation on stocks. (Some say stock prices will rise with inflation, which is true to some extent, but it doesn't account for the rising interest rates that can kill earnings and hurt stocks in the long term.) But pretty much everyone knows that inflation is poison to bonds. If money is losing value quickly, then tying it up for a considerable length of time at a fixed interest rate is a losing proposition. With inflation at 2 percent, a bond with a 3 percent coupon has a *real* interest rate of only 1 percent. But if inflation rises to 5 percent, suddenly your real rate of return is minus 2 percent. You may have more dollars in the end, but you are losing buying power; you are losing wealth. And the picture looks even worse if you've spent your coupon payments along the way. The principal you get back when the bond matures will not be worth nearly as much as it was when you invested it. Now imagine inflation goes to 10 percent annually, or 20 percent, or higher, and you see how destructive inflation can be.

But it is even worse than that. Rising inflation, as we have said repeatedly in earlier chapters, eventually causes interest rates to rise. Rising interest rates only hurts the value of existing bonds even more. Now you have the double whammy of both falling value of your money due to inflation and falling value of your bonds due to rising interest rates.

And, unfortunately, the bad news doesn't stop there. Not only is inflation making your money worth less, rising interest rates are making your bonds worth less, and now you also have to face another rising menace: *increasing credit risk.* You see, the entities that issued your bonds may very well go out of business under these difficult conditions, or at least be unable to repay you. We saw in the last chapter what rising inflation and higher interest rates can do to company earnings. Unable to refinance their debt without paying high interest rates, and caught in a spiral of laying off workers to stay afloat, how will companies generate the new revenues to pay off their existing debt obligations? It is going to become harder and harder to do so.

And the problem will not stop with just corporate bonds from companies that can no longer pay their debts. It will also extend to governments that can no longer pay their debts, whether it is state munis or U.S. Treasuries. Even CDs and money markets will be in trouble.

As we've already said, there are factors delaying the onset of inflation. But once it gets going, it can snowball very quickly. When inflation passes 5 percent, as measured by the CPI, and then approaches 10 percent, it will become impossible to ignore. Interest rates will rise regardless of what the Fed wants, as lenders become cautious to tie up their cash and get it back at a lower value.

We already know that inflation eats away at a bond's value, and the rising interest rates that follow hurt bonds in the secondary market. For example, with 10-year Treasury rates hovering around 2.2 percent as of March 2012, imagine how much the value of these bonds would fall if inflation hit double digits less than halfway into their lives. But this is only the beginning of the problem. In a bubble economy overextended with debt and artificially propped-up markets, inflation is the first big trigger to send it all toppling down.

The first casualty will be the housing market. New home purchases will be out of reach for most at higher interest rates. And homeowners who are already in precarious debt situations will not be able to make payments on adjustable-rate mortgages. When real estate prices fall accordingly, even homeowners who were once in relatively stable positions will find themselves underwater, and new debt defaults will spike upward.

Banks will be forced to write off huge amounts of loans. Mortgage-backed securities will fail. Insurance and derivatives meant to protect against failure will turn out to have little value when everyone is overextended. Failures lead to government bailouts. Bailouts mean more money printing. More money printing means more inflation. And the vicious cycle continues.

Clearly, inflation cannot go up significantly without also raising interest rates. Who in the world will lend anyone any money if they cannot at the very least be compensated for what they will lose to inflation? That means if inflation is 10 percent, interest rates will have to be at least 11 percent for lenders to make even 1 percent on their money. Interest rates will have to exceed inflation.

When interest climbs, in addition to harming businesses, real estate, stocks, and corporate bond values, we will have one other devastating problem: State governments and the federal government will have to make interest payments on their debt with newly borrowed money at the higher and higher interest rate, adding exponentially more and more to the total public debt as time goes on. Eventually, they will not be able to borrow more at any interest rate level because investors will have no confidence in their ability to repay. At that point, the public debt bubble will pop and the borrowing will end. Without newly borrowed money and without the ability to print more money (due to high inflation caused by earlier money printing), state and U.S. governments will not be able to pay on their debt and will be in default—just like overextended homeowners, businesses, consumers, and investors.

Profiting from a Moving Market

As long as the market is moving, there is money to be made. There are many tools built into the market designed so investors can profit from assets moving up or down.

Given our outlook, it's easy to see the advantage of being able to profit from a downward-moving market. And, in fact, when the Aftershock does hit, in spite of rapidly declining asset prices, more money will be made in a shorter time than ever before in history.

But playing around with options and shorts hoping for a price drop can get very complicated, and it can sometimes lead to trouble for investors even if they have the right idea, especially if they're not entirely familiar with the terms of their contracts. As we will explain, the investment vehicles outlined in this chapter come with significant risks, and are not to be employed casually. Due diligence and a sober outlook are critical when playing the market.

Shorting Assets

For any given asset, an investor can be "long" or "short." To be long a certain asset, the investor stands to gain if the asset's value goes up. The simplest method is simply to own the asset outright, though there are other, more complicated methods as well.

To be short an asset is to hold a position by which the investor stands to gain if the asset's value goes down. The prototypical short sell essentially amounts to selling an asset before you own it. For example, say you wanted to short a share of an electronics company. First, you sell borrowed shares of the company at the market price. Then, on or before the agreed-upon date, you would be obligated to buy shares of that company to return to your lender. If the share price goes down during that time, you come out ahead: you buy it for less than you sold it for. If the share price goes up during that time, you lose: you have to buy it at whatever the going rate is. That's where shorts can be truly risky: there is no limit to the potential losses.

Short trading is a less conventional form of investment and can get very, very complicated. Big institutional traders on Wall Street sometimes will even invent new ways to be short an asset no one has ever thought to be short before.

Now let's take a look at the various asset classes and the ways to profit from their movement up or down.

Profiting from Market Moving

Options

One way to benefit from a share price moving up or down without actually owning or borrowing the stock is to purchase an option. To purchase an option, an investor pays a premium—some small fraction of the current share price—and in return has the right to buy or sell the stock at an agreed-upon price (called the strike price) at some specified later date. Once the premium is paid, it is gone. But if the share price moves against the investor's expectations, the option doesn't have to be exercised. The risk is limited to the premium paid up front.

Options come in two basic categories: call options and put options. A call option is meant to take advantage of a rising price.

The investor locks in a strike price to purchase the stock, and if the share price goes up over the length of the option, the investor gets to buy it at a discount.

To take advantage of a declining stock price, an investor can purchase a put option. In this case, the strike price is a selling price. If the share price goes down over the length of the option, the put option owner can buy the stock at the new, lower price and then exercise the option to sell it at the earlier, higher price. Again, if the stock fails to drop, the investor can decline to exercise the option and take the premium paid as a loss—but a smaller loss than shorting the stock would have incurred. Whereas a call option comes with potentially unlimited profits, profits from a put option are limited to the strike price minus the premium paid.

Just like anything else traded on Wall Street, options come with market prices that can move up and down for a lot of reasons. Generally speaking, the more likely the bet you're making is to happen, the higher the price you'll have to pay for it. For example, the farther out an option's expiration date is, the more likely a change in price is. Because of this, longer options typically come with higher price tags, as do options on stocks that are particularly volatile. The way to make money from purchasing options is by having an insight that the rest of the market doesn't—betting on an event the market doesn't see coming.

LEAPS

LEAPS stands for long-term equity anticipation securities. LEAPS are just long-term options. While options generally last between three months and a year, LEAPS often extend as long two years. This is advantageous if the fundamentals underlying an asset will send it up or down eventually, but you aren't sure when that will happen. Just like with options, LEAPS are available as calls (betting on a rise in price) or puts (betting on a drop in price). Of course, the longer term means a higher price tag.

Long Straddles and Strangles

Sometimes rather than betting on just a price rise or just a price drop, an investor may want to bet on both. The investor expects an asset price to move significantly, but isn't sure which way. A typical example of this would be if a company is facing a major court decision, in which a negative outcome would likely make the stock price plummet and a positive outcome would send it soaring. If the market hasn't caught on to this, and the investor wants to take advantage, the most obvious option is a long straddle.

A long straddle amounts to purchasing both a call option and a put option simultaneously, both with the same strike price, which would equal or be close to the current asset's market price. Because you're buying two options, the price tag on a long straddle can get pretty steep, and in order to break even, the asset price has to move a considerable amount: at least as much as the total amount you paid for both the call option and the put option.

A cheaper option is the long strangle. This is basically the same thing as the long straddle, only the strike prices are spread out. For example, if the share price of the security in question is at 50, you might set the strike price for the call option at 55 and the strike price for the put option at 45. The asset price has to move more in order to make it worth it to exercise the option, and the profits are more limited. But it does come with a lower price tag than the long straddle.

Inverse ETFs

Inverse exchange-traded funds (ETFs) can be an effective way to profit from price drops across a whole class of assets. Inverse ETFs can be used to short stock indexes like the Dow or the Standard & Poor's (S&P) 500, or a class of bonds like U.S. Treasuries, corporate bonds, or junk bonds. There are also inverse ETFs that short most major currencies, including the U.S. dollar.

There are two major caveats with inverse ETFs. First, because many of them are reconciled daily, inverse ETFs often have a built-in tracking error. In some cases, if the trend is not consistently moving in one direction—down or up—it can potentially cost you money, even if the overall trend is moving in your favor.

The second is that many inverse ETFs are double- or even triple-leveraged. This can pay off very well when the trend is in your favor, but any movement against your position can be very damaging to your portfolio. Tread with caution.

Shorting in the Aftershock

Under normal circumstances, using shorts, put options and LEAPS, and inverse ETFs would seem like a sound strategy for a declining market. And it is now, too—but only to an extent. There are major pitfalls to be aware of.

First of all, we are already in a heavily manipulated market. Using misleading statistics to make the United States' financial situation appear better than reality is already commonplace. At the time of this writing, the Fed is pumping $85 billion (that we know of) into the economy every month to boost market activity, with no indication that it will be slowing down any time soon. Ben Bernanke has made it clear that he won't tolerate a major, prolonged market decline, and the Fed will continue to manipulate the market for as long as it can.

This doesn't mean we won't see some big drops, but they will likely be short lived. So for those trying to take advantage of those drops, timing is key. It's impossible for us to offer an exact timeline of when to expect a drop in the market, how deep it will be, and how long it will last. This is something we ourselves are always keeping a close eye on—which is why we always stress active management. Buying a put option or an inverse ETF can potentially pay off handsomely, but not if you're taking losses due to poor timing.

Of course, sooner or later the Market Cliff will come—the point past which there is no recovery. Surely, this is a good time to have short positions in your portfolio, right? Well, yes and no.

As we explained in Chapter 4, even after the Fed's firepower has become completely ineffective and the Market Cliff occurs, the Fed still will not tolerate a huge decline—not publicly, anyway. The market will have to be shut down, at first for maybe only a few hours or days, but eventually for a prolonged period of time. In the meantime, financial institutions will be going bankrupt at a rapid pace. There will be a great deal of federal assistance to keep the banking system going, but there certainly won't be much capital to cover the financial system's losses. This brings up an important question for the owner of shorts, put options and LEAPS, and inverse ETFs:

Who's Going to Pay Off on Your Winning Bet?

For any kind of short position you hold, there's always someone on the other end who owes you money if your gamble pays off. But with the financial world in crisis, are any of those people and institutions going to make good on their obligations? Who's going to make them? Is any financial institution facing complete ruin going to care about its reputation and integrity at that point? On top of that, short sellers will probably be one of the prime scapegoats for the financial collapse. Don't expect to see any collective outrage from Wall Street or Washington if the investors who were betting on the collapse don't get their due profits.

Shorting Bonds

Shorting bonds is a more complicated process than shorting stocks. The easiest way is through an inverse ETF. But shorting bonds comes with the same risks as shorting stocks. Even if the bond market isn't formally shut down by the Fed, the market will effectively shut itself down. Individuals and entities on the other end of bond short positions are unlikely to make good on their obligations in the long run.

There is also an added risk to shorting bonds, as the bond market is much more opaque than the public stock market. Nonexpert investors trying to short bonds may find themselves with some very unfavorable contract terms without knowing it, and they might find it very difficult to collect what is owed to them. Any bond shorting strategy must be undertaken with due diligence and consistent monitoring of the situation.

Shorting Real Estate

One doesn't necessarily short real estate outright. But one way to profit from a decline in the housing market is to purchase real estate once it reaches a distressed price level. In fact, profits in real estate can be substantial, and this can be an outstanding market for buyers in the Aftershock period.

The important point here, however, is not to buy too early. If a quarter-million dollar house is selling at $100,000, for example,

The Big Short: A Cautionary Tale

In Michael Lewis's excellent 2010 book *The Big Short*, he illustrates perfectly the advantages and disadvantages of shorting the market in anticipation of a major market meltdown. The story revolves around three groups of investors who were able to see the subprime mortgage crisis in advance. All three groups purchased large amounts of credit default swaps on overrated subprime mortgage–backed bonds for pennies on the dollar. These were essentially insurance policies against a high amount of defaults on these bad loans.

The problem was that, even though they knew these mortgages were almost certain to go bad, the market was able to ignore reality for a long time after the situation started to turn sour, with banks misleading people about the extent of the default problem and manipulating figures to avoid paying off on the credit default swaps they had sold.

As if that weren't bad enough, when reality finally did set in, the biggest dealers in credit default swaps swiftly went bankrupt. Those that did survive did so thanks to heavy government assistance. The investors in the book managed to sell most or all of their credit default swaps (in many cases to the very banks they bought them from in the first place, which were desperate to turn around their terrible bets) in time to each collect a hefty sum. But who knows how it would have turned out if they had waited, and if the banks that sold them the securities had been unable to pay.

For those looking to take advantage of a declining market through short positions, it might mean a lot of waiting while the government boosts the market. And after accumulating losses during that period, the big payday may never come, even when the market does collapse. Again, there are some opportunities for savvy investors to take advantages of declines in the market, but it is important to be aware of the risks and use discretion when allocating your portfolio.

many buyers may be eager to jump on what they think is a great deal. It's not. Only after the Market Cliff has occurred and we've experienced two to three years of economic chaos can buyers expect to purchase real estate at a truly distressed—rather than just corrected—price. With such little capital available in the economy and most investors extremely leery of real estate, that quarter-million-dollar house may be selling for only $5,000. Now that's a bargain, especially to anyone who has invested well in the mean-time. From there, profits can be made either from a quick sale or even as a rental property. At this point, owners can reap rewards even at depressed rental prices, because the purchase was so cheap to begin with.

Shorting Assets Overseas

As we said, there are opportunities to make money using short positions in the Aftershock, but they are limited. And they are not for novice or casual investors.

Aside from the opportunities to take advantage of temporary downswings in the United States before the Market Cliff comes, another potential opportunity is in overseas markets. Although the opportunities to short assets overseas tend to be less than in the United States, it's also less likely that overseas markets will face a shutdown, or that investors holding short positions overseas will be stiffed on their payouts. It still may be a good idea to cash out on your overseas investments when you can, when many people and institutions will be scrambling to buy up short positions to hedge their failing bets (see the sidebar on *The Big Short*). But overseas shorting opportunities are likely to be a more reliable bet than in the United States.

Shorting Currencies

There are shorting opportunities in the foreign exchange market. And the big plus is that, because foreign exchange markets are international, by definition they will not be shut down. Of course, the easiest way to short a currency is by buying other currencies as a hedge against it. One ETF to short the dollar, for example, is UDN, which is simply a basket of foreign currencies that will rise in value as the dollar falls. There are also ETFs available for currencies like the Canadian dollar, the Swiss franc, and many other currencies around the world. While these currencies may suffer in the Aftershock, many will rise relative to the dollar, which will fall precipitously due to the Fed's massive money printing and subsequent pullout of foreign capital.

B

Are the Stock and Gold Markets Manipulated?

POTENTIAL MARKET AND ECONOMIC MANIPULATION BY THE FEDERAL RESERVE

This is a topic that comes up periodically from our readers, and so far we have ignored the issue in our writings. It is sometimes brought up as a reason for short-term movements in the market. There are really two parts to this issue: (1) the manipulation of bonds, foreign exchange, and banking markets; and (2) the manipulation of the stock and gold markets.

In terms of the first part, the Fed clearly and pretty openly manipulates the bond markets and the foreign exchange markets, and directly manipulates the banking markets. Open market operations, in which the Fed buys and sells Treasury bonds, clearly manipulate the bond markets. When the Fed buys Freddie Mac and Fannie Mae mortgage collateralized debt obligations (CDOs), it is clearly manipulating the mortgage market and indirectly the entire bond market.

The Fed uses foreign currency swaps, where the Fed lends money to foreign central banks, to manipulate foreign exchange markets.

The Fed directly manipulates the banking market by making it easier for banks to profit by lending to them at very low interest rates and allowing them to lend to consumers at significantly higher interest rates. The Fed essentially lowers the banks' cost of goods sold—their "goods" being money. This also manipulates the value of their stock and their ability to raise more capital by making them more profitable.

Also, by manipulating the bond, foreign exchange, and banking markets, the Fed also indirectly but powerfully manipulates the United States and world stock markets.

It also clearly manipulated the price of homes through its actions to keep interest rates low and to reduce the speed with which it forces banks to foreclose on mortgage holders. Most important, the government acted to manipulate housing prices by saving Fannie Mae and Freddie Mac. By saving those agencies, the government made mortgage money easier to find, and housing prices were kept much higher than they would have been otherwise.

All of this manipulation is being done to help stabilize the financial markets and thus stabilize the United States and world economy. Of course, if this manipulation also helps maintain asset price bubbles, then ultimately it is stabilizing short-term financial markets at the expense of long-term financial market stability. That's because, ultimately, these asset bubbles cannot be maintained. It is a micro version of the much larger macro problem of the Federal Reserve's printing money and Congress's borrowing massive amounts of money. It stabilizes the short-term economy at the cost of massive destabilization later.

The second part of the question, manipulation of the stock and gold markets, is a source of great interest by conspiracy theorists. However, not long after the first edition of *Aftershock* was published, it jumped to the mainstream media when Charles Biderman, the president of Trim Tabs, a well-respected financial markets research firm, released a report saying that the huge increase in the stock market in 2009 was hard to explain based on the sources of funds moving into the market that normally drive up a stock market.

Trim Tabs made a common-sense analysis of the key flows of funds. An excerpt from their report, which details those flows of funds, follows:

> We cannot identify the source of the new money that pushed stock prices up so far so fast. For the most part, the money did not come from the traditional players that provided money in the past:

- *Companies.* Corporate America has been a huge net seller. The float of shares has ballooned $133 billion since the start of April.
- *Retail investor funds.* Retail investors have hardly bought any U.S. equities. Bond funds, yes. U.S equity funds, no. U.S. equity funds and ETFs have received just $17 billion since the start of April. Over that same time frame bond mutual funds and ETFs received $351 billion.
- *Retail investor direct.* We doubt retail investors were big direct purchases of equities. Market volatility in this decade has been the highest since the 1930s, and we have no evidence retail investors were piling into individual stocks. Also, retail investor sentiment has been mostly neutral since the rally began.
- *Foreign investors.* Foreign investors have provided some buying power, purchasing $109 billion in U.S. stocks from April through October. But we suspect foreign purchases slowed in November and December because the U.S. dollar was weakening.
- *Hedge funds.* We have no way to track in real time what hedge funds do, and they may well have shifted some assets into U.S. equities. But we doubt their buying power was enormous because they posted an outflow of $12 billion from April through November.
- *Pension funds.* All the anecdotal evidence we have indicates that pension funds have not been making a huge asset allocation shift and have not moved more than about $100 billion from bonds and cash into U.S. equities since the rally began.

If the money to boost stock prices did not come from the traditional players, it had to have come from somewhere else.

Their conclusion was that it was possible that the Federal Reserve had acted to directly manipulate the stock market, and was responsible for much of the rise in 2009. They clearly indicated that they didn't have any direct evidence of this, and the evidence was only circumstantial. Hence, they lacked any real proof that would stand up in a court of law or public opinion.

Most people ignored the report as unimportant, even though Trim Tabs is widely used and respected. In fact, they were respected enough that CNBC interviewed them regarding the report. Trim Tabs has a good track record in calling the 2000 bear market and in calling the 2002 bull market. But they missed some of the 2009 bull market by having turned more bearish after the market had risen 40 percent. They said their research had shown that the normal sources of funds to buy stocks were declining and, hence, the bull market was nearing an end.

They were wrong, since the market moved up another 30 percent. Hence, the few people who commented on the report released in January 2010 felt it was partly sour grapes at having missed all of the bull market.

One of the few people who bothered to respond to the report was Barry Ritholtz, certainly no cheerleader, having authored *Bailout Nation* (with Bill Fleckenstein and Aaron Task). He is also one of the more entertaining people to see on Wall Street. He was on a financial authors' panel with *Aftershock* coauthor Bob Wiedemer in New York in March 2010 and was a lot of fun to listen to.

On his web site he made some key points against the Trim Tabs report. First, it would be very hard to cover up such large-scale operations over a long period of time. Second, if the Fed was trying to keep the market up over the last decade, it had sure done a bad job of it. Hence, he didn't give the report any credibility.

Barry took a lot of flak from his readers, many of whom strongly disagreed with him. It is also worth pointing out that the Fed may not be trying to boost the market long term. Instead, its intention would more likely be to save the market from the big collapse of what has been a historic and, we think, very bubblish 1,000 percent increase since the early 1980s.

The manipulation issue has also brought up the issue that had been raised before of whether the government has an informal plunge protection team (PPT). This would be a group of Fed, Treasury, and major bank officials who talk to each other when there is the threat of a major stock market plunge and work to prevent it or counteract a plunge once it happens.

This idea supposedly got going after the huge 20 percent stock market crash of 1987. In that case, as was well documented in a *Wall Street Journal* article written shortly after the crash, the problem the stock market faced was not Black Monday, when the market crashed 20 percent, but Terrible Tuesday, when the markets stopped functioning Tuesday morning after the crash.

The problem, specifically, was that the New York Stock Exchange's market makers had basically run out of capital and couldn't function. There was no market being made in such key stocks as IBM and GM. Market makers on the New York Stock Exchange had been somewhat thinly capitalized and were laid low by their huge losses on Monday and couldn't function on Tuesday.

A 20 percent drop in the stock market is a problem, but a dead stock market is a much bigger problem. So, the Fed and Treasury basically stepped in and told the big banks to lend money to the major market makers, and they would back up the banks if they took any losses. Well, that did the trick. The banks lent the market makers the money they needed, and the stock had one of its biggest one-day rallies in history. Terrible Tuesday became Terrific Tuesday!

After that event, the PPT came into being as an informal group of the same people who worked together to save the market on Terrible Tuesday to deal with any Terrible Tuesdays in the future. Clearly, such direct intervention in the stock market had worked wonders.

Could this same type of thing have happened during the May 2010 flash crash? As further investigations have shown, the flash crash was primarily due to a series of down days culminating in a big down day—the day of the flash crash. It was accentuated by high-frequency traders, who do over 50 percent of the trading in the market now, exiting the market when it got too volatile. Of course, that's part of a broader problem of low volume and little long-term interest in the stock market. But, in many ways, the flash crash wasn't too different from Black Monday of 1987—a big bad day after a series of bad days.

The day of the flash crash had been going badly, but it got worse in the afternoon, partly due to a large trade by the Kansas City–based money management firm Waddell and Reed. After that, some large high-frequency traders pulled out of the market because the volatility was making it difficult for them to trade with any hope of making money. Thus, the flash crash began.

But why did it turn around so suddenly? Did the massive increase in volatility cause the high-frequency traders to come back in? That concept doesn't make sense—the higher volatility of the flash crash would seem likely to push them farther away from the market. Almost like the market makers of 1987, high-frequency traders exited the market because they didn't have the capital or didn't want to risk their capital in such a market. Thus, liquidity was drying up and the market was essentially dying. Seems like a perfect time for another intervention like the one in 1987. Only this time it was much quicker. They didn't act before a 20 percent decline and were able to stop the decline rather quickly and very sharply— a much better performance than 1987. But is it true? And wouldn't we have heard about it by now? You would think so, but it's difficult to be sure. The incredibly sharp turnaround had the telltale signs of a huge intervention.

However, all of the discussion of the flash crash in the media or by financial analysts was on why it went down so fast, not why it went up so fast. In fact, there was almost no discussion at all of why it went up so fast—that was considered normal and not worthy of discussion. The real question was what kind of technical trading error made it happen. Fat finger? Dumb trader? Once the investigations showed it was not a trading error but a big market downturn accentuated by a large trade, people seemed to lose interest. And, again, no one asked why it went up so much so fast.

So we're back to Barry Ritholtz's question. Can something like stock market manipulation remain a secret? To answer that question, let's look at other recent financial community secrets. Enron and Bernie Madoff are obvious examples. However, both remained a secret even though there had been ample warning of problems to anyone looking at them closely. *Fortune* magazine saw something wrong in Enron, and Harry Markopolos (a Chartered Financial Analyst and Certified Fraud Examiner) actually wrote a report to the Securities and Exchange Commission detailing what he thought was going on with Bernie Madoff. So it wasn't a secret, but no one wanted to see it.

In the end, people want to see what they want to see. Even in nonfinancial areas this is true. In the movie *All the President's Men*, someone at the *Washington Post* asked his fellow editors this question: If Watergate is true, why aren't any of the other newspapers like the *New York Times*, *Los Angeles Times*, and *Chicago Tribune* following it? Were staff members at the *Washington Post* the only ones who thought they knew the truth? It did seem hard to believe. But, often, even on big issues, people don't even ask the question.

So is Charles Biderman of Trim Tabs correct in thinking the Fed is intervening? We don't know for sure (and neither does he), but there are clearly a lot of reasons the Fed would want to see the stock market go up. A rising stock market has probably helped out the economy more than any other single positive element in 2009 and 2010. Certainly, it is the only part of our economy that has grown 80 percent. It has put more dollars into people's pockets than even all the borrowed money Congress has spent. It has certainly helped encourage the top 20 percent of our income earners who do over 40 percent of our consumer spending to get back into spending mode.

That puts a lot less pressure on the Fed to do other things like print more money via quantitative easing to boost the economy. You might say pushing up the stock market is probably one of the most cost-effective ways to spur the economy.

People who figure the Fed is manipulating the market mostly assume they are doing it by buying stock futures. That's part of the reason a lot of the upward activity in the market takes place overnight, and there are days when the market opens up with a huge increase despite a complete lack of significant good news. Of course, we really don't know how such manipulation could occur. It could also be via foreign intermediaries. But, again, we don't know the exact mechanism of how this might occur.

All of this could be explained by other factors. And, clearly, the key factor has been that cheerleaders want to see the market go up. However, that cheerleader spirit is also a key reason that manipulation works. With a very skeptical market, such periodic manipulation would fail. Or it would look more like Chinese manipulation of its currency—the currency shows a rock-solid movement up or down, based on what the government wants, with almost no volatility. It is fully manipulated all the time.

With the stock market heavily driven by cheerleaders, it doesn't take much to turn the market around from having a big fall. That's very different from manipulating the market all the time. Key manipulations done at the right time, like turning around the flash crash, greatly helps cheerleader psychology and would be relatively easy to perform.

And everyone wants to see them succeed. Even noncheerleaders. What could be better than a rising stock market and an improving economy? We'd certainly be the first ones to support it if we thought it would work in the long run.

It's only an issue if it is part of maintaining asset bubbles that are unsustainable. And in that broader context, it won't work. Even with a lot of manipulation, it will fail in the end, just as blatant Chinese manipulation of their currency will fail. That's one reason most countries don't manipulate their currencies to anywhere near the extent that the Chinese do. It's not just highly risky; such manipulation never works in the long run. It is just covering up an underlying problem—in China's case, it is a chronic trade surplus that China is using to boost its economy beyond what is economically sustainable. In our case, it is a series of asset bubbles that are unsustainable.

Lacking a smoking gun, stock market manipulation will remain a mystery. And few people will want to investigate because almost no one wants it to be true. Plus, they also hope that it will work.

And that mentality shows up in other ways, such as the lack of interest in a Fed audit. Even though it has received bipartisan support from congressmen as diverse as Republican Ron Paul and Democrat Alan Grayson, it didn't pass. It's almost as if people know the Fed has secrets that they don't really want people to know about. Is direct stock market manipulation one of them? If you don't ask, you'll never find out.

Well, that's probably not true. If the stock market melts down along with much of the economy, like the Enron and Bernie Madoff frauds, people will be mad, and it's likely they will ask these questions, and we will likely find out. But, of course, at that point it will be too late.

This is why we are awarding the ABE Intellectual Courage Award to Charles Biderman, president of Trim Tabs. Not because we think he's right. We don't know. But he did ask the question. And, at this point, that's what's important. He is a long-time well-respected financial analyst who has made good calls in the past, and he backed up his question with good research and exposed himself to ridicule for asking a reasonable question nobody else wants to ask. He is also a Wiley author—a blatant plug for our excellent publisher, which, by the way is a great example of a company that can survive the ups and downs of the American economy and still thrive. They were founded in 1807. That's over 200 years of surviving and thriving—not bad at all.

Statistical Manipulation

We discussed the manipulation of economic statistics in Chapter 1. The key statistics that are easy to manipulate and that the government has a strong motivation to manipulate are the unemployment rate and the inflation rate.

While we can't know for certain how the inflation rate is manipulated, manipulation of the unemployment rate is blatant and generally accepted by the public. The official unemployment rate includes only people who have no job and have been actively looking for work in the past week, and are thus able to receive unemployment benefits.

In a really tough economy, many people will give up searching for work altogether (or will be out of a job long enough that they are no longer eligible for benefits). These discouraged unemployed would be highly reflective of poor economic conditions, and yet the unemployment rate ignores them.

The unemployment rate also does not include the underemployed, people who have been forced by job market conditions to accept work below their skill level or below their desired hours. This group is also ignored by the unemployment rate, even though their situation is a clear indicator of the relative health of the job market.

The official unemployment rate is at somewhat acceptable levels right now—higher than most would like but not alarming. But if we counted the discouraged unemployed and underemployed, it would add up to higher than 18 percent, near Great Depression levels.

This is not a secret. It's not a case of deliberate fraud. It's simply a misleading statistic that the public is largely willing to accept.

In the case of inflation statistics, we don't know exactly what goes on behind closed doors. In many countries—notably China and Argentina—the government can simply pick the inflation rate it wants and make the numbers come out accordingly. The United States is not known for this kind of fraud and would not likely be so blatant in its manipulation. However, that doesn't mean it isn't engaging in some shady practices when it comes to reporting inflation.

The most obvious, and most likely, way the United States could manipulate the inflation calculation is in its definition of the market basket used to measure inflation. This basket of goods and services is very subjective, and it changes over time. Aside from simply giving more weight to certain goods and services, or swapping them out altogether, the government can also make adjustments to the value of goods to offset price changes.

For example, the price of a Honda Civic is going to go up over time. But a 2013 Honda Civic is not quite the same product as a 2003 Honda Civic. How does one measure the change in price versus the change in value? Without outside verification, it's not terribly difficult for the government to skew the numbers in its favored direction. A 10 percent rise in price could easily be recorded as a 10 percent rise in value, with no inflation.

One organization that provides some limited outside verification is Shadow Government Statistics (www.shadowstats.com), which compares current inflation statistics against how they would have been calculated 20 or 30 years ago. In both cases, the number comes out higher than what the government reports today.

In a January 2013 article, Euro Pacific Capital CEO Peter Schiff detailed a survey of various goods over two 10-year periods and compared them to the government's measure of inflation. What he found was that, while his calculations were pretty consistent with the government's inflation figures from 1970 to 1980, the government's reported figures came out significantly lower than his for the years 2000 to 2010.

It's not our place to say that ShadowStats or Peter Schiff is right and that the government is wrong. However, we do think it's significant that people are noting anomalies in the government's measure for inflation.

Given the amount of money printing we've seen, and given what we know about how inflation rises in response to money printing time and time again in countries around the world, we could reasonably expect inflation to be about 6 to 10 percent in 2013— not as high as it will ultimately rise because of the inherent lag factor.

This expectation is pretty consistent with ShadowStats' alternative measures of inflation. And given the government's considerable interest in keeping the number low in order to maintain the stock, bond, and real estate markets, it's not easy to make the leap that it might be using manipulative practices when calculating inflation.

Gold Manipulation

Clearly, gold is not as big a concern for the government as the stock market. However, there is a link between gold and stocks. When investors turn to gold, that pulls money out of stocks and bonds. That's very dangerous when the government is trying to maintain asset bubbles. So by pushing the price of gold down, it leaves investors with few legitimate alternatives other than the traditional markets.

European central banks perform the most active and open buying and selling of gold by governments. European central banks have been selling gold for many years. They have agreed to sell up to about 500 tons of gold a year. This agreement is in effect today, but in 2010 very little gold was sold, whereas in past years the amount of gold sold was often close to the agreed-upon limit. This selling could be considered manipulation, but in theory it is being done so that central banks can sell gold without greatly depressing the market.

The type of manipulation that most people are concerned about would be attempts by the Federal Reserve to push the price of gold down. One potential way to manipulate the price of gold is through swaps.

Gold Swaps

Essentially, gold swaps happen when two central banks literally swap hoards of gold—with the objective of doing nothing more than muddying the accounting waters.

A second type of gold swap involves only one central bank's gold reserves, which are lent for currency to another central bank. The real problem with this tactic is that the banks consider these swaps to be collateralized loans, and thus they don't appear on their balance sheets. No one knows for sure just how much gold and silver the Fed and other central banks have lent to each other in this way, but it would be worth taking a closer look if we could. A serious audit of the Federal Reserve would be a big step forward.

Gold Sales

A final aspect of gold market manipulation would be the sale of gold by the U.S. government. This would be a dramatic step for the government and generally hasn't been taken seriously in the financial community until recently.

Recently, gold has taken some remarkable falls in a very short period of time, and it usually has come after a large amount of gold has been dumped on the market in a very short time. This is suspicious first of all because of the amount of gold sold—larger than most private investors would have. Second, even if an investor did have that much gold to sell, it doesn't make much sense to dump it all at once. Why not spread out the sale to get the best price possible? Unless, that is, making gold prices fall is the goal.

In an article for Sharps Pixley in April, Ross Norman, a former gold trader for NM Rothschild & Son and for Credit Suisse, described the especially unusual circumstances that led to gold's fall in April 2013:

> The gold futures markets opened in New York on Friday 12th April to a monumental 3.4 million ounces (100 tonnes) of gold selling of the June futures contract . . . in what proved to be only an opening shot. . .
>
> Two hours later the initial selling, rumoured to have been routed through Merrill Lynch's floor team, [was followed] by a rather more significant blast when the floor was hit by a further 10 million ounces of selling (300 tonnes) over the following 30 minutes of trading. This was clearly not a case of disappointed longs leaving the market—it had the hallmarks of a concerted "short sale," which by driving prices sharply lower in a display of "shock & awe"—would seek to gain further momentum by prompting others to also sell as their positions as they hit their maximum acceptable losses. . . .

While we don't have definitive proof, events like the one described above are a strong indication that the government is manipulating the price of gold. Note that the sales in question are of futures contracts and not physical gold. Selling physical gold in such large quantities in a short amount of time is much more difficult, and the more manipulation the government engages in, the more it drains the government's resources to continue manipulating in the future. In the short term, manipulation can push the price down even while demand remains high. However, once gold is moving strongly upward, manipulation may not cause the price to fall; it may simply reduce the speed at which the price of gold rises.

Market Manipulation Summary

The fact that there are such strong indicators that the government has been manipulating the gold market is significant. It's a very unusual step, and more complicated than behind-the-scenes manipulation of the stock market, and certainly more complicated than massaging unemployment and inflation statistics. So if the government is taking that step, it's very likely that it is engaging in other, more common types of manipulation, and probably has been for some time.

Terms like moral hazard no longer even exist in the government's vocabulary. As we have said before, that mentality has changed so much that we predict that almost anything that gets into trouble and might threaten the stability of the economy and its asset bubbles will likely be deemed necessary for a bailout, no matter who benefits or whose responsibility it was.

If anything, manipulating the stock market would fit right into what has become an increasing willingness on the part of the government to use its printing and borrowing powers to shore up the economy short term and a tremendous willingness to maintain asset bubbles.

Investment Impact

Long term, if manipulation exists, it will have no impact on the Aftershock scenario other than to make the meltdown that much bigger. Short term, it will certainly have an impact in forestalling the Aftershock, just as the government's other measures of borrowing and printing money will forestall the Aftershock, as we have discussed previously.

Short term, any manipulation certainly makes it harder to time the market. That's part of what manipulation is trying to do. In foreign currency manipulation that is the key impact of manipulation—the central bank manipulates the market in part to scare off manipulators from attacking a currency. A central bank does this with well-timed purchases and lots of mystery surrounding their exact purchases and the timing of those purchases. The central banks want to make the market participants sweat big time and hopefully cause them huge losses if they go against the central bank.

Of course, we don't recommend that most investors try to time the markets too closely. We strongly suggest, for the reasons we mentioned in the book and the reasons we have mentioned in the past, that you make long-term deliberate decisions on where to put your investment capital. You can move short term with the bubbles, but always remember that they are bubbles and your profits depend on your not being in those markets when the bubbles pop.

To make comments on the material in this appendix or enter a discussion thread, please visit our web site at www.aftershockeconomy .com/appendixcomments.

Epilogue

If after reading this book, or any of our books, you think America has made mistakes, you're right. If you think America has somehow lost its ability to change and improve itself, you're wrong. In fact, the United States is still, and will likely be for decades to come, the most resilient, flexible, and dynamic economy in the world. That's due in part to one of the world's most flexible, dynamic, and strongest political systems.

While the short term may be filled with many seemingly insoluble problems, don't be fooled. The long term is very bright, indeed. More than any other country, the United States has been able to forge a path toward greater productivity and higher standards of living. Many countries have benefitted from the groundbreaking work of the United States. China didn't grow so fast because it was able to innovate on its own. It grew so fast because it adopted the methods of free markets and efficient industrial production, many of which were pioneered or perfected by the United States.

Other countries around the world have grown and benefited as well by simply watching the United States and learning how it's done. Not only can they learn directly from our universities, but they can visit our country, see our government, form joint ventures with our corporations, and receive our investment and the business acumen that often comes with it—everything you need to move any developing economy forward.

No, we're not the only country who has pioneered better methods for greater productivity. But no nation has pioneered in more ways than the United States. From our revolution for democracy, which has inspired and changed the world, to our economic system that has led to the most rapid increase in productivity in human history, we have led the world in many of its most important and beneficial changes.

That we have been distracted by our economic bubbles and away from our relentless focus on productivity in the pursuit of easy money is understandable. It's a regrettable and costly mistake. But, it's a mistake we will learn from.

By focusing back on improving productivity, the economy will rebound to a much, much higher standard of living than today. The United States has shown time and again it can lead itself, and the world, forward in improving both productivity and quality of life. The two are by no means mutually exclusive. In fact, they are mutually dependent.

But, like all our changes in the past, the ones in the future will be no different. They will not be bestowed on us. We will have to make them. They will be difficult and controversial. That's nothing new for the United States. We have done it before, and we will do it again.

What's new for the United States is that in this bubble economy, we have lost that willingness to change and to be controversial. To throw out a king and establish a democracy in 1776 was about as controversial as any country had ever been. Now, we have become more like other countries. It's not that all other countries have done poorly, but they surely haven't done as well as the United States. Our ability to change quickly, effectively, and beneficially has been far beyond what any other country has shown in the past two centuries.

That ability is still there, but will need to be rekindled. When this bubble economy ends, the rekindled spirit of America will begin.

Index